MACROECONOMIC
THEORY
AND POLICY

PRENTICE-HALL, INC., Englewood Cliffs, New Jersey

FRANK ZAHN
Associate Professor of Economics
Bowling Green State University

MACROECONOMIC THEORY AND POLICY

Library of Congress Cataloging in Publication Data

ZAHN, FRANK.
  Macroeconomic theory and policy.

  Includes bibliographies.
  1. Macroeconomics. 2. Economic policy. I. Title.
HB171.5.Z34   339   74-19151
ISBN   0-13-542555-7

10 9 8 7 6 5 4 3 2 1

Printed in the United States of America

PRENTICE-HALL INTERNATIONAL, INC., *London*
PRENTICE-HALL OF AUSTRALIA, PTY. LTD., *Sydney*
PRENTICE-HALL OF CANADA, LTD., *Toronto*
PRENTICE-HALL OF INDIA PRIVATE LIMITED, *New Delhi*
PRENTICE-HALL OF JAPAN, INC., *Tokyo*

For Katy

Contents

Preface

This book is organized on the premise that once the basic theoretical (and technical) materials which make up a macroeconomic model are familiar to students, analysis of macroeconomic problems and consideration of remedial policy alternatives can be undertaken with relative ease. As each sector of the basic or skeleton model is developed it is interrelated with those previously developed. Once the skeleton model is complete, it is used to help explain the impacts of some of the important means (policy instruments) whereby the fiscal authority, the monetary authority, business, and labor precipitate changes in the system implied by the model. Subsequently, the skeleton model is extended in order to improve its ability to explain current economic phenomena and to further explain the impacts of forces which precipitate changes in the system implied by the model.

Hopefully, the book provides a more efficient, as well as a more effective, means of learning macroeconomic theory and policy. The method of presentation permits a rigorous treatment of the subject matter and thereby aids student comprehension and stimulates student interest. It was the positive response of my students over the last six years and the substantial improvement in their ability to analyze macroeconomic problems and to evaluate policy alternatives that prompted the expansion of my notes into a textbook.

In Part I an introduction to the structure of economic analysis is provided. The basic terminology and concepts used in macroeconomic analysis are defined and examples of each are provided. Subsequently, a simple model for macroeconomic analysis (which will be a review for students who have completed principles of macroeconomic theory) is developed and used to demonstrate the usefulness of model building technique in evaluating national economic policy issues. As the simple model is developed, care is taken to further clarify the basic terminology and concepts of macroeconomic analysis.

In Part II a general equilibrium model which helps to explain some of the more important aspects of both the demand and supply side of a modern macroeconomy is developed. The model is fully interrelated by use of multiple diagrams. Subsequently, the complete model is used to help explain the impacts of various policy alternatives whereby the fiscal authority, the monetary authority, business, and labor influence the system implied by the model.

In Part III theoretical extensions of the skeleton model which help to explain more completely some of our current macroeconomic problems are developed. Of particular importance are the chapters on the inflation process, capital theory and economic growth, and recent developments in monetary economics. Care is taken in developing the material to present basic theoretical, empirical, and policy questions raised by the Keynesian-Monetarist controversy. Moreover, the new interpretation of Keynesian economics, as primarily disequilibrium dynamics, is explained. The new look not only helps in our understanding of the inflation process, but helps bridge the gap in our understanding of the Keynesian-Monetarist rivalry.

A writer is indebted to more persons than can be acknowledged adequately in a preface. But there are those whose special contributions must be mentioned. Among these are Robert M. Weintraub, R. Robert Russell, Robert L. Crouch, and William R. Hosek who introduced me to the subject. Michael T. Rabbitt, Lloyd M. Valentine, David Cantor, Robert Burton, Bevars D. Mabry, James R. Ostas, Donald L. Sternitzke, and John H. Hoag provided valuable comments during various stages of the preparation of the manuscript. Special thanks go to Delores Reynolds who typed much of the manuscript and to my former students, particularly Michael Arthur, David Roberts, and Paul Watro, who also provided helpful comments. Very special thanks go to my wife, Roberta, and our children, David and Deborah, for their patience and understanding. As is traditional, the sole responsibility for any shortcomings of the book and errors is mine.

Frank Zahn

MACROECONOMIC
THEORY
AND POLICY

PART I

The Structure
of the
Analysis

CHAPTER 1

Introduction

1.1 AGGREGATE ECONOMIC ANALYSIS

A study of our economy is a necessary prerequisite to achieving socioeconomic progress, however conceived. More than ever before, we must be able to understand and evaluate a barrage of related economic problems, as well as possible solutions to those problems suggested by modern-day activists, the news media, and would-be government representatives. Self-interest, inexorably intertwined with the general welfare, requires that we give considerable attention to the subject of economics.

Economics is the study of the relation of man's wants to scarce resources. Microeconomics emphasizes the working dimension of the individual parts of the whole or aggregate economy. It is the economic study of individual households, firms, and industries. It deals with the division of output, the allocation of resources among competing ends, income distribution, and relative prices. The prefix "micro" implies concentration on the parts of the whole economy.

On the foundations of microeconomics has been built the study of macro- or aggregate economics. Aggregate economics deals with economic affairs *in the large*. It looks at the total economic experience rather than the individual parts. As a result, aggregate economics deals with some of the most controversial issues of our time, including inflation, taxes, unemployment, and the role of government. Thus, on the one hand, a basic understanding of the subject might permit us to decide issues on a less emotional basis, regardless of whether our perspective is conservative, liberal, radical, or what have you. On the other hand, it may lead us to conclude that these nebulous divisions merely disguise a community of mutual ignorance.

1.2 THE SCIENTIFIC METHOD

Mankind acquires knowledge by two means: On the one hand, knowledge is acquired by way of revelation. Revealed knowledge is either accepted or rejected on the basis of faith, and it is capable neither of proof nor disproof. Revealed knowledge and its implications fall within the realm of theology. On the other hand, knowledge is also acquired by way of reason. Such knowledge and its implications fall within the realm of science. Scientists formulate theories which attempt to explain and predict physical and social phenomena; these theories are capable of disproof. Economics is one of the social sciences.

All sciences, whether physical or social, order their legitimate arguments within the structure of the scientific method. The only difference between the application of the scientific method for the physical scientist and the social scientist is that the latter can only apply it less exactly than the physical scientist. That is, the margin of explanatory and predictive error is greater for the social scientist.

An economist, like any other scientist, (1) begins with certain simplifying assumptions, (2) derives relationships that are inherent in the body of assumptions, (3) proceeds logically to the conclusions implied from the relationships, and (4) tests to see if these conclusions are verified or substantiated by what actually happens in the "real world." Parts (1), (2), and (3) of the scientific method comprise the structure of a theory. A theory is a deductive process of reasoning capable of falsification or disproof. Part (4), verification, is an inductive process of reasoning which gives the theory empirical content; that is, it integrates theory with the real world to see if the theory explains and/or predicts some aspect of the economy.

Unfortunately, experiments cannot be conducted in an economy in advance to determine potential solutions to our economic problems. The alternative is to experiment with a model exhibiting the basic characteristics of an economy. Such procedures allow economists to test their theories before subjecting the economy to possible errors. Thus, the more adequately a model depicts the actual economy, the lower the probability of inappropriate policy decisions. Despite the problems involved in model building techniques, a model can represent the basic behavior of an economy and can be useful not as the end of economic analysis but as a means for analyzing economic problems and evaluating policy alternatives.

The economist attempts to help society reach its economic goals. Models are employed in positive economics to provide explanations about what *has* or what *will* take place; models are employed in normative economics to help decide what *should* take place. Since World War II and more specifically since the implementation of the 1946 Employment Act, the government has become active in attempts to solve national economic problems, including balance of payments deficits, unemployment, inflation, and economic growth. While generally letting market forces determine prices and outputs of goods and services, monetary and fiscal policies are used to manipulate the economy so as to achieve national policy goals. Aggregate economic models play an increasingly indispensable role.

1.3 THE LANGUAGE OF ECONOMISTS

Mathematics has played an important role in the development of scientific knowledge. It has developed a universal language of symbols that minimizes ambiguity. It is the most efficient means of organizing an argument; inconsistencies and logical errors are more easily detected. The role of mathematics in building aggregate economic models is that of providing a language for the development of successive degrees of approximations of the real world within which we can examine the impact of various policy alternatives.

Although there is little question that mathematics is an indispensable language of economic analysis, it is not a complete language. It requires "connective tissue" in the form of "common" language such as English or Russian. Economists must have an ability to understand and express that from which they abstract (the real world) as well as the abstraction itself (the model).

This text will employ elementary mathematics along with a common language to explain basic aggregate economic theory and policy.

SELECTED READINGS

BOULDING, K. E., *Economics as a Science*, New York: McGraw-Hill, 1970.

FRIEDMAN, M., "The Methodology of Positive Economics," in *Essays in Positive Economics*, Chicago: University of Chicago Press, 1955.

NAGEL, E., "Assumptions in Economic Theory," *American Economic Review, Proceedings*, 53 (May 1963), 211–19.

SAMUELSON, P. A., "Problems in Methodology-Discussion," *American Economic Review, Proceedings*, 53 (May 1963), 231–36.

CHAPTER 2

Basic Terminology

2.1 NATIONAL INCOME ACCOUNTING

Acting in various productive capacities, individuals earn income and purchase goods and services produced in the economy. The exchanges are facilitated with the medium of exchange, money. These aggregate economic activities interrelate in a repetitive process of mutual accommodation and stimulus. National income accounting is the means of identifying and measuring aggregate economic activities. Although a more detailed explanation of the national income accounts is given in any principles text which discusses aggregate economic theory, we shall spend some time at this point in reviewing the system in a simplified manner.

Let us begin with a summary of the gross national product accounts for a hypothetical economy much like the United States. Gross national product, GNP, is the sum of new goods and services (valued at their market prices) that an economy produces in a time period of, say, one year. Table 2.1.1 shows the GNP account for our hypothetical economy. In general, the account is similar to the production statement for an individual firm. The left-hand side shows the total costs and profits of producing current output. The right-hand side shows how the total value of final goods and services is distributed among consumption, investment, government, and net foreign expenditures in the economy.

The first item shown on the right-hand side of Table 2.1.1 is personal consumption expenditures of $640 billion. The personal (or household)

TABLE 2.1.1

National Income and Product Account (billions of dollars)

Wages, salaries, supplements		$600	Personal consumption expenditures		$640
Social insurance contributions		30	Durable	$90	
Proprietors' income		70	Nondurable	270	
Rental income		20	Services	280	
Net interest		30	Gross private domestic investment		150
Corporate profits		90	Residential construction	$40	
Profit taxes	$40		Business fixed investment	100	
Dividends	35		Net change in inventory	10	
Undistributed profits	20		Net exports of goods and services		10
Inventory valuation adjustments	−5		Government purchases of goods and services		220
National income		$840	Federal	$100	
Indirect business taxes		90	State and local	120	
Net national product		$930			
Capital consumption allowance		90			
Gross national product		$1020	Gross national product		$1020

sector purchases durable, nondurable, and service goods. Durable goods (appliances, automobiles, etc.) are those that generally last more than a year, nondurables (food, clothing, etc.) are generally consumed within a year, while service goods (medical attention, laundry and dry cleaning, etc.) are consumed momentarily.[1]

The second item on the right-hand side of Table 2.1.1 is gross private domestic investment of $150 billion. The business sector retains a portion of output produced including additions to the capital stock (nonresidential construction, machines, trucks, etc.), inventories, and the stock of residential housing. These goods represent both net additions to the capital stock (net investment) and replacement due to depreciation, obsolescence, and destruction (capital consumption). Since residential construction represents additions to the stock of housing, it is treated as investment. It is inappropriate to treat the cost of housing as consumption because it is not consumed during the period of purchase. Rather, the part of housing which is consumption is estimated as the implicit rental value of all housing.

The third item on the right-hand side of Table 2.1.1 is net foreign (or net export) expenditures of $10 billion. This is the difference between receipts from exports of currently produced domestic goods and services (merchandise, insurance, transportation, etc.) and payments for imports of foreign-produced goods and services. Since consumption, investment, and government expenditures include import expenditures, total import expenditures are subtracted from the right-hand side of the GNP account so that it will reflect only current domestic production (valued at market prices). This is accomplished when import expenditures are subtracted from export expenditures, and the result, net foreign expenditures, is included on the right-hand side of the GNP account.

The final item on the right-hand side of Table 2.1.1 is government expenditures of $220 billion. They are divided into the purchases of federal and state and local governments. These expenditures include public construction of highways, government purchases of buildings and equipment, and payments to government employees. No distinction is made between public investment and public consumption.

The left-hand side of Table 2.1.1 gives a breakdown of the production costs for the economy and the difference between the market value and the cost of production, that is, profits. Most of the items are self-explanatory. Producers in the economy pay $600 billion in wages, salaries, and supplements. Social insurance contributions are $30 billion. Noncorporate or proprietors' income in the economy is $70 billion. Rental income of $20 billion is the implicit annual rental income homeowners pay for renting

---

[1] Some economists argue that household purchases of consumer durables are investment and that only the depreciation of these goods per time period should be included in consumption expenditures.

housing; on the left-hand side of the GNP account rental income balances the flow of services from the stock of housing included in personal consumption expenditures on the right-hand side of the account. Individuals in the economy earn $30 billion in net interest income. Corporate profits, which include profit taxes, dividends, undistributed profits, and an adjustment for changes in the value of inventories, are $90 billion.[2] National income of $840 billion is the sum of income earned in the economy. Indirect business taxes, which include sales, excise, and property taxes, are $90 billion; although such taxes are associated with the employment of factors of production, they are not received by factors as a part of national income. Since indirect business taxes are a part of the sales price of final product and appear on the right-hand side of the accounts, the sum of national income and indirect business taxes, net national product, is $930 billion. Producers in the economy charge $90 billion against their receipts as a capital consumption allowance; when this nonfactor cost is added to the left-hand side, it balances the gross flow of investment on the right-hand side. When the capital consumption allowance is added to net national product, GNP is $1020 billion and the left- and right-hand sides of the account balance.

Figure 2.1.1 is a diagram corresponding to the information in Table 2.1.1 that illustrates the circular flow of income-expenditures and therefore the national product of the economy. The diagram begins on the left with GNP − $1020 billion. The business sector charges $90 billion against GNP for capital consumption allowance; this amount flows into gross business saving. The remainder is a net national product of $930 billion. The government sector charges $90 billion in indirect business taxes against net national product such that national income is $840 billion. However, the personal (or household) sector does not receive $840 billion; $30 billion is paid for social insurance and $40 billion is paid in profit taxes. Also, businesses retain $15 billion in undistributed profits. Hence, the personal sector directly received $840 − $30 − $40 − $15 = $755 billion and another $120 billion in government transfer payments, to make personal income $875 billion. Governments collect $184 billion in personal taxes, leaving $875 − $184 = $691 billion in personal disposable income. In the diagram, households allocated their personal disposable income by spending $640 billion on consumption and saving $51 billion. In our example, $3 billion of saving becomes import expenditures and $48 billion flows into investment.

Notice that gross business saving of $105 billion plus personal saving of $51 billion is $156 billion. Gross investment just equals total saving less

[2] The inventory valuation adjustment is inserted under corporate profits to account for gains (or losses) resulting from sales of goods from inventory during periods of rising (or falling) prices. Profits (or losses) from inventory goods produced in previous periods due to rising (falling) prices should not be included in current national product. Since net changes in inventory are valued at current prices on the right-hand side of the account, the inventory valuation adjustment merely ensures that the right- and left-hand sides balance.

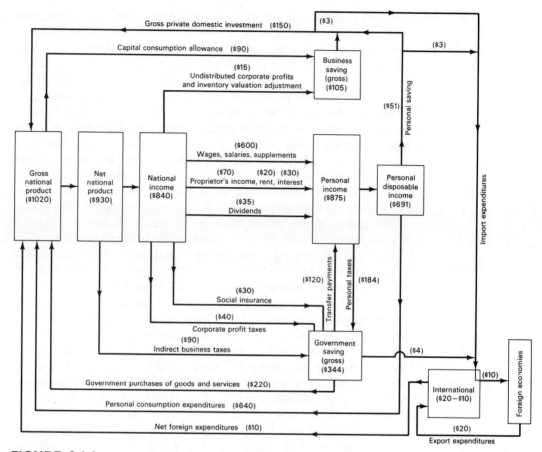

FIGURE 2.1.1

Circular Flow in the Aggregate Economy (billions of dollars)

personal and business import expenditures, $156 − $3 − $3 = $150 billion.
Also notice that total government receipts of $344 billion just equal govern-
ment transfer payments to persons of $120 billion plus government purchases
of $220 billion plus $4 billion for import expenditures, $120 + $220 +
$4 = $344 billion.

Government, business, and personal import expenditures are $4 +
$3 + $3 = $10 billion. These expenditures flow through the international
sector to foreign economies. Foreigners spend $20 billion for domestic
exports. Thus, net foreign expenditures of $20 − $10 = $10 billion are
added to domestic GNP.

One can readily see in Fig. 2.1.1 that the economy can be stimulated
in various places by government action to achieve desired economic goals.
First, as we shall see more clearly later on, monetary policy can be brought to

bear in stimulating or discouraging investment through the capital and money markets. Second, government expenditures and tax policies can alter the circular flow system. And third, government negotiation of international trade and exchange rate policies can alter our net foreign expenditures and thereby the circular flow of the economy. In the chapters to come each of these potential policy areas will be explored.

We can derive (in algebraic form) some of the basic national income identities from Table 2.1.1 or from Fig. 2.1.1. The following notations are used to simplify the presentation:

GNP = gross national product

NNP = net national product

Y = national income

PY = personal income

DY = personal disposable income

C = personal consumption expenditures

GI = gross private domestic investment

D = capital consumption allowance

I = net private domestic investment

G = government purchases of goods and services

F = net foreign expenditures (export minus import expenditures)

TR = government transfer payments to persons

SI = social insurance contributions

BS = gross business saving

NBS = net business savings, $BS - D$

PS = personal saving

S = net saving, $NBS + PS$

GS = gross saving, $S + D$

IBT = indirect business taxes

CT = corporate profit taxes

PT = personal taxes

T = net taxes (total taxes less transfer payments)

GNP can be calculated from either the right- or left-hand side of the GNP account. The expenditure approach yields

$$GNP \equiv C + GI + G + F \qquad \text{(gross national product) (2.1.1)}$$
$$1020 \equiv 640 + 150 + 220 + 10$$

and since

$$I \equiv GI - D \qquad \text{(net domestic investment)} \qquad (2.1.2)$$
$$60 \equiv 150 - 90$$

then

$$NNP \equiv GNP - D \qquad \text{(net national product)} \qquad (2.1.3)$$
$$930 \equiv 1020 - 90$$

or

$$NNP \equiv C + I + G + F \qquad (2.1.4)$$
$$930 \equiv 640 + 60 + 220 + 10$$

National income is the difference between NNP and indirect business taxes,

$$Y \equiv NNP - IBT \qquad \text{(national income)} \qquad (2.1.5)$$
$$840 \equiv 930 - 90$$

A portion of national income is directed to gross business saving and the government for social insurance and corporate profit taxes; also the government transfers a portion of its receipts to persons in the economy such that

$$PY \equiv Y - NBS - SI - CT + TR \qquad \text{(personal income)} \qquad (2.1.6)$$
$$875 \equiv 840 - 15 - 30 - 40 + 120$$

A portion of personal income is directed to personal taxes such that

$$DY \equiv PY - PT \qquad \text{(personal disposable income)} \qquad (2.1.7)$$
$$691 \equiv 875 - 184$$

Disposable income is directed to personal saving and consumption so that

$$PS \equiv DY - C \qquad \text{(personal saving)} \qquad (2.1.8)$$
$$51 \equiv 691 - 640$$

Alternatively, net national product can be calculated by summing disposable income, net business saving, and net taxes,

$$NNP \equiv DY + NBS + T \qquad \text{(net national product)} \qquad (2.1.9)$$
$$930 \equiv 691 + 15 + 224$$

where

$$T \equiv PT + CT + SI + \text{IBT} - TR \qquad \text{(net taxes)} \qquad (2.1.10)$$
$$224 \equiv 184 + 40 + 30 + 90 - 120$$

or by substituting (2.1.8) into (2.1.9),

$$\text{NNP} \equiv C + PS + \text{NBS} + T \qquad\qquad (2.1.11)$$
$$930 \equiv 640 + 51 + 15 + 224$$

or

$$\text{NNP} \equiv C + S + T \qquad \text{(value of output)} \qquad (2.1.12)$$
$$930 \equiv 640 + 66 + 224$$

where

$$S \equiv PS + \text{NBS} \qquad \text{(net saving)} \qquad (2.1.13)$$
$$66 \equiv 51 + 15$$

By equating like terms [Eqs. (2.1.4) and (2.1.12)],

$$C + I + G + F \equiv C + S + T \qquad\qquad (2.1.14)$$
$$640 + 60 + 220 + 10 \equiv 640 + 66 + 224$$
$$930 \equiv 930$$

we see that the net claims against the value of output (net expenditures) just equals the net value of output (net income). Notice that in our example with no government deficit or surplus net taxes exceed government expenditures by government import expenditures and net saving exceeds net investment by personal and business import expenditures.

If we add the capital consumption allowance to both sides of (2.1.14),

$$C + GI + G + F \equiv C + GS + T \qquad\qquad (2.1.15)$$
$$640 + 150 + 220 + 10 \equiv 640 + 156 + 224$$
$$1020 \equiv 1020$$

we see that gross claims against the value of output (gross expenditures) just equal the gross value of output (gross income).

The national income accounts are often misinterpreted. Although there is some correlation between social welfare and GNP, the accounts were not devised to measure social welfare. They were devised to measure changes in the level of economic activity. Increases in GNP are associated with pollution of environment, and all these social costs are not included in the national income accounts.   Growth in GNP does not necessarily reflect growth in the quality of life.   Many economists believe that we should deflate the national income accounts by some measure of social cost associated with the reduction in the quality of our environment so that we have a measure of not only economic activity but also social welfare.

Moreover, for one reason or another, all economic activity is not recorded in the national income accounts.   For example, illegal gambling and prostitution, "do-it-yourself" labor (on your home, automobile, or yard) at home, and housewife labor provide social value but are not included in the income accounts.   For another example, although business interest payments are considered a purchase of financing services, consumer and government interest payments are not and are excluded from the income accounts.

One of the most important shortcomings of national income accounting is that it measures the level of economic activity without any measure of changes in the quality of goods and services.   The statement (although probably not too well founded) that the quality of goods has decreased with increases in GNP means that increasing GNP does not reflect changes in the quality of goods and therefore is misleading.

2.2   AGGREGATE ECONOMIC VARIABLES

The specification of a model includes both variables and parameters.   Variables explained within the structure of a model are called *endogenous variables*.   Endogenous variables are those economic variables whose determination is the purpose of the model.   For example, if the model provides an explanation of how national income is determined, then national income is an endogenous variable.   Variables which are not explained, but are taken as given from outside the model, are called *exogenous variables*.   Exogenous variables may be either noneconomic or economic in nature and are determined independently of the system implied by the model; they are included in the model in order to show how their changes influence the system but are not themselves determined within the system.   For example, if the money stock is assumed to be determined by the monetary authority and its value given to the system implied by the model, then the money stock is an exogenous variable.   *Parameters* of the model are constant magnitudes, the statistical estimates of which give specific empirical content to the relationships between economic variables; they help specify the empirical form that an economic relationship *has* taken or *will* take in the real world.   For example, if we estimate from the data (a record of the real world) that there is a proportional relationship, a, between consumer expenditures and disposable income, then *a* is a parameter, the estimate of which gives empirical content to the relationship.

Whether endogenous or exogenous, a variable is either *stock* or *flow*. A stock variable is a quantity measurable at a specific point in time. A flow variable is a quantity measurable for a specific period of time. For example, the stock of capital is a quantity measurable on January 1, 1972. But investment (a flow) is the change in capital stock from January 1, 1972 to January 1, 1973. Money is another stock variable, but the spending of money is a flow. Individuals frequently confuse stocks and flows. This confusion over money often leads to the conclusion that increases in money (a stock) imply an equal increase in spending (a flow). This is not necessarily true, since it is possible for individuals to have more money but spend less and vice versa. The stock-flow distinction is clearly made in business accounting. The balance sheet or *stock statement* summarizes the assets and liabilities of a business firm at a *point* in time. The profit and loss statement or *flow statement* summarizes the receipts and expenses incurred in a *period* of time.

The variables used in economic models are expressed in either *real* or *nominal* terms. To say that our dollar income is $200 per week is a statement about our nominal income. But to say that our nominal dollar income of $200 per week relative to the price index, say 110, for a basket of goods and services is $200/110 or approximately $182 is a statement about our real income. Real income is the collection of goods and services we can command with our money incomes and is simply estimated relative to some other period by use of a price index. That is, the real value or purchasing power of our nominal income is less than $200 (relative to the price index— 100 in a base year). The use of real variables permits a more meaningful comparison of economic magnitudes over time. That is, GNP is most conveniently valued at market prices. But prices fluctuate from year to year. Hence, an increase in the value of GNP may reflect merely an increase in prices instead of an increase in physical output. Real GNP and the values of its real components provide more realistic measures of economic growth than nominal GNP and the values of its nominal components.

2.3 AGGREGATE ECONOMIC EQUATIONS

Whether expressed verbally or symbolically, a model is structured by using three basic types of equations. *Identities*, such as those expressed in Section 2.1, are equations which define economic variables; they are true by definition. *Functional equations* specify economic relationships between economic variables. There are two types, *behavioral equations* and *technical equations*. Behavioral equations embody behavioral relationships between economic variables. For example, to say that consumer expenditures are a function of disposable income is to say that consumers' behavior is such that the amount they spend on goods and services depends on the level of their disposable income. Technical equations embody technological or institutional relationships between economic variables. For example, to say that output produced is a function of the capital and labor is to say that due to the technical nature of the production process the quantity of output supplied depends on the quantities of labor and capital employed.

Equalities are statements of the equilibrium conditions (or states) of a model. Equilibrium is a concept used to describe a condition toward which, or away from which, the interaction between economic relationships tends to move. That is, the simultaneous interaction of the equations of the model determines the equilibrium values of the endogenous variables. For example, to say that the equilibrium price and quantity of a good is determined when supply equals demand is to say that the suppliers and demanders of a good come together in the market, haggle over the price and quantity of the good to be exchanged between them, and agree finally on a price and quantity. When the equilibrium price exists (and the equilibrium is stable) there is no tendency for it to change since all who wish to buy at that price do buy and all who wish to sell can sell. At any other price, some who wish to buy or some who wish to sell at those prices cannot.

All three of the above types of equations are called *structural equations* because they form the theoretical structure of the model. If we wish to analyze the determination of an endogenous variable as the various sectors of the model interact, we must express the endogenous variable in terms of only the parameters and the exogenous variables of the model. These equations are called the *reduced forms* (or solutions) of the model; they are derived from the structural equations. Reduced forms are nothing new in stating an argument. They are used all the time, but in verbal form. An attempt to explain that which is unknown in terms of that which is unknown, or to explain that which is known in terms of that which is known, or to explain that which is known in terms of that which is unknown would be ridiculous. Since a reduced form is a statement of an unknown (an endogenous variable) in terms of the known (the exogenous variables and parameters of the model), only an appropriate reduced form is capable of determining the value of, and explaining changes in, an endogenous variable.

2.4 TYPES OF ECONOMIC ANALYSIS

There are three basic types of economic analysis: statics, comparative statics, and dynamics. *Static analysis* considers the equilibrium state of the model when the values of the exogenous variables are held fixed. *Comparative static analysis* compares different equilibrium states associated with different sets of values of the exogenous variables. *Dynamic analysis* is concerned with the study of specific time paths of economic variables regardless of whether they are equilibrium or disequilibrium values.

Static analysis is limited since the adjustment process to an equilibrium state may not be instantaneous. An equilibrium state may have lost its relevance before it is established if the exogenous variables in the model should change in the meantime. Furthermore, even if the adjustment process is undisturbed by changes in the exogenous variables, the equilibrium state may be unattainable; that is, some equilibrium states may be unstable, in which case the adjustment process will tend to move the system away from equilibrium. Changes in the equilibrium state due to changes in exogenous variables are considered in comparative statics, while the question of attainability and stability fall within the realm of dynamic analysis.

An analogy may help make the distinction more clear. Take a strip of motion picture film. Look at one frame. Analyze the properties of the state toward which the activity in the frame will be at rest. An analysis of that state is static analysis. Now look at two or more frames and compare the different states at which the same variables will be at rest given a change in some physical constant. A comparison of those two or more states is comparative static analysis. Finally, put the film in the projector and watch the motion picture. An analysis of the movement of the variables in the film over time whether in states of rest (equilibrium) or not (disequilibrium) is dynamic analysis.

All three types of analysis may be qualitative and/or quantitative. For example, if we are only interested in whether one variable increases or decreases given a change in another variable in the model, the analysis is qualitative since we consider only the direction of change. But when the magnitude of the change is considered, the analysis is obviously quantitative. One can readily see that quantitative analysis implies qualitative analysis, but the reverse is not true. In the remainder of the text quantitative aspects of the model dictated by the data are assumed. Emphasis is placed on the qualitative aspects of the model. Furthermore, the text will emphasize the static and comparative static character of the economy with reference to the dynamic aspects, particularly in Chapters 9 and 11.

SELECTED READINGS

BEECH, E. F., *Economics Models*, New York: Wiley, 1957.

BUSHAW, D. W., and R. W. CLOWER, *Introduction to Mathematical Economics*, Homewood, Ill.: Irwin, 1957, Chap. 2.

KOGIKU, K. C., *An Introduction to Macroeconomic Models*, New York: McGraw-Hill, 1968.

SAMUELSON, P. A., "The Evaluation of Social Income," in F. Lutz and D. C. Hague (eds.), *The Theory of Capital*, New York: Macmillan, 1961, pp. 32–57.

——, *Economics*, 8th ed., New York: McGraw-Hill, 1970.

SHAPIRO, E., *Macroeconomic Analysis*, 3rd ed., New York: Harcourt Brace, 1973.

CHAPTER 3

A Simple Aggregate Model

3.1 THE MODEL

At this point it is useful to construct a model similar to the one developed in the principles course in aggregate economics. In addition to providing a review, the model will be used here to identify examples of the basic components of models just described in Chapter 2. The model is a simple approximation of the aggregate economy capable of the following: (1) the static determination of national income, consumption, and disposable income; and (2) a comparative static evaluation of the impact of changes in investment, I, government expenditures, G, and net taxes, T, on consumption, C, disposable income, DY, and national income, Y.

First, let us specify that consumption depends on disposable income. Second, disposable income is defined to be the difference between national income and net taxes. And third, equilibrium is established when national income generated from output supplied is just equal to the sum of intended consumption, investment, and government expenditures generated from output demanded.

Formally the model is structured by the following equations:

$$C = f(DY) \qquad \text{(a behavioral equation)} \qquad (3.1.1)$$

$$DY = Y - T \qquad \text{(an identity)} \qquad (3.1.2)$$

$$Y = C + I + G \qquad \text{(an equality)} \qquad (3.1.3)$$

The endogenous variables of the model are C, DY, and Y because their values are determined within the model. The exogenous variables are T, I, and G because their values are given from outside the model. Equation (3.1.1) is a functional relationship which implies that aggregate consumer behavior depends on (or is a function of) disposable income. Equation (3.1.2) is an identity, true by definition. Equation (3.1.3) is an equality stating the equilibrium condition of the model.

Now assume that the empirical form of the consumption function is linear,

$$C = a_0 + a_1 DY \qquad (3.1.4)$$

where a_0 and a_1 are parameters, the estimates of which would be obtained from actual data. (See the appendix to this chapter to see how parameter values can be estimated from the data.) The parameter a_0 is the value of consumption if disposable income is zero and its value is constant. The parameter a_1 is the slope, dC/dDY, of the consumption function, or the marginal propensity to consume from disposable income, or the percent of the change in disposable income that is consumed. Since disposable income is either consumed or saved, $1 - (dC/dDY)$ is the marginal propensity to save. If individual consumption and saving are constrained by disposable income, $0 < (dC/dDY = a_1) < 1$.

3.2   A GRAPHICAL ANALYSIS

Figure 3.2.1 is a graphical representation of the model. Any point on the 45° line from the origin is equidistant from the two axes such that the distance from the origin to a point on the horizontal axis will be the same as the vertical distance from that point to the 45° line. Since national income is on the horizontal axis, the vertical distance from any point on the horizontal axis to a point on the 45° line is the measure of national income as well. Hence, the 45° line reflects the sum of actual consumption, saving, and net taxes generated from output supply.

If net taxes are some value $\bar{T}$, then substituting Eq. (3.1.2) into (3.1.4) gives an expression of the consumption function in terms of national income,

$$C = a_0 - a_1 \bar{T} + a_1 Y \qquad (3.2.1)$$

where the slope of the consumption function is a_1 and the vertical axis intercept is $a_0 - a_1 \bar{T}$.

To the consumption function we may add the exogenous values of

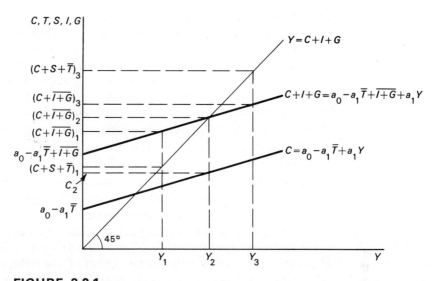

FIGURE 3.2.1

Income and Expenditures Equilibrium

investment and government spending, $\overline{I + G}$, and thereby derive the aggregate spending curve,

$$C + I + G = a_0 + \overline{I + G} - a_1\overline{T} + a_1 Y \qquad (3.2.2)$$

Equation (3.1.3) states that in equilibrium national income generated from output supplied just equals intended expenditures generated from output demand. Thus, equilibrium consumption, C_2, and national income, Y_2, are determined simultaneously with an equilibrium level of aggregate spending, $(C + \overline{I + G})_2$.

If income were Y_1, intended expenditures, $(C + \overline{I + G})_1$, would be greater than national income, $(C + S + \overline{T})_1$. Stated differently aggregate demand would be greater than aggregate supply. Producers of goods and services would increase the quantity of output supplied until intended expenditures were realized, $(C + S + \overline{T})_2 = (C + \overline{I + G})_2$. If income were Y_3, $(C + S + \overline{T})_3 > (C + \overline{I + G})_3$ and producers would have accumulated excess inventories. Consequently, they would cut back production until the excess inventories were disposed of. As a result, income generated from the production of goods and services would decrease until it just equaled intended expenditures, $(C + S + \overline{T})_2 = (C + \overline{I + G})_2$. In disequilibrium, since government expenditures, investment, and net taxes are fixed, it is consumption and saving that will adjust until equilibrium is established.[1]

On the right-hand side in Fig. 3.2.2, Fig. 3.2.1 is extended to determine simultaneously the equilibrium value of disposable income, DY_2, consistent with the equilibrium values of consumption, C_2, and national income, Y_2.

To illustrate the comparative statics of the model, suppose that in Fig. 3.2.2 investment and/or government spending were increased to a value of $\overline{\overline{I + G}} > \overline{I + G}$. The aggregate spending curve would shift upward from $C + I + G$ to $(C + I + G)'$. The new equilibrium value of aggregate spending would increase from $C_2 + \overline{I + G}$ to $C_3 + \overline{\overline{I + G}}$. The equilibrium values of consumption, national income, and disposable income would increase from C_2, Y_2, and DY_2 to C_3, Y_3, and DY_3, respectively.

Now assume that net taxes were increased to $\overline{\overline{T}} > \overline{T}$. The consumption function and the aggregate spending curve on the left-hand side of Fig. 3.2.2 would shift downward from C to C'' and from $(C + I + G)'$ to $(C + I + G)''$, respectively. The new equilibrium values of the endogenous variables would be C_1, Y_1, and DY_1; aggregate spending would be $C_1 + \overline{I + G}$.

We may conclude from the comparative static analysis that increases (decreases) in net taxes decrease (increase) consumption and national and disposable income. Further, increases (decreases) in investment and/or government expenditures increase (decrease) consumption and national and disposable income.

3.3　AN ALTERNATIVE METHOD OF ANALYSIS

By deriving the reduced-form equations of the model, we can determine more precisely the equilibrium values of the endogenous variables of the model and examine the relative impact of changes in net taxes, investment, and/or government spending on the endogenous variables of the model.

Substituting (3.2.1) into (3.1.3) and factoring gives the reduced form for national income,

$$Y = \frac{a_0}{1 - a_1} - \frac{a_1}{1 - a_1} T + \frac{1}{1 - a_1} (I + G) \qquad (3.3.1)$$

---

[1] The dynamic properties inherent in the model indicate that the equilibrium depicted in Fig. 3.2.1 is stable. That is, upon small displacement from equilibrium there is a tendency to return to it. This will occur because the slope of the consumption function, and therefore the slope of the total spending curve is less than the slope of the 45° line and intersects the 45° line from above. The model does not tell how the system moves toward the equilibrium if temporarily displaced, but $0 < a_1 < 1$ ensures that the system will continue to adjust until equilibrium is established.

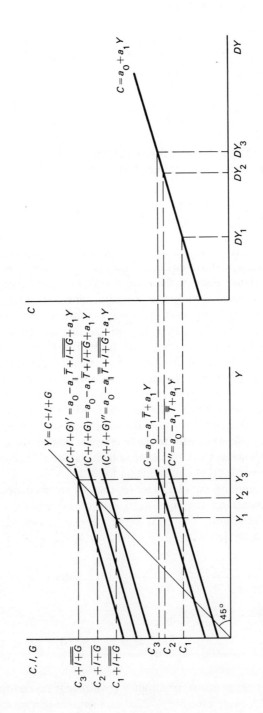

FIGURE 3.2.2

Changes in the Exogenous Variables

This is a reduced form since it states an endogenous variable, Y, in terms of only exogenous variables and the parameter values of the model.

Substituting (3.3.1) into (3.1.2) gives

$$DY = \frac{a_0}{1 - a_1} - \frac{1}{1 - a_1} T + \frac{1}{1 - a_1} (I + G) \qquad (3.3.2)$$

the reduced-form equation for disposable income.

Substituting (3.3.2) into (3.1.4) gives

$$C = \frac{a_0}{1 - a_1} - \frac{a_1}{1 - a_1} T + \frac{a_1}{1 - a_1} (I + G) \qquad (3.3.3)$$

the reduced-form equation for consumption.

The reduced-form equations may be used more precisely to determine the equilibrium values of the endogenous variables given the values of net taxes, investment, government spending and estimates of the parameter values. Further, they may be used to answer some comparative static questions. What will happen to national income, disposable income, and consumption given changes in net taxes, investment, and/or government expenditures? Which of the exogenous variables will have the greater impact?

Denote a change in national income given a change in net taxes and investment plus government spending in Eq. (3.3.1) as $\partial Y/\partial T$ and $\partial Y/\partial(I + G)$, respectively. There is no need for panic at the sight of partial derivatives. Partial derivatives are merely questions expressed in symbolic form. They ask what will be the magnitude and/or the direction of change in a variable when there is a change in the value of one of its determinants while holding all other determinants fixed.

By examining Eq. (3.3.1) we see that Y can be changed only by changes in the elements on the right-hand side of the equation. Since only one (composite) variable, $I + G$, is being allowed to change, the others go to zero and we are left with $\partial Y = \left[1/(1 - a_1)\right] \partial(I + G)$ or

$$\frac{\partial Y}{\partial(I + G)} = \frac{1}{1 - a_1} > 0 \qquad \text{since } 0 < a_1 < 1$$

and, similarly,

$$\frac{\partial Y}{\partial T} = \frac{-a_1}{1 - a_1} \leq 0 \qquad \text{since } 0 < a_1 < 1$$

Hence, changes in investment and/or government expenditures affect changes in national income positively. That is, increases (decreases) in $I + G$ result in increases (decreases) in Y by a multiple, $1/(1 - a_1)$. And increases (decreases) in T result in decreases (increases) in Y by the multiple $a_1/(1 - a_1)$. The factors which are multiplied by the exogenous variables in the reduced-form equations are the *reduced-form multipliers*, indicating the multiples at which changes in exogenous variables change the endogenous variables. The sign of each multiplier indicates the direction of change.

By comparing the absolute values of the net taxes and the investment-government spending multipliers, we note that the impact on national income of increases (decreases) in investment and/or government spending is greater than independent decreases (increases) in net taxes. This is true since only a percent, a_1, of the increases (decreases) in disposable income due to decreases (increases) in net taxes will affect total spending through consumption, while increases (decreases) in $I + G$ will have a unit impact on spending.

Similarly, in Eq. (3.3.2)

$$\frac{\partial DY}{\partial (I + G)} = \frac{1}{1 - a_1} > 0, \qquad 0 < a_1 < 1$$

$$\frac{\partial DY}{\partial T} = \frac{-1}{1 - a_1} < 0, \qquad 0 < a_1 < 1$$

Although the signs of these reduced-form multipliers are opposite, their absolute values are the same. Hence, increases (decreases) in investment and/or government spending or decreases (increases) in net taxes by the same amount have the same absolute impact on disposable income.

From Eq. (3.3.3) we note that

$$\frac{\partial C}{\partial (I + G)} = \frac{a_1}{1 - a_1} > 0, \qquad 0 < a_1 < 1$$

and

$$\frac{\partial C}{\partial T} = \frac{-a_1}{1 - a_1} < 0, \qquad 0 < a_1 < 1$$

such that increases (decreases) in investment and/or government spending have the same absolute impact on consumption as decreases (increases) in net taxes.

3.4 A NUMERICAL EXAMPLE

By substituting into each of the reduced-form equations a set of values for the exogenous variables and parameter values of the model, we may determine equilibrium values of the endogenous variables. Assume, for example, the following information:

$$a_0 = \$50 \qquad T = \$10$$
$$a_1 = .8 \qquad I + G = \$20$$

Then by Eqs. (3.3.1), (3.3.2), and (3.3.3), respectively,

$$Y = \frac{\$50}{1 - .8} - \frac{.8}{1 - .8} \$10 + \frac{1}{1 - .8} \$20$$
$$= \$310$$

$$DY = \frac{\$50}{1 - .8} - \frac{1}{1 - .8} \$10 + \frac{1}{1 - .8} \$20$$
$$= \$300$$

and

$$C = \frac{\$50}{1 - .8} - \frac{.8}{1 - .8} \$10 + \frac{.8}{1 - .8} \$20$$
$$= \$290$$

Now suppose that taxes increased from \$10 to \$15 and that the government does not spend the increased revenue; Y, C, and DY would change (let Δ denote a discrete change in):

$$\Delta Y = -\frac{.8}{1 - .8} \Delta T$$
$$= -\frac{.8}{1 - .8} \$5$$
$$= -\$20$$

and

$$\Delta DY = -\frac{1}{1 - .8} \$5$$
$$= -\$25$$

and

$$\Delta C = -\frac{.8}{1 - .8} \$5$$
$$= -\$20$$

Changes in exogenous investment and/or government expenditures can be calculated in a similar fashion. The impact of combination of changes in the exogenous variables can be evaluated as well. Do it.

3.5   SUMMARY

This chapter has presented a simple model of national income, consumption, and disposable income determination. Subsequently, a comparative static analysis was developed in both graphical and equation forms. Further, a numerical example was used to actually calculate the equilibrium values of the endogenous variables as well as to demonstrate what would happen to the values of the endogenous variables if the values of the exogenous variables were to change. Examples of the basic components of economic models were identified along the way.

The chapter has provided some basic understanding of the principles of model building. Now we are ready to move on to a model which more closely approximates the structure of the aggregate economy. The higher the level of approximation, the lower the margin of predictive and explanatory error.

APPENDIX
Estimating the Parameters
of a Function

In Chapter 3 we assumed that the form of the consumption function that best fits the disposable income, DY_t, and consumption, C_t, data was linear. The form that actually best fits the data for any relationship can be determined by statistical techniques (primarily regression analysis). Although it is beyond the scope of this text to expound on these techniques, it will be helpful to show a simplified means of fitting a function to the data and estimating its parameter values. In this way we may understand more clearly how economists put theory and fact together as a means of explaining economic activity.

Let us begin by finding the parameter values of a short-run consumption function when the form of the function is known to be linear,

$$C_t = a_0 + a_1 DY_t \tag{3.A.1}$$

A single observation will include both a value for disposable income and consumption. The pair of values (DY_1, C_1) is an observation of disposable income and consumption for year 1. The pair of values (DY_2, C_2) is an observation for year 2. Two observations are sufficient to determine the parameter values a_0 and a_1 in (3.A.1). We first find a_1, the slope of the line or the marginal propensity to consume, by dividing the change in consumption between any two observations by the change in disposable income:

$$a_1 = \frac{C_2 - C_1}{DY_2 - DY_1} = \frac{\Delta C}{\Delta DY} \qquad (3.A.2)$$

After solving (3.A.1) for a_0,

$$a_0 = C_t - a_1 DY_t \qquad (3.A.3)$$

we may substitute the value of a_1 calculated by (3.A.2) along with the value of average consumption and disposable income into (3.A.3) and sum to give the value of a_0.

A numerical example will make the means of estimation more clear. Suppose that $(DY_1, C_1) = (900, 900)$ and that $(DY_2, C_2) = (920, 916)$. Then the marginal propensity to consume is

$$a_1 = \frac{C_2 - C_1}{DY_2 - DY_1} = \frac{916 - 900}{920 - 900} = \frac{16}{20} = .8$$

And by substituting a_1 and the average values of $DY = 920 + 900 \div 2 = 910$ and $C = 916 + 900 \div 2 = 908$ into (3.A.3) we find that

$$a_0 = 908 - .8(910) = 180$$

Since there are only two observations in this example, each observation will also give the same value for a_0 as do the averages.

Table 3.A.1 provides another example of consumption and disposable income data which is used to estimate the parameter values of the consumption function, (3.A.1). The table lists ten observations. The values have been chosen to give a picture that includes both falling and rising levels of consumption and disposable income. When there are more than two observations, we must use Eq. (3.A.2) to calculate the values of $\Delta C / \Delta DY$ between each period as shown in the fourth column of Table 3.A.1. By taking the average of the fourth column we estimate the marginal propensity to consume, $a_1 \approx 7.3 \div 9 \approx .8$.

By substituting $a_1 \approx .8$ along with the average values of consumption and disposable income shown at the bottom of Table 3.A.1 into Eq. (3.A.3), we find that

$$a_0 = 882 - .8(878) = 882 - 702 = 180$$

Thus, we may write the estimated consumption function,

$$C_t = 180 + .8DY_t$$

To obtain a still clearer picture of what has been done, we may plot the observations of disposable income and consumption as shown in Fig. 3.A.1. The linear form of the relationship does not fit the observations perfectly. What is wrong?

There are three possibilities: (1) A mistake in estimation has been made; (2) another form of the function, i.e., some type of curvilinear form, would provide a better fit to the data; or (3) observations do not always lie exactly on the function. Mistakes can be corrected and a better fit to the data may be obtained by selecting a different form of the function by means of trial and error. Furthermore, there

TABLE 3.A.1

An Example of Data on Consumption and Disposable Income

t	DY_t	C_t	$\Delta C/\Delta Y$
1	940	930	
			$-20/-28 =$ .71
2	912	910	
			$-30/-35 =$ .86
3	877	880	
			$-30/-42 =$ .71
4	835	850	
			$-40/-45 =$ .89
5	790	810	
			$10/14 =$ .71
6	804	820	
			$40/45 =$ .89
7	849	860	
			$40/47 =$ .85
8	896	900	
			$40/48 =$ .83
9	944	940	
			$-20/-23 =$ .87
10	921	920	
Total	8768	8820	7.32
Average	877	882	.81

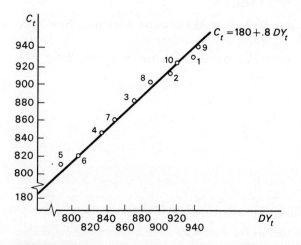

FIGURE 3.A.1

Illustration of Fitting a Linear Function to Consumption and
Disposable Income Data from Table 3.A.1

are statistical measures which help to evaluate the form of the function that best fits the data.

Even if there have been no mistakes and no other form of the function gives a better fit to the data, all observations generally will not lie exactly on the function. Part of the problem is rounding errors in calculation. But another more important explanation is that there are factors other than disposable income that determine consumption, i.e., personal wealth, political events, and income distribution. Economists recognize that changes in these factors will cause relatively minor short-run changes in consumption compared with changes caused by variation in the level of disposable income. But they accept the small probability that consumption will be very much above or very much below the "true" short-run consumption function and a larger probability that it will deviate by smaller amounts. Furthermore, these other factors are assumed to cause consumption to deviate from the consumption function in a random fashion. These unexplained random deviations limit the explanatory and predictive ability of the consumption function. But every little change in consumption does not have to be explained. Something less than 100 percent explanatory and predictive ability in the social sciences appears to be inevitable since human behavior is, at best, difficult to explain and predict in any exact manner.

SELECTED READINGS

BENAVIE, A., *Mathematical Techniques for Economic Analysis*, Englewood Cliffs, N.J.: Prentice-Hall, 1972, Chap. 1.

CHIANG, A. C., *Fundamental Methods of Mathematical Economics*, New York: McGraw-Hill, 1967.

DRAPER, N. R., and H. SMITH, *Applied Regression Analysis*, New York: Wiley, 1966.

PART II

A Skeleton Model
of the
Aggregate Economy

CHAPTER 4

Aggregate Income and Expenditures

4.1 CONSUMPTION, SAVING, AND NET TAXES

Since about 65 percent of total expenditures on goods and services produced and sold in the United States are consumption expenditures, our model must include a theory of consumption. Many factors influence aggregate consumption expenditures. The primary factor is the level of aggregate household income. Others include changes in tastes, the distribution of income, the availability of credit, expectations of prices and future income, a household's past standard of living, income relative to the income of others, and a household's stock of wealth. Changes in these other factors will be considered in later chapters, particularly in Chapter 10. But for now, we shall assume that they are constant in the short run and that the most important determinant of consumption, C, is the level of disposable income, DY. Formally,

$$C = C(DY) \qquad (4.1.1)$$

For simplification purposes, assume that consumption is a linear function of disposable income,

$$C = a_0 + a_1 DY \qquad (4.1.2)$$

as we did in Chapter 3. As disposable income increases, consumers purchase additional consumer goods. Their marginal propensity to consume is

33

$dC/dDY = a_1$. The parameter a_0 is the amount of consumption which would take place if disposable income were zero.

Since disposable income is defined as the sum of saving, S, and consumption, saving is defined as the difference between disposable income and consumption,

$$S \equiv DY - C \qquad (4.1.3)$$

We may substitute Eq. (4.1.2) into (4.1.3) and thereby derive the saving function,

$$S = -a_0 + (1 - a_1)DY \qquad (4.1.4)$$

A comparison of the saving and the consumption functions indicates that their intercepts are equal but opposite in sign; if disposable income were zero, saving would be negative $(S = -a_0)$ and consumption would be positive $(C = a_0)$. Changes in disposable income change consumption, but by less than the increment in disposable income. The remainder is saved. Because disposable income is the sum of consumption and saving, the percent of changes in disposable income consumed or the marginal propensity to consume, dC/dDY, plus the percent of changes in disposable income saved or the marginal propensity to save, dS/dDY, equals 100 percent or unity $[(1 - dC/dDY) = 1 - a_1 = dS/dDY$ and $0 < a_1 < 1]$.

Figure 4.1.1 illustrates the comparative properties of the consumption and the saving functions of a hypothetical economy. Along the 45° line from the origin, consumption on the vertical axis is just equal to disposable income on the horizontal axis; the line is the *all-consumption line*. If disposable income were $40 billion, all of disposable income would be spent on consumer goods and services, and saving would be zero because at this level of disposable income the consumption function intersects the all-consumption line. If disposable income were less than $40 billion, say $20 billion, consumption would be greater than disposable income by $5 billion and saving or dissaving would be −$5 billion. If disposable income were greater than $40 billion, say $80 billion, consumption would be less than disposable income by $10 billion and saving would be $10 billion.

In our illustration the values of the vertical axis intercepts of the consumption and saving function are equal ($10 billion) but opposite in sign. If disposable income were zero, consumption would be $10 billion, and saving would have to be −$10 billion. Because the marginal propensity to consume, $dC/dDY = a_1 = 7.5/10 = .75$, 75 percent of the changes in aggregate disposable income is the change in consumption. Because the marginal propensity to save, $dS/dDY = 1 - a_1 = 2.5/10 = .25$, 25 percent of changes in aggregate disposable income is the change in saving. It follows that $(dC/dDY) + (dS/dDY) = (1 - a_1) + a_1 = .75 + .25 = 1$ and

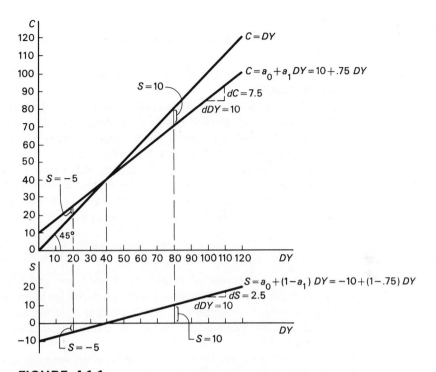

FIGURE 4.1.1

Consumption and Saving Functions (billions of dollars)

$0 < a_1 = .75 < 1$. The marginal propensities to consume and save are constant because the forms of the consumption and saving functions are linear.

Disposable income has been defined inclusive of saving and consumption. There is a difference between total income earned or national income and disposable income. The difference is net taxes, that is, the amount that individuals pay in taxes to local, state, and the federal governments net of the amount that governments return directly to the public in the form of transfer payments (welfare payments or subsidies to individuals, farmers, and businesses). This difference implies that disposable income can be defined alternatively as national income, Y, less total net taxes,

$$DY \equiv Y - T \qquad (4.1.5)$$

Substituting (4.1.5) into both Eqs. (4.1.2) and (4.1.4) gives

$$C = a_0 - a_1 T + a_1 Y \qquad (4.1.6)$$

and

$$S = -a_0 - (1 - a_1)T + (1 - a_1)Y \qquad (4.1.7)$$

consumption and saving, respectively, expressed in terms of national income and net taxes.

Certain taxes, such as property taxes, are exogenous since property owners pay a fixed amount regardless of the level of their personal or aggregate income. However, other taxes, such as personal income taxes, are endogenous since they depend on the level of income. Sales and excise taxes are determined similarly. Tax rates among individuals will vary with individual income as well as with the type of tax being collected. Moreover, transfer payments are likely to vary with income. In the aggregate we may specify an equation for total net tax revenues as

$$T = t_0 + t_1 Y \qquad (4.1.8)$$

where t_0 is the exogenous component of net taxes, and t_1 is the aggregate rate of net taxation from national income. A change in net taxes may occur if the exogenous component, t_0, changes and/or if the net tax rate, t_1, changes and/or if income changes. Changes in income are said to induce changes in net taxes.

Figure 4.1.2 illustrates the relationship between net taxes and income given changes in the values of t_0, t_1, and Y. The exogenous net tax, $\bar{t}_0$, is the vertical axis intercept and $\bar{t}_1$ is the slope of the net tax equation, T'. If the level of income were to increase from Y_1 to Y_2, then there would be an induced change in total net taxes by $T_2 - T_1$.

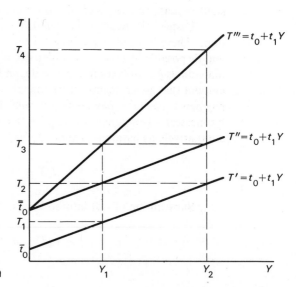

FIGURE 4.1.2

Net Tax Function

Suppose that exogenous net taxes were to increase from $\bar{t}_0$ to $\bar{\bar{t}}_0$. The net tax equation would shift upward to T''. For any given level of income net taxes would be greater by $\bar{\bar{t}}_0 - \bar{t}_0$. For example, if the level of income were Y_1, net taxes would increase from T_1 to T_2, where $T_2 - T_1 = \bar{\bar{t}}_0 - \bar{t}_0$.

Now suppose that the net tax rate were to increase from $\bar{t}_1$ to $\bar{\bar{t}}_1$. The net tax equation would pivot to T'''. If the level of income were Y_1, net taxes would increase from T_2 to T_3. If income were to increase from Y_1 to Y_2, at the new tax rate there would be an induced increase in net taxes by $T_4 - T_3$.

Alternatively, substituting Eq. (4.1.8) into Eqs. (4.1.6) and (4.1.7) gives

$$C = a_0 - a_1 t_0 + a_1(1 - t_1)Y \tag{4.1.9}$$

and

$$S = -a_0 - (1 - a_1)t_0 + (1 - a_1)(1 - t_1)Y \tag{4.1.10}$$

consumption and saving, respectively, in terms of national income.

Figure 4.1.3 interrelates the consumption (4.1.9), saving (4.1.10), and net taxes (4.1.8) functions. Along the corresponding consumption, saving, and net tax functions, we may identify for every level of national income the corresponding values of consumption, saving, and net taxes. For example, if the consumption, saving, and net tax equations are C', S', and T', respectively, then $Y_1 \equiv C_1 + S_1 + T_1$; similarly, $Y_2 \equiv C_2 + S_2 + T_2$, and $Y_3 \equiv C_3 + S_3 + T_3$.

Moreover, Fig. 4.1.3 illustrates simultaneous changes in the consumption, saving, and net tax functions, given alternative changes in the exogenous component of net taxes and the rate of net taxation. If, for example, the exogenous component of net taxes were increased from $\bar{t}_0$ to $\bar{\bar{t}}_0$, then the consumption, saving, and net tax functions shift to C'', S'', and T'', respectively. Net taxes will be greater for any given level of income by $\bar{\bar{t}}_0 - \bar{t}_0$; saving will be less for any given level of income by $(1 - a_1)(\bar{\bar{t}}_0 - \bar{t}_0)$; and consumption will be less for any given level of income by $a_1(\bar{\bar{t}}_0 - \bar{t}_0)$. The decrease in saving and consumption for any given level of income will be equal to the increase in taxes. Should the average tax rate be increased from $\bar{t}_1$ to $\bar{\bar{t}}_1$, the slope of the net tax function will increase as shown by T'''; the slopes of the consumption and saving functions or the marginal propensities to consume and save net of the marginal propensity of governments to tax out of national income will decrease as shown by C''' and S''', respectively.

Hence, for any given level of income, since the marginal propensity of governments to net tax will be greater by $\bar{\bar{t}}_1 - \bar{t}_1$, the marginal propensity to consume will be less by $a_1[1 - (\bar{\bar{t}}_1 - \bar{t}_1)]$ and the marginal propensity to save will be less by $(1 - a_1)[1 - (\bar{\bar{t}}_1 - \bar{t}_1)]$. The total decrease in consumption and saving for any particular level of income will be equal to the increase in net taxes.

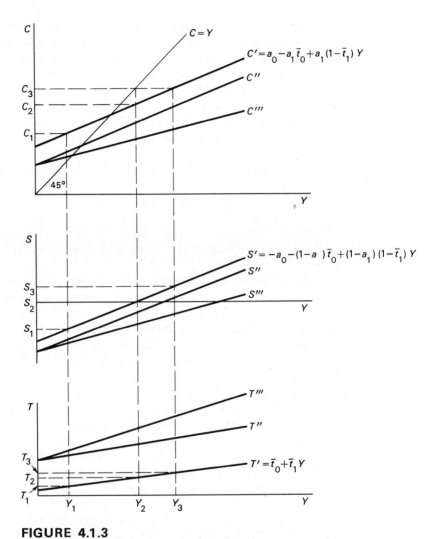

FIGURE 4.1.3

Consumption, Saving, and Net Tax Functions

The diagrams in Fig. 4.1.3 may be condensed by summing vertically the saving and net tax functions. In Fig. 4.1.4 for a level of income Y_1, net taxes would be T_1 and saving would be S_1. Hence, $S + T = S_1 + T_1$. For a level of income Y_2, net taxes would be T_2 and saving would be S_2. Hence, $S + T = S_2 + T_2$. By vertically summing saving and net taxes for all levels of income, we derive the $S + T$ curve as shown in the lower diagram.

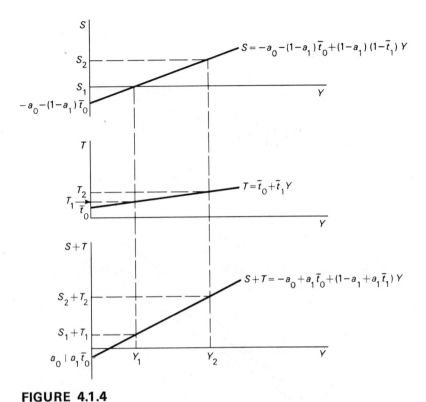

FIGURE 4.1.4

Derivation of the Saving Plus Net Tax Curve

Alternatively we may add the saving function (4.1.10) and the net tax function (4.1.8) algebraically. This yields

$$S + T = -a_0 + a_1 t_0 + (1 - a_1 + a_1 t_1)Y \qquad (4.1.11)$$

Figure 4.1.5 illustrates the relationship between the consumption function (4.1.9) and the $S + T$ curve (4.1.11). The consumption function is drawn with a vertical intercept, $a_0 - a_1 \bar{t}_0$, where $t_0 = \bar{t}_0$, and a slope of $a_1(1 - \bar{t}_1)$, where $t_1 = \bar{t}_1$. The $S + T$ curve is drawn with a vertical axis intercept, $-a_0 + a_1 \bar{t}_0$, and a slope of $1 - a_1 + a_1 \bar{t}_1$.

Suppose that exogenous net taxes are increased from $\bar{t}_0$ to $\bar{\bar{t}}_0$; then consumption would be less by $a_1(\bar{\bar{t}}_0 - \bar{t}_0)$ for any given level of income; that is, the consumption function will shift to C'. The $S + T$ curve will shift to $(S + T)'$; that is, for any given level of income net taxes plus saving would

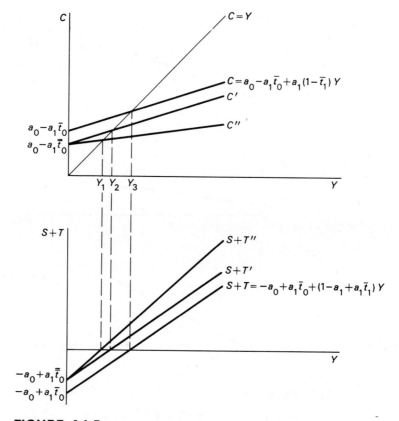

FIGURE 4.1.5

Relationship between the Consumption Function and the Saving Plus Net Taxes Curve

be more by $a_1(\bar{\bar{t}}_0 - \bar{t}_0)$. As shown in Fig. 4.1.4, increases in exogenous net taxes decrease both consumption and saving. So when the $S + T$ curve shifts to $(S + T)'$, net taxes increase by an amount greater than the decrease in saving; that amount is the decrease in consumption.

Now suppose that the average net tax rate increases from $\bar{t}_1$ to $\bar{\bar{t}}_1$. The consumption function and the $S + T$ curve will pivot to C'' and $(S + T)''$, respectively, because the slope or marginal propensity to consume from national income has decreased by $a_1[1 - (\bar{\bar{t}}_1 - \bar{t}_1)]$ and the slope of the $S + T$ curve has increased by $a_1(\bar{\bar{t}}_1 - \bar{t}_1)$. The slope of the $S + T$ curve is greater, since the decrease in the marginal propensity to save is less than the increase in the marginal propensity to net tax by the decrease in the marginal propensity to consume; this is true for any given level of income.

One can readily see that our model need not include both a saving and a consumption function. This would be redundant since aggregate saving behavior automatically reflects aggregate consumption behavior and vice versa. Moreover, the influence of net tax changes on aggregate saving automatically reflects the influence of net tax changes on aggregate consumption. Thus, we shall continue the analysis of economic aggregates using only the $S + T$ curve in Fig. 4.1.5.

The $S + T$ curve diagram and corresponding equation (4.1.11) will now be placed on the next page. This page will be called the Summary Page. It will be duplicated throughout Part II. As each part of the model is developed, it will be added to the summary page and interrelated to those previously developed. Thus, at the end of Part II the graphical form of the model will be fully assembled and interrelated.

4.2 INVESTMENT EXPENDITURES

Capital assets (plant, equipment, and inventories) are employed as a factor input in the production of aggregate output. At any point in time an economy possesses a stock of capital assets. These assets result from prior investment expenditures which took place for two reasons: (1) to replace that part of the stock of capital assets used up through depreciation, destruction, and obsolescence, and (2) to increase the stock of capital assets and thereby augment the productive capacity of the economy. Gross investment is the total expenditure for new capital assets within a time period. Net investment is gross investment less replacement. Hence, net investment results in net increases in the stock of capital. Net investment can be zero or negative as well. When gross investment just replaces used up capital, then net investment is zero and the stock of capital does not change. When gross investment is insufficient to provide for replacement of used up capital, net investment is negative and the stock of capital decreases; that is, net disinvestment occurs.

Investment expenditures are heterogeneous. As such, no single investment theory can reasonably apply to the various forms of investment. Potential expenditures for owner-occupied housing are not dominated by profit considerations as are business expenditures for plant, equipment, and inventory. Moreover, even though the profit motive dominates in cases of business expenditures, inventory investment probably responds to factors which are different from those factors determining plant and equipment expenditures. However, since business expenditures make up about two thirds of gross private investment, they will be given primary consideration in developing a theory of investment.

Investment spending for a new capital asset at its purchase price occurs because the investor expects the net return from purchasing and operating the asset to at least equal its opportunity cost. The opportunity cost of an investment outlay is the net return from the next best alternative earning asset. Thus, the problems that a businessman encounters in an

SUMMARY PAGE

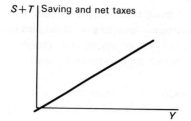

$S+T$ | Saving and net taxes

Y

Equation

1. $S+T = -a_0 + a_1 t_0 + (1 - a_1 + a_1 t_1)Y$

investment decision are problems of portfolio management. As a portfolio manager, he must decide what combination of earning assets maximizes his profit. Similarly, he must decide whether the expected returns over the life of the capital asset will cover the purchasing and operating cost plus yield a net return at least equal to the cost of borrowing the investment funds. Even if he does not have to borrow (say he plans to use retained earnings to finance the investment) he must expect to realize a net return at least equal to the net return he could earn by lending his money to someone else.

One approach in making the decision to invest is to calculate the present market value of the expected net return of an additional capital asset and compare it to the purchase price of the additional capital asset. If the present market value is at least as great as the price, it is profitable to invest. Another approach is to calculate the marginal efficiency of investment, MEI, or the rate of return which an investment expenditure is expected to earn and compare it to the rate of return on the next best alternative earning asset. If the MEI is at least as great as the rate of return on the next best alternative, it is profitable to invest. In the analysis to follow the interest rate on a one-year bond will be considered representative of the opportunity cost of investment, that is, the yield on the next best alternative earning asset; it will be called the market rate of interest.

The investment decision-making process may be formalized by beginning with the equation for the growth of a sum at compound interest. A lender will receive at the end of one year

$$X_1 = PV(1 + R) \qquad (4.2.1)$$

where X_1 is the expected return at the end of one year, PV is the amount lent (the present value of the loan), and R is the rate of interest. If he lends the same amount for two years, he will expect a total return, X_2, at the end of the second year of

$$X_2 = PV(1 + R)(1 + R) = PV(1 + R)^2 \qquad (4.2.2)$$

If, for example, $PV = \$1082.64$ and $R = .10$,

$$X_2 = \$1082.64(1 + .10)^2 = \$1310$$

We may generalize this process by saying that the amount lent, PV, at an interest rate, R, for n number of years will grow at the end of nth years to

$$X_n = PV(1 + R)^n \qquad (4.2.3)$$

Now look at the decision-making process from the standpoint of an investor (a potential borrower of funds for investment). Suppose that an investor expects net returns from the purchase and operation of a capital asset to grow to X_n at the end of the nth year. He will pay R percent on the amount borrowed to finance the purchase during the first year and then for the second year again R percent on the amount borrowed plus another R percent on the first year's interest and then for the third year again R percent on the amount borrowed plus another R percent on the first and second years' interest and so on up through the nth year. Thus, the amount PV is the present market value of the capital asset or the maximum amount the investor will be willing to borrow from a lender based on the expected return to be realized at the end of n years discounted by the rate of interest. Solving (4.2.2) for PV gives

$$PV = \frac{X_n}{(1 + R)^n} \tag{4.2.4}$$

an equation for estimating the present market value of the purchase. If the present value of the purchase is at least as great as the purchase price of the asset, then it is profitable to invest. If, for example, $n = 2$ years, $X_2 = \$1310$, and $R = .10$, then

$$PV = \frac{\$1310}{(1 + .10)^2} = \$1082.64$$

where the investor is willing to purchase the capital asset and finance $1310 at 10 percent for two years if the purchase price of the capital asset or the investment outlay is at most less than $1082.64. The interest paid would equal ($1310 - \$1082.64) = \$227.36$.

More generally, if a capital asset is expected to yield returns at the end of each year of its discounted life,[1] we can find the present value of a series of expected returns, $E_1^e, E_2^e, \ldots, E_n^e$, by discounting each back to the present by the rate of interest,

$$PV = \frac{E_1^e}{1 + R} + \frac{E_2^e}{(1 + R)^2} + \cdots + \frac{E_n^e}{(1 + R)^n} \tag{4.2.5}$$

If, for example, $n = 2$ years, $E_1^e = \$1100$, $E_2^e = \$1210$, and $R = .10$, then

$$PV = \frac{\$1100}{1 + .10} + \frac{\$1210}{(1 + .10)^2} = \$2000$$

---

[1] The discounted life of an asset reasonably would be considered a length of time in which the asset would be fully depreciated, that is, its productive life. However, some firms will decide that the risks associated with capital expansion require that they realize their net return in a period of time that is less than the productive life of a capital asset. Thus, the discounted life of an asset may be less than its productive life.

If the investment outlay or price of the capital asset is at most less than its present value, the investor will purchase the capital asset and pay interest of $2310 − $2000 = $310.

Since the purchase price of a capital asset, P^I, is generally known in advance of the potential purchase, an alternative means of making an investment decision is to estimate the rate of return that will make the cost of an additional capital asset equal to the expected net return stream. This rate of return is called the marginal efficiency of investment, MEI, since it equates expected net return (efficiency) from one additional (marginal) capital asset to the cost of purchasing (investment) the new asset.[2] Formally,

$$P^I = \frac{E_1^e}{1 + \text{MEI}} + \frac{E_2^e}{(1 + \text{MEI})^2} + \cdots + \frac{E_n^e}{(1 + \text{MEI})^n} \qquad (4.2.6)$$

Consider a purchase price of $2000 on a capital asset which will be fully discounted in two years. At the end of the first year, net return is expected to be $1100 and at the end of the second year $1210. Then,

$$\$2000 = \frac{\$1100}{1 + \text{MEI}} + \frac{\$1210}{(1 + \text{MEI})^2}$$

and

$$\text{MEI} = .10 \quad \text{or} \quad 10 \text{ percent}$$

This example illustrates that the expected net return at the end of the first year is $1000 plus a 10 percent rate of return on the $1000 (or $100). And at the end of the second year the expected net return is $1000 plus the $100 for the first year when $1000 is committed plus 10 percent of the $100 for the first year (or $10) plus 10 percent of $1000 committed for two years. Thus, a 10 percent rate of return is expected on each dollar per year committed to the investment outlay.

Whether an asset will be purchased using the MEI approach depends on the market rate of interest relative to the MEI. Investment will occur if the MEI is at least as great as the rate of interest. That is, if MEI $\geq R$, investment will take place: if MEI $< R$, investment will not take place.

In any particular time period, any number of potential investment

---

[2] Some economists define the discounting rate of return as the marginal efficiency of capital, MEC. Others, beginning with A. P. Lerner, *The Economics of Control*, 1963 (see the Selected Readings at the end of this chapter), recognize that the expected net return refers to the investment outlay instead of the total stock of capital at any point in time and argue, therefore, that the concept of MEI is more consistent in the analysis. See also R. G. D. Allen, *Macro-Economic Theory*, pp. 62–66 and pp. 108–112. In Chapter 11, a theory of capital relating to the theory of investment presented here will be discussed in more detail.

opportunities may exist. Each is associated with a MEI. If the investment opportunities are ranked in order of decreasing profitabilities, we obtain the demand schedule for investment. Figure 4.2.1 shows an example of an investment schedule where both the MEI and the opportunity cost of investment or the market rate of interest are measured on the vertical axis and investment on the horizontal axis. If, for example, the rate of interest was 8 percent, investment would be $80 billion, where MEI $= R =$ .08. That is, all capital assets where MEI $\geq R =$ .08 would be profitable. If the rate of interest were to decrease to 5 percent, then $120 billion in investment would take place, since additional capital assets with lower MEIs will become profitable at the lower interest rate. Changes in R disturb the equality between MEI and R. Thus, changes in investment will occur until the equality is restored.

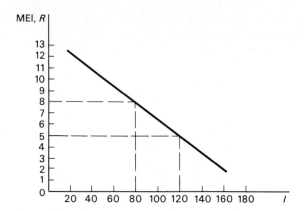

FIGURE 4.2.1

MEI Schedule (billions of dollars)

Whether we use the present value approach or the MEI approach, investment spending clearly depends on the rate of interest,

$$I = g(R) \qquad (4.2.7)$$

where decreases in the rate of interest increase investment spending. In the present value approach [Eq. (4.2.5)], decreases in the opportunity cost of investment, R, increase the present value of new capital assets, and investors will be willing to pay a higher purchase price (investment) for new capital assets. And investment spending increases. In the MEI approach [Eq. (4.2.6)], decreases in the opportunity cost of investment, R, increase investment spending, since more capital assets previously considered unprofitable become profitable; their MEIs are at least as great as the new rate of interest. Since there is no simple way that permits MEI to be calculated in Eq. (4.2.6) because the terms in the numerator are not equal, MEI is sometimes replaced by the rate of interest. The result of summing the series then is the present value of the expected return stream. If the present value is at least as great as the cost of purchase, investment takes place. It follows also that the MEI $\geq R$. Conversely, if the cost of purchase exceeds the present value, MEI $< R$ and additional investment will not take place.

Whether one uses the present market value or MEI approach to determine investment demand, Eqs. (4.2.5) and (4.2.6) show that revisions in expectations about future net returns will influence investment spending. Expectations about the future demand for products are periodically optimistic, and additional productive capacity may be required to handle future demand. Noncapital costs may fall if firms can increase the productive efficiency of noncapital factors of production, such as labor. Technical progress will affect the firm's ability to compete more effectively and thereby render part of the stock of capital obsolete. In the aggregate these factors may cause expected net returns to be revised upward, and the present market value of an asset will be higher at any given market rate of interest. Hence, additional investment will become profitable. Alternatively, with increases in expected net returns, additional investment will be profitable at any given value of the MEI and market rate of interest.

Because net returns are highly correlated to expected net returns, which are in turn highly correlated to current income, economists include income in the net investment function such that

$$I = I(Y, R) \qquad (4.2.8)$$

Assume that the net investment function is linear,

$$I = b_0 + b_1 Y - b_2 R \qquad (4.2.9)$$

where the expected signs of the relationships between the rate of interest and net investment is negative and the relationship between income and net investment is positive. That is, as the opportunity cost of investment falls, capital assets with lower expected yields become profitable, and net investment will increase. As net return expectations become more optimistic for higher levels of income, net investment will be greater for any given rate of interest.

Figure 4.2.2 illustrates how changes in the net investment demand occur. If the level of income is Y_2, a picture of Eq. (4.2.9) can be drawn where the horizontal axis intercept (or value of net investment if the rate of interest were zero) is $(b_0 + b_1 Y_2)$ and the slope of the net investment function

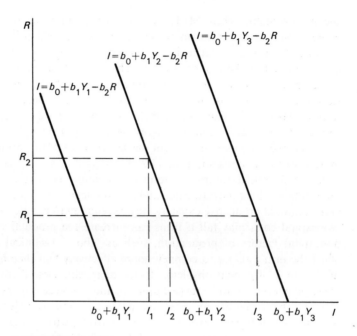

FIGURE 4.2.2

Net Investment Function

is $\partial I/\partial R = -b_2$. The exogenous component of net investment is b_0, since it is the value of net investment if both the rate of interest and income were zero. The marginal propensity to invest or the percent of total spending for net investment is $\partial I/\partial Y = 0 < b_2 < 1$. For the level of income, Y_2, if the market rate of interest falls from R_2 to R_1 net investment will increase from I_1 to I_2. For lower levels of income, for example, Y_1, the net investment demand curve shifts to the left; net investment will be less at any given rate of interest. For higher levels of income, for example, Y_3, the net investment demand curve lies to the right; net investment will be greater at any given rate of interest. If the interest rate falls from R_2 to R_1 and income simultaneously increases from Y_2 to Y_3, net investment will increase from I_2 to I_3. Hence, in addition to the decrease in the interest rate stimulating net investment demand, the simultaneous increase in income further stimulates net investment.

The relationships among the rate of interest, capital demand, and net investment demand is not as simple as the foregoing implies, but for the skeleton model they will suffice. These relationships will be expanded in Chapter 11. We may now add the net investment equation (4.2.9) and Fig. 4.2.2 to the summary page.

SUMMARY PAGE

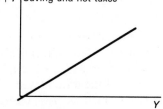

$S+T$ | Saving and net taxes

Y

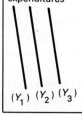

R | Investment and government expenditures

(Y_1) (Y_2) (Y_3)

$I+G$

Equations

1. $S+T = -a_0 + a_1 t_0 + (1-a_1 + a_1 t_1) Y$

2. $I+G = b_0 + G + b_1 Y - b_2 R$

4.3   GOVERNMENT EXPENDITURES AND FINANCE

At every political level governments purchase new goods and services such as war materials, transportation, schools, and highways. Governments also disburse money for purposes other than new goods and services, for example, to provide transfer payments to farmers, the poor, and the unemployed.

Government expenditures are financed externally by three basic means, tax revenues, borrowing from the public, and creating new money. Governments may finance expenditures through taxation, the influence of which was illustrated in Section 4.1. Governments, particularly the federal government, may also elect to finance expenditures up to the limit imposed by Congress by incurring a deficit. Deficit spending is merely spending financed by going into debt. The government can issue certificates of debt or bonds. These bonds are simply government I.O.U.s. The Treasury may sell the bonds directly to commercial banks and the nonbank public. Or the Treasury may sell the bonds to the Federal Reserve Banking System. When the Federal Reserve accepts those bonds it can do two things with them. First, it can sell them to the public. This effectively means that money is borrowed from the public to finance government expenditures. Second, the Federal Reserve can hold on to the bonds. This effectively means that the Federal Reserve creates a demand deposit (a checking account) for the federal government in exchange for the bonds. The second alternative is called monetizing the

FIGURE 4.3.1

Derivation of the Investment Plus Government Expenditures Curve

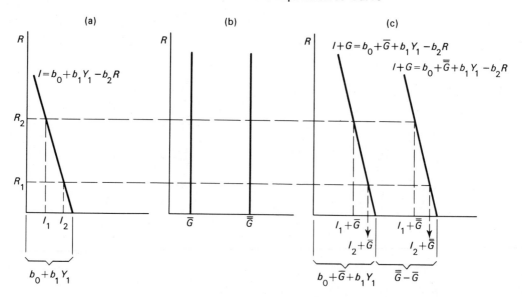

debt; the result is not only increases in government spending and debt but net increases in the stock of money since demand deposits are one component of the stock of money.

Although government expenditures are partly induced by changes in the level of income, we may reasonably assume that they are primarily exogenous. To simplify our graphical representation of the economy, let us combine government and investment spending into one equation and one diagram of the model.

Figure 4.3.1(a) shows the investment function (4.2.9) described in the previous section for a level of income, Y_1. Figure 4.3.1(b) shows that government expenditures are given at some value $\bar{G}$ and invariant with respect to the market rate of interest. By horizontally summing the quantities of investment and government spending at all rates of interest, we may derive the $I + \bar{G}$ curve shown in Fig. 4.1.1(c). For example, at the rate of interest R_2, investment would be I_1 and government expenditures would be $\bar{G}$. The sum of $I + G = I_1 + \bar{G}$, as shown in Fig. 4.3.1(c) for $R = R_2$. Similarly, for $R = R_1$, investment plus government spending is $I_2 + \bar{G}$. For each level of income there is an investment curve. Hence, there are a host of $I + G$ curves, one for every level of income.

An alternative way of deriving the $I + G$ curve is to add exogenous government spending to the investment function (4.2.9),

$$I = b_0 + b_1 Y - b_2 R$$

and obtain

$$I + G = b_0 + G + b_1 Y - b_2 R \qquad (4.3.1)$$

The $I + G$ equation may then be plotted for any given level of income by varying the values of R and calculating corresponding values of $I + G$. If income is Y_1 and government spending increases from $\bar{G}$ to $\bar{\bar{G}}$, the $I + G$ curve will shift to the right. The horizontal distance between the old and new $I + G$ curve at any given rate of interest equals $\bar{\bar{G}} - \bar{G}$ as measured along the horizontal axis; e.g., in Fig. 4.3.1, $I + G = I_1 + \bar{G}$ at $R = R_2$ and $I + G = I_2 + \bar{\bar{G}}$ at $R = R_1$. Furthermore, since there is an investment schedule for each level of income (see Fig. 4.2.2), it follows that there is an $I + G$ schedule for each level of income.

As we shall see more clearly in a later section, changes in government spending changes the level of income. Shifts in the $I + G$ curve occur with initial changes in government expenditures. And further shifts occur due to the secondary effect of a change in income which results from the initial change in government expenditures. Figure 4.3.2 shows an increase in government expenditures from $\bar{G}$ to $\bar{\bar{G}}$. The $I + G$ curve initially shifts from $I + G$ to $(I + G)'$ where the change in government expenditures is measured

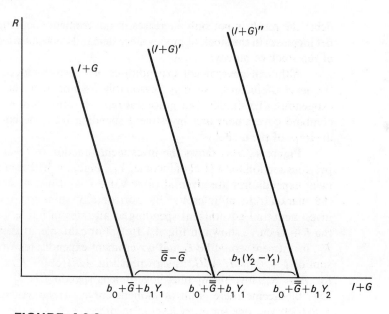

FIGURE 4.3.2

Investment Plus Government Expenditures Curve

on the horizontal axis by $\bar{\bar{G}} - \bar{G}$. If government expenditures increase income from Y_1 to Y_2, the $I + G$ curve will again shift to $(I + G)''$; the difference between the horizontal intercepts is $b_1(Y_2 - Y_1)$, as shown in Fig. 4.3.2. Thus, the total increase in $I + G$ for any given rate of interest is $\bar{\bar{G}} - \bar{G} + b_1(Y_2 - Y_1)$.

We may now replace the investment equation and diagram with the $I + G$ equation and diagram on the summary page of the skeleton model and proceed in the next section to discuss foreign expenditures.

4.4 FOREIGN EXPENDITURES

Foreign expenditures on exports of goods and services produced domestically are the smallest purchasing component of the U.S. economy; they account for only 4–6 percent of the total expenditures. In other economies the volume of export expenditures ranges from 10 percent of total expenditures to more than 35 percent. Despite its relatively small percentage in some economies, export expenditures have an important influence on the level of income in all market economies.

Export expenditures depend on domestic prices and interest rates relative to foreign prices and interest rates, tariff and trade policies between

SUMMARY PAGE

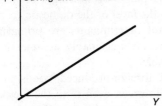

$S+T$ | Saving and net taxes

Y

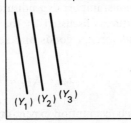

R | Investment expenditures

(Y_1) (Y_2) (Y_3)

I

Equations

1. $S+T = -a_0 + a_1 t_0 + (1-a_1+a_1 t_1)\, Y$

2. $I = b_0 + b_1 Y - b_2 R$

trading economies, foreign exchange rates, surpluses or shortages between trading economies, foreigners' incomes, and the level of the domestic economy's imports. Some of the more important determinants are primarily determined by external factors. Hence, we may reasonably assume that export expenditures, X, is an exogenous variable.

Domestic expenditures on imports of foreign-produced goods and services are determined by similar factors. However, even if all the factors mentioned were to remain unchanged, import expenditures, IM, would largely depend on the level of income, Y, in the domestic economy. Since income is endogenous, import expenditures are endogenous.

The expenditures discussed in the preceding sections are those for both domestic and foreign goods and services. That is, the consumption function (4.1.9),

$$C = a_0 - a_1 t_0 + a_1(1 - t_1)Y \tag{4.4.1}$$

implicitly includes consumption expenditures for both foreign and domestic goods and services. The foreign (f) and domestic (d) components are explicit if we rewrite,

$$C = C_d + C_f$$
$$= (a_0^d + a_0^f) - (a_1^d + a_1^f)t_0 + (a_1^d + a_1^f)(1 - t_1)Y \tag{4.4.2}$$

where

$$C_d = a_0^d - a_1^d t_0 + a_1^d(1 - t_1)Y \tag{4.4.3}$$

and

$$C_f = a_0^f - a_1^f t_0 + a_1^f(1 - t_1)Y \tag{4.4.4}$$

The marginal propensity to consume domestic goods $dC_d/dY = a_1^d(1 - t_1)$, and the marginal propensity to consume foreign goods

$$\frac{dC_f}{dY} = a_1^f(1 - t_1)$$

The investment function (4.2.9),

$$I = b_0 + b_1 Y - b_2 R \tag{4.4.5}$$

can be rewritten as

$$I = I_d + I_f = (b_0^d + b_0^f) + (b_1^d + b_1^f)Y - b_2 R \tag{4.4.6}$$

where

$$I_d = b_0^d + b_1^d Y - b_2 R \tag{4.4.7}$$

and

$$I_f = b_0^f + b_1^f Y \tag{4.4.8}$$

Government expenditures are best considered exogenous with domestic and foreign goods components, $G = G_d + G_f$.

Total import expenditures are implicitly considered as both endogenously determined by domestic income and exogenously by government expenditures. The import expenditure, IM, function,

$$\begin{aligned} IM &= C_f + I_f + G_f \\ &= a_0^f - a_1^f t_0 + b_0^f + G_f + (a_1^f(1 - t_1) + b_1^f)Y \end{aligned} \tag{4.4.9}$$

is simply the sum of the consumption (4.4.4), investment (4.4.8), and government spending, G_f, components of domestic import expenditures. Figure 4.4.1 shows the import expenditure function. Import expenditures are on the vertical axis, and income is measured on the horizontal axis. Where $G_f = \bar{G}_f$, $t_0 = \bar{t}_0$, and $t_1 = \bar{t}_1$ the vertical axis intercept is $a_0^f - a_1^f \bar{t}_0 + b_0^f + \bar{G}_f$ and the slope of the import expenditure function or marginal propensity to spend on imports, $dIM/dY = a_1^f(1 - \bar{t}_1) + b_1^f$.

If we superimpose onto Fig. 4.4.1 an exogenous value of foreign expenditures on exports produced domestically, $X = \bar{X}$, we can identify the level of income sufficient to achieve the import-export expenditure balance. If the level of income is Y_1, then export expenditures outweigh import

FIGURE 4.4.1

Import Expenditures Function

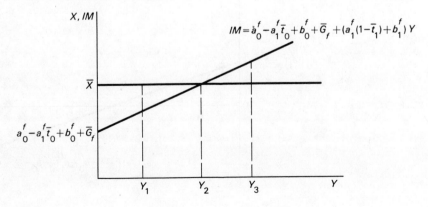

expenditures. If income is Y_3, import expenditures are greater than export expenditures.

Since consumption, investment, and government spending implicitly include components of import expenditure, we need only add net foreign expenditures, $F = X - IM$, to other expenditures such that

$$Y = C + I + G + F$$

That is, since $C + I + G$ overstates expenditures on domestically produced goods and services by a lump sum, IM, and understates them by X, we must add F to obtain total expenditures on domestic goods and services. By substracting the import expenditure function (4.4.9) from export expenditures, X, we derive

$$F = X - IM$$
$$= X - a_0^f + a_1^f t_0 - b_0^f - G_f - (a_1^f(1 - t_1) + b_1^f)Y \quad (4.4.10)$$

the net foreign expenditure function.

Figure 4.4.2 shows the net foreign expenditure function for given values of the parameters and exogenous variables. Net foreign expenditures are measured on the vertical axis and income on the horizontal axis. The slope of the net foreign expenditure function or the marginal propensity to net export is $dF/dY = -(a_1^f(1 - \bar{t}_1) + b_1^f)$. The vertical intercept is $\bar{X} - a_0^f + a_1^f \bar{t}_0 - b_0^f - \bar{G}_f$. Note that the net foreign expenditure function is the vertical difference between the export and import expenditures for any given level of income shown in Fig. 4.4.1. If $Y = Y_1$, export expenditures exceed

FIGURE 4.4.2

Net Export Expenditures Function

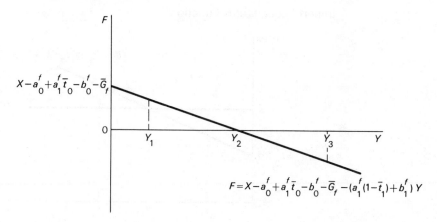

import expenditures and $F > 0$; if $Y = Y_3$, import expenditures exceed export expenditures and $F < 0$; if $Y = Y_2$, import and export expenditures are equal and $F = 0$.

We can combine investment, government, and net foreign expenditures into one equation and one diagram. By recognizing the foreign and domestic components of expenditures we can add the $I + G$ function (4.3.1) to the net foreign expenditure function (4.4.10),

$$I + G + F = b_0^d - a_0^f + a_1^f t_0 + G_d + X + (b_1^d - a_1^f (1 - t_1)) Y - b_2 R$$

$$(4.4.11)$$

Figure 4.4.3 shows the relationship between $I + G + F$ and R for increasing levels of income Y_1 to Y_2 to Y_3 and for given values of the exogenous variables, G and X. Increases (decreases) in income for any given combination of values for the interest rate, export expenditures, and government spending will increase (decrease) net total expenditures (investment and import expenditures) as long as $b_1^d > a_1^f (1 - t_1)$. For any given interest rate and income level, increases (decreases) in government and/or export expenditures increase (decrease) total expenditures; i.e., the $I + G + F$ curve shifts rightward (leftward). The slopes of the I, $I + G$, and $I + G + F$ relationships with respect to the rate of interest are the same.

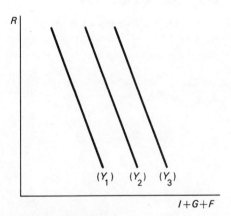

FIGURE 4.4.3

Investment Plus Government Plus
Net Foreign Expenditures Curve

Now replace the $I + G$ curve on the summary page with the $I + G + F$ curve and proceed to the next section where we shall interrelate it with the $S + T$ curve.

SUMMARY PAGE

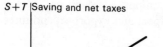

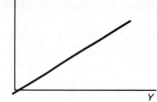

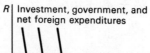

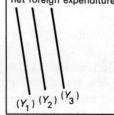

Equations

1. $S+T = -a_0 + a_1 t_0 + (1-a_1+a_1 t_1)Y$

2. $I+G+F = b_0^d - a_0^f + a_1^f t_0 + G_d + X$
$$+ (b_1^d - a_1^f(1-t_1))Y - b_2 R$$

4.5 INCOME-EXPENDITURES EQUILIBRIUM

By now you should have some basic understanding of the determinants of aggregate expenditures. Until we develop a theory of aggregate supply we shall assume that producers merely accommodate the quantity of income demanded in the economy by generating changes in income from output supplied so that individuals may realize intended expenditures. Thus,

$$Y = C + S + T \qquad (4.5.1)$$

As the income-expenditures relationships explained in this chapter interact, aggregate income and intended aggregate expenditures tend toward the equality

$$Y = C + I + G + F \qquad (4.5.2)$$

or

$$C + S + T = C + I + G + F \qquad (4.5.3)$$

If $C + S + T > C + I + G + F$, income is greater than the intended expenditures of consumers, investors, and foreigners. Producers have built up excess inventories of goods and services that are greater than the demand for those goods and services. Hence, there is an excess supply of income. Producers will cut back production until those excess inventories are depleted. *For a given rate of interest*, income will fall until individuals just realize intended expenditures. If $C + S + T < C + I + G + F$, income is less than intended expenditures. Hence, there is an excess demand for income. Producers will increase their production of goods and services to satisfy the excess demand. *For a given rate of interest*, the increased production will generate the income necessary to realize the intended expenditures.

In Eq. (4.5.2) by subtracting consumption from both sides of the equation,

$$Y - C = I + G + F \qquad (4.5.4)$$

Recognizing that income not consumed is saving and net taxes and substituting $S + T$ into (4.5.4) gives

$$S + T = I + G + F \qquad (4.5.5)$$

an alternative form of the income-expenditures equality (4.5.2). Alternatively, we could have canceled out consumption on both sides of (4.5.3) to obtain the same thing.

Figure 4.5.1 illustrates the equality (4.5.5). At all points along the 45°

line from the origin, $S + T$ on the vertical axis just equals $I + G + F$ on the horizontal axis. At all points below the 45° line $S + T < I + G + F$. For example, at point A, $(S + T)_1 < (I + \bar{G} + F)_2$. Intended investment, government, and net foreign expenditures exceed the income that is not consumed. Producers will increase production and thereby income until individuals can consume, save, and pay sufficient net taxes to realize total intended expenditures. Since investment and net foreign expenditures are positively related to income, as income increases, so will total intended expenditures. Hence, *for a given interest rate*, the economy will move toward some point to the right of *a* on the income-expenditures equilibrium curve as indicated by the arrows.

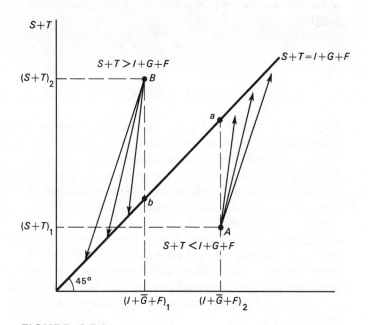

FIGURE 4.5.1

Income-Expenditures Equilibrium

At all points above the 45° line $S + T > I + G + F$. For example, at point B, $(S + T)_2 > (I + G + F)_1$. Producers are producing unintended inventories such that income exceeds intended expenditures. Producers will cut back production until those unintended inventories are disposed of; income falls. Since income and expenditures are positively related, expenditures will decrease as well. *For any given interest rate*, the economy will move toward some point to the left of *b* on the income-expenditures equilibrium curve as indicated by the arrows. Thus, the income-expenditures sector is not in equilibrium until $S + T = I + G + F$.[3]

Now place the equality and Fig. 4.5.1 on the summary page and proceed with the next section where a condensed version of the income-expenditures sector is illustrated.

4.6 THE *IS* SCHEDULE

We may derive an alternative picture of the income-expenditures sector. The purpose is simple. It will be more convenient to interrelate this sector with the rest of the model if we condense it into one equation. The condensed version is called the *IS* schedule and it is defined as a locus of points representing combinations of interest rates and income levels, all of which satisfy the income-expenditures equilibrium condition, $S + T = I + G + F$.

Figure 4.6.1 graphically shows the derivation of the *IS* schedule. If income is Y_1, the $S + T$ curve in the upper left-hand quadrant shows that $(S + T)_1$ is saving plus net taxes. If the income-expenditures equilibrium condition is to be satisfied, investment, government, and net foreign expenditures must be $(I + G + F)_1$, as indicated in the upper right-hand quadrant. If income is Y_1, for expenditures to be $(I + G + F)_1$ the interest rate must be R_2, as shown in the lower right-hand quadrant. Hence, (Y_1, R_2) is a combination of an interest rate and level of income which satisfies the income-expenditures equilibrium condition, $(S + T)_1 = (I + G + F)_1$. The combination can be mapped into the lower left-hand quadrant. If investment and net foreign expenditures were *not* functions of income, (Y_2, R_1) would be another combination of an income level and an interest rate which satisfies the equilibrium condition, $(I + G + F)_2 = (S + T)_2$. This combination is also mapped in the lower left-hand quadrant. Together with other such combinations the *IS'* locus or schedule is formed.

But since investment and net foreign expenditures depend on income, the $I + G + F$ curve shifts when income changes. If the level of Y is Y_3, the corresponding interest rate is R_1, where $(S + T)_3 = (I + G + F)_3$. Thus, the condensed version of the income-expenditures sector is more horizontal,

---

[3] We have briefly explained adjustments to equilibrium in the income-expenditure sector of our model in terms of changes in income and intended expenditures for a given interest rate. As we shall soon see, the interest rate is an endogenous variable and it changes when the income-expenditure sector is not in equilibrium. Thus, in Fig. 4.5.1. adjustments from positions above or below the 45° line can involve several combinations of change in income and intended expenditures. Depending on the relative influences of changes in income and the interest rate on expenditures, net adjustments from position *A* may be to positions on the 45° line to the right or left of *a* and from *B* to positions to the left or right of *b*. In Chapters 5 and 6 we shall explore the possibilities more thoroughly.

SUMMARY PAGE

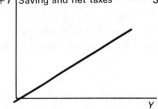

$S+T$ | Saving and net taxes

Y

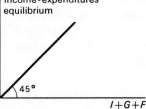

$S+T$ | Income-expenditures equilibrium

45°

$I+G+F$

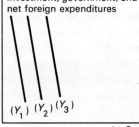

R | Investment, government, and net foreign expenditures

(Y_1) (Y_2) (Y_3)

$I+G+F$

Equations

1.　$S+T = -a_0 + a_1 t_0 + (1 - a_1 + a_1 t_1) Y$

2.　$I+G+F = b_0^d - a_0^f + a_1^f t_0 + G_d + X$
$$+ (b_1^d - a_1^f (1 - t_1)) \ Y - b_2 R$$

3.　$S+T = I+G+F$

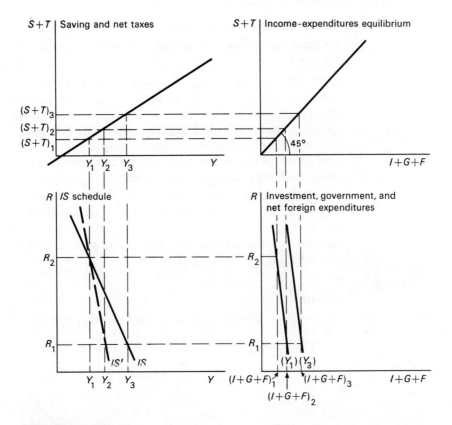

FIGURE 4.6.1

Derivation of the *IS* Schedule

as shown by *IS* in the lower left-hand quadrant. Note that the greater the influence of income on $I + F$, the more responsive income is to changes in the interest rate.

Alternatively, the *IS* schedule can be derived algebraically. Equating the $S + T$ (4.1.11) and the $I + G + F$ (4.4.11) curves and solving for Y in terms of R gives

$$Y = \frac{b_0^d + a_0^d - a_1^d t_0}{1 - a_1^d + a_1^d t_1 - b_1^d} + \frac{1}{1 - a_1^d + a_1^d t_1 - b_1^d} X$$

$$+ \frac{1}{1 - a_1^d + a_1^d t_1 - b_1^d} G_d - \frac{b_2}{1 - a_1^d + a_1^d t_1 - b_1^d} R \quad (4.6.1)$$

the equation for the *IS* curve which was graphically derived in Fig. 4.6.1.

Any changes in the exogenous variables of the income-expenditures sector will change the *IS* schedule as well. For example, suppose that domestic government expenditures increased from $\bar{G}_d$ to $\bar{\bar{G}}_d$. As shown in Fig. 4.6.2 the $I + G + F$ curve shifts from $(Y_1)\bar{G}_d$ to $(Y_1)\bar{\bar{G}}_d$, and the *IS* schedule shifts from $IS'\bar{G}_d$ to $IS''\bar{\bar{G}}_d$. At any given interest rate, say R_1, $I + G + F$ increases to $(I + G + F)_2$. However, for any given interest rate a shift in the $I + G + F$ curve due to the increase in government expenditures increases income as well. Thus, the complete increase in $I + G + F$ depends not only on the increase in government expenditures but also on the responsiveness of net import and investment spending to changes in income. In the lower left-hand quadrant income increases to Y_2 and the complete shift in the $I + G + F$ curve is from $Y_1\bar{G}_d$ to $Y_2\bar{\bar{G}}_d$ in the lower right-hand quadrant of Fig. 4.6.2. At the interest rate, R_1, $I + G + F$ increases from $(I + G + F)_1$ to $(I + G + F)_3$. Similarly, we can show graphically the influence of changes in export expenditures and the tax parameters on the *IS* schedule. Do it.

FIGURE 4.6.2

Effect of an Increase in Government Expenditures on the *IS* Schedule

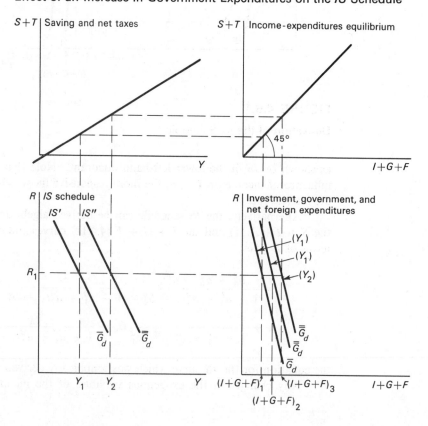

There is an easier way of determining the effect of changes in the exogenous variables on the *IS* curve. If we wish to know what will happen to income for every interest rate given that only domestic government expenditures increase (decrease), we take a partial derivative of the *IS* curve, Eq. (4.6.1),

$$\frac{\partial Y}{\partial G_d} = \frac{1}{1 - a_1^d + a_1^d t_1 - b_1^d}$$

For any given interest rate income increases (decreases) given an increase (decrease) in domestic government spending by the factor of $1/1 - a_1^d + a_1^d t_1 - b_1^d$. The *IS* curve shifts to the right (left).

Similarly,

$$\frac{\partial Y}{\partial X} = \frac{1}{1 - a_1^d + a_1^d t_1 - b_1^d}$$

Increases (decreases) in net foreign expenditures increase (decrease) income for any given interest rate. The *IS* curve shifts rightward (leftward). Furthermore, by differentiating income with respect to any of the parameters in the *IS* equation, e.g., the tax rate, t_1, or the fixed tax, t_0, we are able to show what the change in income will be for any given rate of interest. Convince yourself by doing it.

We may now add the *IS* diagram in Fig. 4.6.2 to the summary page. The *IS* schedule does not represent additional information. It is merely a condensed version of the structural equations of the model already presented. It is an alternative picture of the income-expenditures sector of the model.

4.7 SUMMARY

The income-expenditures sector of our skeleton model is now complete in terms of words, diagrams, and equations. The sector is interrelated as well. Income is supplied by producers of goods and services in exchange for factor input services into the production process. Factor services are owned by individuals in the economy who consume, save, and pay net taxes depending on the amount of income they receive. However, income may not equal intended expenditures. Government and export expenditures are assumed to be exogenous. Intended consumption and import expenditures depend primarily on income, and intended investment depends not only on income but also on the interest rate (the opportunity cost of investment). Changes in income and the interest rate (and, therefore, intended expenditures) will occur until income generated from output supply is sufficient to realize intended expenditures generated by output demand.

SUMMARY PAGE

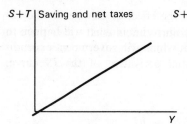

$S+T$ | Saving and net taxes

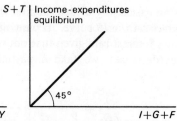

$S+T$ | Income-expenditures equilibrium

45°

$I+G+F$

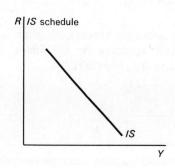

R | IS schedule

IS

Y

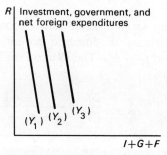

R | Investment, government, and net foreign expenditures

(Y_1) (Y_2) (Y_3)

$I+G+F$

Equations

1. $S+T = -a_0 + a_1 t_0 + (1 - a_1 + a_1 t_1) Y$

2. $I+G+F = b_0^d - a_0^f + a_1^f t_0 + G_d + X$
    $+ (b_1^d - a_1^f (1 - t_1)) Y - b_2 R$

3. $S+T = I+G+F$

Since the primary determinants of the endogenous variables of the income-expenditures sector are income and the interest rate, there are various combinations of the two variables which will satisfy the equilibrium condition. A locus of such combinations is called the *IS* schedule. Just as changes in the exogenous variables of the model change the income and intended expenditure relationships, so will they change the *IS* schedule.

For any given interest rate increases in government or export spending and/or decreases in the tax parameters will shift the *IS* schedule rightward and thereby increase income. Conversely, decreases in government and export spending and/or increases in the tax parameters will have the opposite result.

REVIEW QUESTIONS

1. Given: $C = a_0 + a_1 DY$

   $T = t_0 + t_1 Y$

   (a) Derive the saving plus net taxes equation.
   (b) What is the marginal propensity to save from national income?
   (c) Assume the value of consumption if disposable income were zero is $50, the *MPC* is .5, fixed net taxes are $10, the marginal rate of net taxation is .1, and national income is $1000. How much will individuals consume, save, and pay in net taxes?
   (d) If the marginal rate of net taxation is increased from .1 to .2, what will be the change in consumption, saving, and net taxes for a given level of national income, $1000?

2. The Pot Corporation takes as given three investment projects each with a two year discounted life where:

Project	Expected Return per Period	Cost
A	$ 5.00	$ 8.68
B	$10.00	$10.00
C	$ 4.00	$ 7.43

   If the interest rate is 10 percent, calculate the present value of each project; then calculate the *MEI* of each project. How much investment will be undertaken? If the interest rate falls to 5 percent what will be the change in investment?

3. Assume firms X, Y, and Z are the only three firms in the economy. The costs and *MEI*s of the investment projects each firm is considering are given below:

Firm X			Firm Y			Firm Z		
Project	Cost	MEI	Project	Cost	MEI	Project	Cost	MEI
1	$ 800	.11	1	$700	.13	1	$1000	.10
2	$1200	.08	2	$800	.08	2	$ 800	.12
						3	$1200	.05

(a) On a sheet of graph paper draw the *MEI* curve for each firm and the aggregate *MEI* curve.
(b) At the different interest rates shown in the table below, calculate the amount of investment that will be undertaken by each firm individually and all three firms aggregately.

Rates of Interest

	.15	.13	.11	.06
Firm X				
Y				
Z				
All Firms				

4. Given $I + G = b_0 + b_1 Y - b_2 R + G$ where $b_0 = \$150$, $b_1 = .3$, $b_2 = \$2000$, $G = \$250$, $Y = \$1000$, $R = .09$

(a) Calculate investment and investment plus government expenditures.
(b) If national income increases to \$1200 and the interest rate increases to 10 percent, what will happen to investment?
(c) Using the information in this problem and the information given in 1(c), derive and calculate the government spending multiplier. Assume the interest rate is exogenous. What information do multipliers provide?
(d) On a sheet of graph paper draw the $I + G$ curve in this problem when $Y = \$1000$.

5. Given $F = X - a_0^f + a_1^f t_0 - b_0^f - G_f - (a_1^f(1 - t_1) + b_1^f)Y$ where $X = \$119$, $a_0^f = \$10$, $a_1^f = .1$, $t_0 = \$10$, $b_0^f = \$5$, $b_1^f = .01$, $G_f = \$20$, $t_1 = .1$, $Y = \$1000$

(a) Calculate net foreign expenditures and import expenditures.
(b) Given the information in 1(c), 4, and 5(a), show that income equals expenditures.
(c) If income would have exceeded expenditures, would the system be to the right or left of the *IS* schedule? If the interest rate were exogenous, explain the process of adjustment to income-expenditure equilibrium.
(d) Under what condition(s) in the income-expenditure sector will a change in the interest rate leave income unchanged?

SELECTED READINGS

ACKLEY, G., *Macroeconomic Theory*, New York: Macmillan, 1962.

ALLEN, R. G. D., *Macro-Economic Theory*, New York: Macmillan, 1968, Chaps. 2, 4, 6, and 7.

Council of Economic Advisers, "Financing a Federal Deficit," and "Formulating Fiscal Policy," in W. L. Smith and R. L. Teigen (eds.), *Readings in Money, National Income and Stabilization Policy*, Homewood, Ill.: Irwin, 1974, pp. 323–30.

HICKS, J. R., "Mr. Keynes and the Classics," *Econometrica*, 5 (April 1937), 147–59.

KEYNES, J. M., *The General Theory of Employment, Interest and Money*, London: Macmillan, 1936, Chaps. 8, 9, 11, and 12.

LERNER, A. P., *The Economics of Control; Principles of Welfare Economics*, New York: Macmillan, 1944.

MUSGRAVE, R. A., *The Theory of Public Finance*, New York: McGraw-Hill, 1973.

PERRY, G. L., "Consumer Demand in the United States" (a Review Article), *American Economic Review*, 57 (Sept. 1967), 832–40.

SAMUELSON, P. A., "The Simple Mathematics of Income Determination," in L. A. Metzler (ed.), *Essays in Honor of Alvin H. Hansen*, New York: Norton, 1948.

Also see Chapters 10 and 11 of this book.

CHAPTER 5

The Money Market

5.1 MONEY SUPPLY

The Stock of Money

The Board of Governors of the Federal Reserve Banking System (Fed) is located in Washington, D.C. They are the major policy-making officials of the Fed. Each of the seven members, including a chairman, is appointed by the president for a term of 14 years subject to Senate confirmation. The Fed consists of 12 Federal Reserve Banks located in 12 districts across the United States and numerous commercial banks which hold membership in the system. Although the system is owned by the member banks, the primary function of the Fed is to act as the nation's chief monetary authority and to provide the economy with a supply of money consistent with the economic goals of the 1946 Employment Act, e.g., maximum growth, full employment of resources, price stability, and a favorable balance of payments.

Money is an asset which serves as the medium of exchange and a store or value. It consists of coin and currency held by the nonbank public and demand deposits (checking accounts) held by commercial banks. That is,

$$MS = C^P + DD \qquad (5.1.1)$$

where MS is the money stock, C^P is coin and currency, and DD is demand deposits. Other assets such as saving deposits are not included in our definition of money since generally they must first be converted into either coin, currency, or demand deposits before they are acceptable in exchange for goods and services.

As we shall soon demonstrate, money is created by the banking system. It is generated from base or high-powered money. Base money can be defined in terms of those who hold base money. That is,

$$B = C^P + \text{RES} \tag{5.1.2}$$

where B is base money, C^P is coin and currency held by the nonbank public, and RES is the total unborrowed reserves held by commercial banks.

Unborrowed reserves are simply the total amount of base money commercial banks hold against their total deposit liabilities less borrowed reserves. They are required by the Fed to hold reserves against both demand deposits and time deposits, TD (required reserves). Further, they may hold reserves in excess of requirements (excess reserves) as well as borrowing additional reserves. Thus, by definition

$$\text{RES} = \text{RRD} + \text{RRT} + ER - BR \tag{5.1.3}$$

where RRD is total required reserves held against demand deposits, RRT is total required reserves held against time deposits, ER is total excess reserves held by commercial banks, and BR is the borrowed reserves of commercial banks. The difference between ER and BR is called net free reserves.

The required reserves held against demand deposits is a percent, r_D, of demand deposits,

$$\text{RRD} = r_D DD \tag{5.1.4}$$

and the required reserves held against time deposits is a percent, r_T, of time deposits,

$$\text{RRT} = r_T TD \tag{5.1.5}$$

The reserves held in excess of what is required can be expressed as a percent, e, of total deposit liabilities,

$$ER = e(DD + TD) \tag{5.1.6}$$

Also, borrowed reserves can be expressed as a percent, br, of total deposit liabilities,

$$BR = br(DD + TD) \tag{5.1.7}$$

By subtracting (5.1.6) from (5.1.7) we see that net free reserves can be expressed as a percent, $e - br$, of total deposit liabilities,

$$ER - BR = (e - br)(DD + TD) \tag{5.1.8}$$

The percents r_D and r_T are called the required reserve ratios on demand deposits and time deposits, respectively. The percents, e, br, and $e - br$ are called the excess reserve, the borrowed reserve, and the net free reserve ratios, respectively. By substituting Eqs. (5.1.4), (5.1.5), (5.1.6), and (5.1.8) into (5.1.3) we derive an alternative expression for total unborrowed reserves (hereafter called total reserves),

$$\text{RES} = r_D DD + r_T TD + (e - br)(DD + TD) \qquad (5.1.9)$$

Some bank customers will deposit cash and checks drawn on other banks, while others will withdraw cash from their deposits, either directly or by a check drawn on their bank. Normally, the volume of withdrawals and deposits are approximately equal in a time period. Because only a portion of the deposit liabilities of banks are required by the Fed to be held in reserve, banks may make loans to the public. It is this fractional reserve system which permits the banking system to create money.

A naive version of the money creation process assumes that public preference for currency and time deposits is constant, $C^P = \bar{C}^P$ and $TD = \overline{TD}$. Furthermore, it assumes that banks will loan out all excess reserves (stay "loaned up") and do not borrow any reserves so that the net free reserve ratio is zero. This means that Eq. (5.1.9) becomes

$$\text{RES} = r_D DD + r_T \overline{TD} \qquad (5.1.10)$$

Solving (5.1.2) for total reserves,

$$\text{RES} = B - \bar{C}^P \qquad (5.1.11)$$

equating like terms in (5.1.10) and (5.1.11), and solving for DD gives

$$DD = \frac{-\bar{C}^P}{r_D} - \frac{r_T \overline{TD}}{r_D} + \frac{B}{r_D} \qquad (5.1.12)$$

By substituting (5.1.12) into (5.1.1)

$$MS = \left(1 - \frac{1}{r_D}\right)\bar{C}^P - \frac{r_T \overline{TD}}{r_D} + \frac{B}{r_D} \qquad (5.1.13)$$

or since (5.1.2) states that $B = C^P + \text{RES}$,

$$MS = \bar{C}^P - \frac{r_T \overline{TD}}{r_D} + \frac{\text{RES}}{r_D} \qquad (5.1.14)$$

Thus, the money stock equation can be expressed in terms of base money or in terms of total reserves because total reserves are a component of base money. Base money and total reserves differ by a constant, $\bar{C}^P$. If we wish to know the change in the stock of money in a time period given only a change in base money or a change in total reserves, we may partially differentiate either (5.1.13) or (5.1.14). Let us work with (5.1.14) for now, where

$$\frac{\partial MS}{\partial \mathrm{RES}} = \frac{1}{r_D} \tag{5.1.15}$$

or

$$\partial MS = \frac{1}{r_D}\,\partial \mathrm{RES} \tag{5.1.16}$$

Given a change in total reserves, the change in the stock of money depends on the reciprocal of the required reserve ratio on demand deposits. Thus, in a time period $1/r_D$ is the total reserve as well as the base money multiplier, i.e., the multiple at which changes in total reserves or base money change the stock of money. The Fed can change the stock of money by effecting changes in the total reserve position of commercial banks. If, for example, $r_D = .25$ and there is a discrete change in reserves by $\Delta \mathrm{RES} = \$10$ million,

$$\Delta MS = \frac{1}{.25}\,\$10\ \text{million} = \$40\ \text{million}$$

Moreover, the Fed can change the stock of money for a given level of total reserves by changing only the required reserve ratio on demand deposits. By partially differentiating (5.1.14) with respect to $1/r_D$,

$$\frac{\partial MS}{\partial(1/r_D)} = -r_T\overline{TD} + \mathrm{RES} \tag{5.1.17}$$

or

$$\partial MS = (\mathrm{RES} - r_T\overline{TD})\,\partial\frac{1}{r_D} \tag{5.1.18}$$

If, for example, $\mathrm{RES} = \$10$ million, $r_T = .1$, and $\overline{TD} = \$1$ million and the Fed decreases r_D from .25 to .2, $\Delta(1/r_D) = 1$ and

$$\Delta MS = (\$10\ \text{million} - .1(\$1\ \text{million}))(1) = \$9.9\ \text{million}[1]$$

---

[1] If we use the money stock equation expressed in terms of base money (5.1.13),

$$\partial MS = -\bar{C}^P\,\partial\frac{1}{r_D} - (r_T\overline{TD})\,\partial\frac{1}{r_D} + B\,\partial\frac{1}{r_D}$$

And in our example the change in the money stock is the same. If $\bar{C}^P = \$1$ million and $\mathrm{RES} = \$10$ million such that $B = \$11$ million and $r_T\overline{TD} = \$.1$ million,

$$\Delta MS = -\$1\ \text{million}(1) - \$.1\ \text{million}(1) + \$11\ \text{million}(1)$$
$$= \$9.9\ \text{million}$$

Changes in only the required reserve ratio on time deposits also change the money stock. Equation (5.1.14) indicates that $\partial MS / \partial r_T = -\overline{TD}(1/r_D)$.

We have stated that the Fed can change the stock of money by effecting changes in total reserves and the required reserve ratios. But how is this accomplished? The Fed has three primary tools at its disposal to effect changes in the stock of money: *open market operations*, *discount policy*, and *changes in reserve requirements*.

Reserve Requirements

The Fed sets the percents of demand and time deposit liabilities that must be held in reserve. A decrease in reserve requirements increases banks' excess reserves and thereby provides inducements for them to expand bank credit. If, for example, the Fed decreases the required reserve ratio on demand deposits, banks can make additional loans even though their total reserves do not change; Eq. (5.1.18) indicates that the money stock will increase by $(RES - r_T \overline{TD}) \, \partial (1/r_D)$. Conversely, increases in the required reserve ratio on demand deposits means that the money stock will decrease by $(RES - r_T \overline{TD}) \, \partial (1/r_D)$.

Discount Policy

The Fed sets the interest rate or discount rate charged to member banks for borrowing at the Federal Reserve Bank in their district. The discount rate is called the cost of member banks borrowing at the Fed. Member banks may have made loans to the public in return for notes or I.O.U.s. If member banks find it profitable or if they find it necessary to borrow funds in case they are caught short of required reserves, they may take acceptable notes to the Fed and borrow. If, for example, the loan value of the note is $100 and the discount rate is 10 percent per annum, the Fed will loan the member bank the $100 for one year less an interest charge of $10 or $100 - $10 = $90. This transaction is called discounting a note. Most borrowing is done by the *advance* technique where the bank borrows on its own note using government securities as collateral.

When the Fed decreases the discount rate, the cost of borrowing is less. And if member banks borrow additional funds, they increase their reserves. As shown in (5.1.16) the money stock will increase by $(1/r_D) \, \partial RES$. When the discount rate is raised, banks are discouraged from borrowing.

Open Market Operations

We have learned by experience that changes in reserve requirements and the discount rate are not the primary tools by which the Fed initiates changes in the stock of money. Changes in reserve requirements have too abrupt an impact on the economy. It is primarily for this reason that this tool of monetary policy is not used as a short-run instrument for changing the money stock. Reserve requirements have been decreased in the long run to increase the potential of the money creation process. Changes in the discount rate are not considered to be an effective tool of monetary policy any more. Historically, banks have been reluctant to borrow from the Fed even when it is profitable to do so. In recent years changes in the discount rate have been used by the Fed to signal future intentions of monetary ease or restraint and to support open market operations.

Open market operations or the buying and selling of mostly government securities by the Fed has proved to be the most desirable and effective means of changing the stock of money. At the trading desk of the Federal Reserve Bank in New York, a team of traders phone the government securities dealers to buy or sell whatever the Fed decides is desirable. The buying and selling of government securities, which are widely held by banks and large corporations, changes the reserve (and base money) position of member banks and thereby provides inducement to create additional bank credit. Banks and other bondholders are not forced to buy or sell. But since the Fed is a large supplier and demander of securities, it can provide inducement for voluntary response through the market. That is, the Fed can either make bonds more or less attractive by varying their profitability to other buyers and sellers.

Figure 5.1.1 summarizes the workings of the government securities market and the means whereby the Fed provides inducement for either buying or selling. Government securities, GS, are on the horizontal axis and the price of government securities, BP, is on the vertical axis. We begin our analysis where an upward-sloped supply curve, S, and a downward-sloped demand curve, D, determine the equilibrium price, BP_2, and the equilibrium quantity of government securities, GS_1.

If the Fed decides to sell government securities, it increases the supply in the market to, say, S'. The price falls to BP_1 and the quantity demanded by banks and others increases to GS_2. Even if securities are not purchased by banks, but rather nonbanks, such as individuals or corporations, the nonbanks pay with checks drawn on commercial banks. Consequently, the sale decreases commercial banks' reserves. Purchasers are encouraged to buy securities because the price of them is lower and the yield higher.[2] Conversely, if the Fed decides to buy securities, it increases the demand for securities to, say, D'. The price rises to BP_3 and the yield on securities falls. Holders of securities are thereby encouraged to increase the quantity supplied in the

---

[2] The price and yield or interest rate on a bond is inversely related. If, for example, you buy a $100 security or bond for $99 maturing in one year at 4 percent interest, you would receive $100 upon maturity plus $4 in interest, making the effective yield about 4.8 percent. If, however, you bought the bond for $101, you would receive $100 upon maturity plus $4 in interest. But the effective yield or rate of interest would be about 2.9 percent.

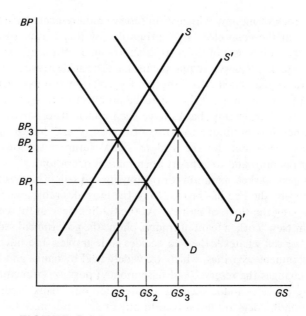

FIGURE 5.1.1

Government Bond Market

market to GS_3. Again, if the Fed buys from nonbanks instead of banks, it pays with checks drawn on itself that are deposited by the seller in commercial banks. Thus, bank reserves increase.

The Money Creation Process

Up to now we have had some idea of what money is, what determines changes in the stock of money in the economy, and the primary tools that the Fed can use to change the money stock. But the actual creation process needs additional illustration. Suppose, for example, that the Fed decides to provide reserves for net additions to the stock of money. In all probability it will use its most important tool, open market operations. More specifically, it will increase its demand for government securities and buy the increase in the quantity supplied which results as the price of securities rises.

Figure 5.1.2 is a flow chart which illustrates the money creation process. The octagon represents the Fed, the boxes represent the commercial banks, and the circles represent members of the nonbank public. We begin with a purchase of government securities, $GS = \$10$ million, by the Fed from bank 1. The purchase leaves bank 1 with additional reserves, $\Delta ER = \$10$ million. Our assumption that banks stay loaned up still holds. So bank 1 creates bank credit, $BC = \$10$ million, in exchange for notes, $N = \$10$ million. Our assumption that public preference for currency and time deposits remains fixed still holds. Let us assume that public 1 spends the money it borrowed and that the money is deposited in bank 2. In return for cash, bank 2 creates a demand deposit, $DD = \$10$ million. Bank 2 is required to hold 20 percent of the deposits received as required reserves,

FIGURE 5.1.2

Flow Chart of the Money Creation Process Given Fed Purchases of Government Securities (millions of dollars)

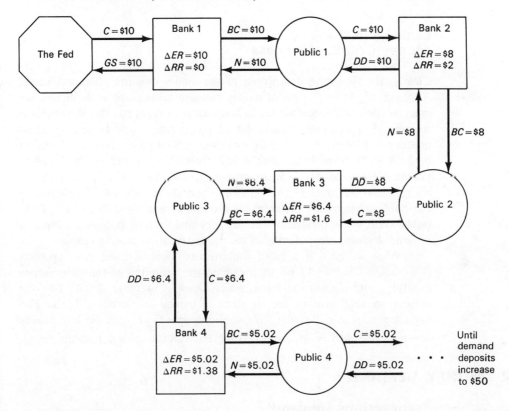

GS = government securities
C = cash
BC = bank credit
N = notes
DD = demand deposits
ER = excess reserves
RR = required reserves

.2 × \$10 million = ΔRR = \$2 million, and is prepared to loan out the change in excess reserves, ΔER = \$8 million. It creates bank credit, BC = \$8 million, in return for notes, N = \$8 million, from public 2. In exchange for cash, bank 3 creates a demand deposit, DD = \$8 million. Bank 3 then holds required reserves, .2 × \$8 million = ΔRR = \$1.6 million, and loans out its change in excess reserves, ΔER = \$6.4 million. In exchange for notes, N = \$6.4 million, from public 3 it creates bank credit, BC = \$6.4 million. The process continues, and demand deposits, a component of money, increase by a multiple of the initial increase in excess reserves. By Eq. (5.1.16), demand deposits (money) increase by $(1/r_D)\,\Delta RES = (1/.2)$ × \$10 million = \$50 million.

Leakage in the Money Creation Process

Clearly, the foregoing description of the money creation process is naive. Although the basic process of money creation takes place as described, we must recognize that member banks hold excess reserves and that they borrow reserves. For example, if bank 4 held excess reserves of 10 percent of its new demand deposits or .1 × \$6.4 million = \$.64 million, then in addition to ΔRR = \$1.38 million, bank 4 will create bank credit of BC = \$4.38 million instead of BC = \$5.20 million. Thus, by banks holding excess reserves, the potential of the expansion process is reduced. Furthermore, the public changes its preference for currency and time deposits. If the public changes its preference for currency and/or time deposits relative to demand deposits, the potential of the money creation process changes.

What we need is a more sophisticated view of the money creation process. In Chapter 13 we shall expand the definition of the base money multiplier and discuss the forces which shape it in more detail. For the present, we shall assume that the stock of money is determined by the Fed and exogenous to our model. We need only specify that the stock of money is some value, $MS = \overline{MS}$, and that the Fed can change it if it so desires.

5.2   MONEY DEMAND

Transactions Demand

Money facilitates the expenditures of income for goods and services offered for sale in the economy. Money is held for transactions purposes because there is a lack of correspondence between money inflows and outflows. Households hold money between paydays and draw down these balances to facilitate expenditures. They purchase such items as food, clothing, and shelter. Similarly, businesses hold money for transactions which occur between receipt of payments for their product and outlays when their bills become due. Money is held for both planned transactions and as a precaution against unexpected circumstances which require unplanned purchases, e.g., auto repairs or doctor bills. Total transactions balances are the sum of unplanned and planned transactions balances.[3]

Money held for both planned and unplanned transactions purposes, MT, primarily depends on the level of income, Y,

$$MT = MT(Y) \tag{5.2.1}$$

Transactions balances are expected to be positively related to income. As income increases, larger numbers and dollar magnitudes of planned transactions generally occur. Moreover, with higher income a person will generally have an increased need to ensure against unplanned transactions.

Professors Baumol and Tobin (see the Selected References) have pointed out that transactions demand is primarily considered a means of facilitating exchange. The inability of individuals to make prompt payments out of transactions balances entails a penalty cost. They can ensure against the penalty by holding larger average cash balances. The price of the insurance is the opportunity cost of holding these balances or the earnings foregone on an alternative short-term asset, such as short-term government bonds. Consequently, the demand for transactions balances entails a choice between a means of payment and the nearest money substitute. The higher the opportunity cost of holding transaction balances, for example, the 30 or 60 day treasury bill rate, the higher the marginal cost of insurance and the less the amount of transactions balances desired. Thus, planned transactions balances depend inversely on the bill rate. Precautionary balances for unplanned transactions are also held for insurance purposes and are therefore influenced by the bill rate in a similar manner.

The Baumol-Tobin type of model may exaggerate the importance of the short-term rate in explaining transactions demand, particularly for planned transactions. The transaction cost of moving in and out of short-term financial investments for very short periods is often too high to be economical. Typically, in modern macromodels the interest elasticity of goods inventories is considered negligible. The interest elasticity of transactions balances (a cash inventory) may be considered negligible as well. Further, the penalty cost of running out of cash instead of being constant may be the cost of utilizing credit or overdraft facilities. The credit or

---

[3] Traditionally the distinction is made between transactions and precautionary balances. However, since precautionary balances are but reserves for unexpected transactions and since their determinants are similar, we shall classify both of them as transaction-motivated.

overdraft rate of interest may vary in proportion to the short-term rate such that the penalty cost of a lack of cash will rise in proportion to the opportunity cost of holding cash.[4] Further, only individuals with large transactions balances would benefit from managing transactions cash in the interest-sensitive manner suggested by the Baumol-Tobin model. But these same individuals are also likely to have credit and overdraft facilities readily available; these facilities reduce their precautionary needs. In an analysis involving the three alternatives of credit, short-term financial investment, and transactions cash, it is not evident that interest elasticity of transactions balances is quantitatively significant.[5] Consequently, our primary consideration of the impact of the interest rate on money demand will be deferred to the next part of this section.

Assume that the transactions money demand function (5.2.1) is proportional to income,

$$MT = g_1 Y \qquad (5.2.2)$$

where in Fig. 5.2.1 the intercept of the transactions money demand curve is zero and the slope is $\partial MT/\partial Y = g_1$. If income is Y_1, the quantity demanded of transactions balances is MT_1. If income increases to Y_2, $MT_2 - MT_1$ additional money will be demanded for transaction purposes.

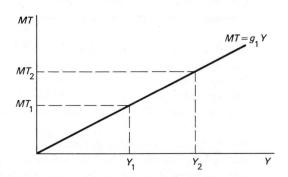

FIGURE 5.2.1

Transactions Money Demand

We may now add the transactions money demand equation (5.2.2) and Fig. 5.2.1 to our summary page of the skeleton model and proceed to a more complete discussion of the influence of the interest rate on the demand for money.

---

[4] One should not confuse money and credit. Credit is a means of intermediate exchange, but only money serves as a means of final exchange. If you doubt this, pay for goods with credit and forget to pay your bill with money. Such action will convince you that money and credit are not the same.
[5] See A. Leijonhufved, *On Keynesian Economics and the Economics of Keynes,* New York: Oxford University Press, Inc., 1968, pp. 358–59.

SUMMARY PAGE

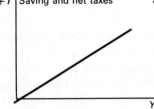

$S+T$ | Saving and net taxes

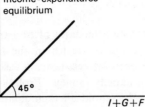

$S+T$ | Income-expenditures equilibrium

45°

$I+G+F$

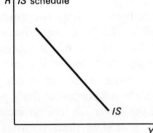

R | IS schedule

IS

Y

R | Investment, government, and net foreign expenditures

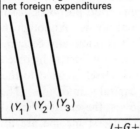

(Y_1) (Y_2) (Y_3)

$I+G+F$

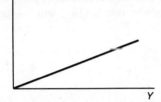

MT | Transactions money demand

Y

Equations

1. $S+T = -a_0 + a_1 t_0 + (1 - a_1 + a_1 t_1)Y$

2. $I+G+F = b_0^d - a_0^f + a_1^f t_0 + \bar{G}_d + X$
   $$+ (b_1^d - a_1^f (1-t_1))Y - b_2 R$$

3. $S+T = I+G+F$

4. $MT = g_1 Y$

81

Asset Demand

Money is not only a medium of exchange but an asset which permits individuals to accumulate wealth in the form of money balances. Financial assets include both interest-bearing assets, such as bonds, and non-interest-bearing assets, namely money. Professor Tobin has shown that individuals will not necessarily hold all their financial assets in excess of transaction requirements in the form of interest-bearing assets. They will hold asset balances in the form of money.

For simplification purposes, assume that there are only two financial assets, money and bonds. Although the capital value of money varies with the price level, it is nominally certain. But the capital value of a bond is uncertain. Bonds earn interest income but expose the holder to risk because the bond price (inversely related to the rate of interest) can rise or fall and thereby create capital gain or loss. The larger the proportion of one's portfolio held in bonds, the greater the risk and the larger the interest income. Thus, risk and interest income are inversely related to the proportion of one's portfolio held in money balances.

A bondholder observes the current price of a particular bond, $1/R$.[6] He is uncertain whether the future price of the bond, $1/R_f$, will go higher or lower. The percentage gain, g, will be

$$g = \frac{1/R_f - 1/R}{1/R} \tag{5.2.3}$$

Tobin assumed that although the actual value of g is given by (5.2.3), its expected value $E(g) = 0$ because a portfolio manager is uncertain about future interest rates with symmetrical expectations of loss or gain.[7] They

---

[6] We assume that a bond is a perpetuity with an annual contract return of $1.

[7] The asset holder has a whole spectrum of expected capital gains (and losses), g. He has an implicit distribution of gains around a mean value, $E(g)$. We assume that $E(g) = 0$. If the probabilities of gain (loss) are normally distributed, a natural measure of risk is

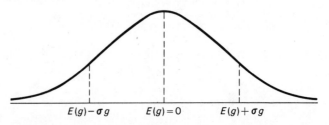

obtained by use of the standard deviation, σg, of the probability distribution. Since two-thirds of the area under the curve is between $E(g) - \sigma g$ and $E(g) + \sigma g$, an asset holder has 66.7 percent chance that the actual value of g will be between $E(g) \pm \sigma g$. For example, if $\sigma g = 2$ percent, the asset holder has a two-thirds chance that actual g will be between -2 and 2 percent.

associate g with a probability distribution which has a mean or expected value equal to zero. The standard deviation about the mean, σg, measures the variability of g. Tobin assumes that σg is an index of the risk of holding one bond.[8]

The nominal value of an individual's asset portfolio, A, equals the sum of money balances, MA, and bonds, B,

$$A = MA + B \qquad (5.2.4)$$

Dividing through by A gives

$$1 = \frac{MA}{A} + \frac{B}{A} \qquad (5.2.5)$$

or

$$1 = m + b \qquad (5.2.6)$$

where m is the proportion of total portfolio held in money and b is the proportion held in bonds. A decision to increase the proportion of asset portfolio held in bonds means the proportion held in money must decrease because $m + b = 1$.

Total return per dollar on an individual's portfolio, TR, will be

$$TR = (R + g)b \qquad (5.2.7)$$

That is, the interest rate plus the capital gain rate times the proportion of portfolio held in bonds is the actual total return on portfolio. Money is not included because holding money yields no return.

Since $E(g) = 0$, Eq. (5.2.7) can be rewritten as

$$E(TR) = R \cdot b \qquad (5.2.8)$$

where TR is associated with a probability distribution which has a mean or expected value, $R \cdot b$, and a standard deviation, σTR, which is used as an index of risk on total portfolio.[9] The foregoing implies that total risk, σTR, is equal to the risk associated with holding one bond, σg, times the proportion of asset portfolio held in bonds, b,

$$\sigma TR = \sigma g \cdot b \qquad (5.2.9)$$

---

[8] Tobin also makes the strong assumption that σg and R are independent. This implies that asset holders feel that any given change in the interest rate is just as probable at low as at high rates of interest.

[9] The standard deviation of the probability distribution associated with total expected return may be interpreted in a manner similar to σg.

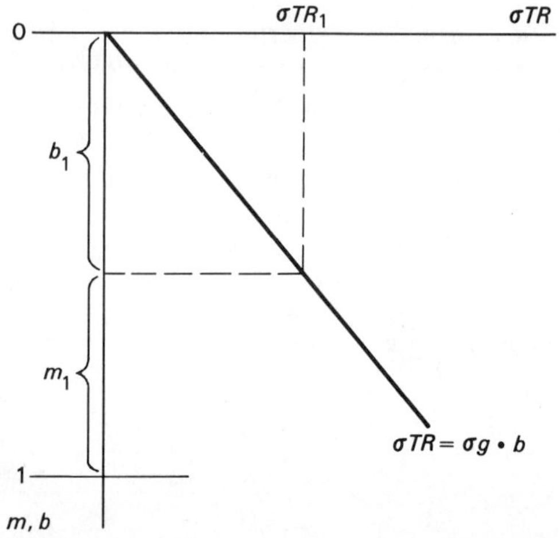

FIGURE 5.2.2

Relationship between Risk and the Proportion of Asset Portfolio Held in Bonds and Money

Both Eqs. (5.2.6) and (5.2.9) are shown in Fig. 5.2.2. Risk on total portfolio, σTR, is on the horizontal axis, and the proportion held in bonds, b, is on the vertical axis; b is constrained between unity and zero and $1 = m + b$. The slope of the relationship between σTR and b is $d\,\sigma TR/db = \sigma g$. If σTR_1 risk is taken, $b = b_1$ and $m = m_1$ such that $b_1 + m_1 = 1$.

We now have a rationale for portfolio decisions once a portfolio manager decides on how much risk to take. But this begs the question—how does he decide how much risk to take?

There are two sides to the decision-making process, the subjective and the objective sides. By solving (5.2.9) for b,

$$b = \frac{1}{\sigma g}\,\sigma TR \tag{5.2.10}$$

and then substituting the results into (5.2.8) we derive

$$E(TR) = \frac{R}{\sigma g}\,\sigma TR \tag{5.2.11}$$

an expression of expected return as a linear function of risk. Given σg, $R/\sigma g$ will be constant at a given interest rate. For example, for $R = R_1$ in Fig. 5.2.3 the slope of the relationship specified in (5.2.11) is $dE(TR)/d\,\sigma TR = (R_1/\sigma g)$. Since the interest rate is given information to the portfolio manager, (5.2.11) is an objective constraint on the decision process. Increases in risk are incurred as the opportunity for expected returns increases.

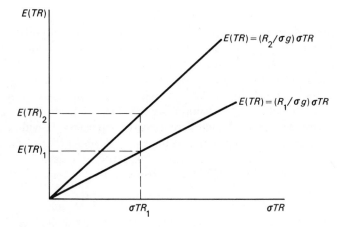

FIGURE 5.2.3

Relationship between Expected Return and Risk

As the interest rate increases, opportunity for higher expected return is associated with any given level of risk. If, for example, the interest rate increases from R_1 to R_2, for $\sigma TR = \sigma TR_1$ the opportunity for expected return is higher, that is, $E(TR)_1 < E(TR)_2$. Conversely, decreases in the rate of interest decrease the slope of the interest rate constraint, and for any given level of risk expected return is less.

The subjective side of the decision-making process can be shown by use of an indifference map. We shall assume that most individuals in the economy are risk averters. That is, the trade-off for any given level of expected satisfaction between risk and expected return is positive or the marginal rate of substitution is greater than zero. If an individual is expected to take additional risk, he must be compensated with higher expected return.

The total expected satisfaction (or utility) function is specified by

$$E(U) = L(E(TR), \sigma TR) \qquad (5.2.12)$$

where $E(U)$ is total expected satisfaction expressed as a function of expected return on asset portfolio and risk. $\partial E(U)/\partial E(TR) > 0$ because increases in expected returns increase expected satisfaction for any given level of risk. $\partial E(U)/\partial\,\sigma TR < 0$ because increases in risk decrease expected satisfaction or increase expected dissatisfaction for every level of expected return. Solving (5.2.12) for expected return in terms of risk and total expected satisfaction yields

$$E(TR) = L^{-1}(E(U), \sigma TR)^{10} \qquad (5.2.13)$$

---

[10] We assume that the hypothesis of the implicit function therein is satisfied so that we may solve (5.2.12) for $E(TR)$ as a function of $E(U)$ and σTR.

For every level of expected satisfaction, we may derive a locus of combinations of expected return and risk among which an individual is indifferent or expecting equal satisfaction; the locus is called an indifference curve. One such curve for $E(U) = E(U)_2$ is shown in Fig. 5.2.4. For each level of expected satisfaction, (5.2.13) can be used to derive an indifference curve, including $E(U)_3 > E(U)_2 > E(U)_1$. The higher the indifference curve, the greater the expected level of satisfaction because for any given level of risk, expected return is greater. An indifference *curve* depicts an individual's preference or willingness to accept combinations of risk and levels of expected return in order to maintain a constant level of expected satisfaction. An indifference *map* shows an individual's preferences at various levels of expected satisfaction.

The indifference curves drawn in Fig. 5.2.4 show that the marginal rate of substituting expected return for risk is greater than zero. The individual is a *risk averter* because he is only willing to take additional risk if expected return increases. But movement along the curves shows that the individual's marginal rate of substitution is increasing. That is, this person requires larger and larger units of expected return if he is to incur additional units of risk. Tobin called this individual a *risk diversifier*. Had the indifference curves been concave from below where the marginal rate of substitution would be decreasing, the person would be willing to accept smaller and smaller units of expected return for additional units of risk. He is a *risk plunger*. Of course, if an individual were a *risk lover*, he would have a marginal rate of substitution less than zero. That is, he would derive positive

FIGURE 5.2.4

Indifference Curves Relating Expected Return on Asset Portfolio and Risk

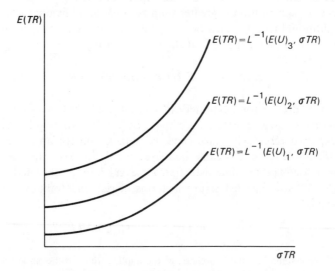

expected satisfaction from taking the risk and would be willing to accept less expected return with additional units of risk.

Although the cases of the risk plunger and risk lover are interesting, in the rest of our analysis we shall assume that people are risk diversifiers. You may want to proceed with the other two assumptions and examine their implications for the theory of money demand. Try it.

Now we are ready to put the subjective indifference map (Fig. 5.2.4) and the objective opportunity constraint (Fig. 5.2.3) together as shown in Fig. 5.2.5. For $R = R_1$ maximum expected satisfaction is achieved where the opportunity constraint is tangent to the indifference curve, $E(U) = E(U)_1$. The equilibrium combination of expected return, $E(TR)_1$, and risk, σTR_1, is the one that the individual is both *able* and *willing* to choose. And $E(U)_1$ is the highest level of expected satisfaction that is attainable given $R = R_1$. If the interest rate increases to R_2, the opportunity constraint pivots upward and a higher level of expected satisfaction, $E(U)_2$, is attainable. The individual is both able and willing to accept $E(TR) = E(TR)_2$ and $\sigma TR = \sigma TR_2$, the expected satisfaction maximizing solution.

We have rationalized a portfolio decision-making process, that is, the proportion of asset portfolio our portfolio manager is both willing and able to hold in money and in bonds. Figure 5.2.5 shows the combinations of

FIGURE 5.2.5

Equilibrium Expected Return on Asset Portfolio and Risk

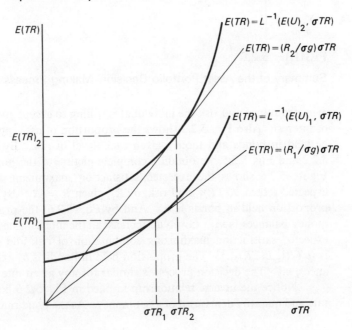

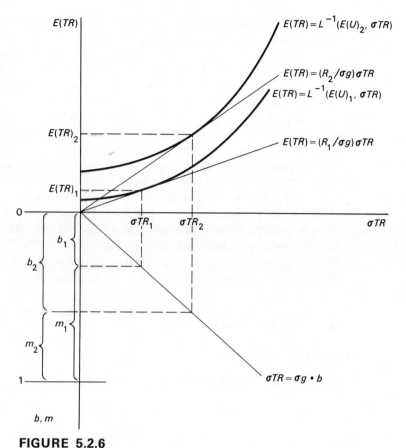

FIGURE 5.2.6

Summary of the Asset Portfolio Decision-Making Process

expected return and risk the individual is willing to accept given various rates of interest. Also Fig. 5.2.2 shows the proportion of asset portfolio that will be held in bonds and money given each level of risk. By combining Fig. 5.2.2 and Fig. 5.2.5, we obtain a complete picture of the portfolio decision. Figure 5.2.6 shows the expected satisfaction maximizing combination of expected return, $E(TR)_1$, and risk, σTR_1, given $R = R_1$. By Eq. (5.2.10) the proportion held in bonds is b_1. And by Eq. (5.2.6) the proportion held in money balances is m_1. Given an increase in the interest rate to $R_2 > R_1$, the expected satisfaction maximizing combination of risk and expected return is $(\sigma TR_2, E(TR)_2)$.[11] The proportion held in bonds is b_2 and in money balances, m_2. The decision process is similar for any given rate of interest.

Notice the inverse relationship implied in Fig. 5.2.6 between the bond rate and quantity demanded of asset money. As the bond rate or opportunity

---

[11] This assumes that the substitution effect of an increase in R outweighs the income effect.

cost of holding money increases the proportion of asset portfolio held in idle balances falls and individuals purchase additional bonds. When they do so they incur additional risk and higher expected return. Conversely, when the bond rate falls, the demand for money balances increases; less risk is incurred and less return expected. Such behavior for each individual implies an aggregate relationship between asset money balances, MA, and the rate of interest, R,

$$MA = MA(R) \qquad (5.2.14)$$

Moreover, there is an inverse relationship implied by the foregoing analysis. Let us assume that (5.2.14) is linear,

$$MA = e_0 - e_1 R \qquad (5.2.15)$$

Figure 5.2.7 shows a picture of (5.2.15). Asset money balances are on the horizontal axis and the rate of interest is on the vertical axis. The horizontal axis intercept is e_0 and the slope of the relationship, $\partial MA/\partial R = -e_1$. As the interest rate rises, additional risk associated with additional bond purchases is taken and less is demanded in asset money balances.[12]

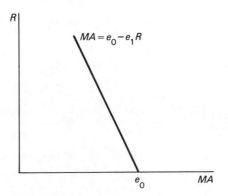

FIGURE 5.2.7

Asset Demand for Money

Again we may add another equation and diagram to the summary page. This time we add the asset money demand equation (5.2.15) and the diagram in Fig. 5.2.7.

---

[12] Similarly, the demand for bonds can be derived simultaneously with the demand for asset money balances. The demand for bond holdings is positively related to the interest rate or inversely related to the price of bonds, $1/R$. The bond market will be developed in the appendix to this chapter.

SUMMARY PAGE

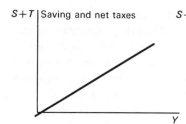

$S+T$ | Saving and net taxes

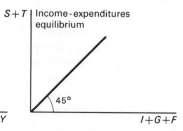

$S+T$ | Income-expenditures equilibrium

45°

$I+G+F$

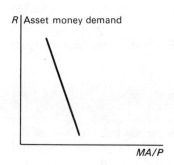

R | Asset money demand

MA/P

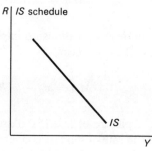

R | IS schedule

IS

Y

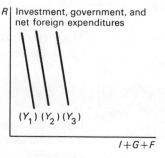

R | Investment, government, and net foreign expenditures

$(Y_1) (Y_2) (Y_3)$

$I+G+F$

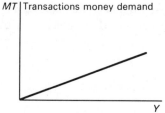

MT | Transactions money demand

Y

Equations

1. $S+T = -a_0 + a_1 t_0 + (1 - a_1 + a_1 t_1) Y$

2. $I+G+F = b_0^d - a_0^f + a_1^f t_0 + G_d + X$
     $\qquad + (b_1^d - a_1^f (1 - t_1)) Y - b_2 R$

3. $S+T = I+G+F$

4. $MT = g_1 Y$

5. $MA = e_0 - e_1 R$

Total Money Demand

The foregoing implies that the total money demand, MD, is defined by the sum of transactions and asset components of money demand,

$$MD = MT + MA \qquad (5.2.16)$$

The dichotomy is somewhat arbitrary, but it helps to emphasize the motives that individuals have in demanding money balances.

Substituting Eqs. (5.2.2) and (5.2.15) into (5.2.16) gives the total demand equation for money,

$$MD = e_0 + g_1 Y - e_1 R \qquad (5.2.17)$$

Figure 5.2.8 shows a picture of the total money demand equation. Given income Y_1, the horizontal axis intercept is $e_0 + g_1 Y_1$ and the slope is $\partial MD / \partial R = -e_1 < 0$. At higher levels of income the interest rate is higher for any given quantity of money demanded. Thus, there is a whole family of total money demand curves, one for each level of income. Given the money stock $\overline{MS}$ and income Y_1, the interest rate is R_1; as income increases to Y_2 and Y_3, the equilibrium interest rate rises to R_2 and R_3, respectively.

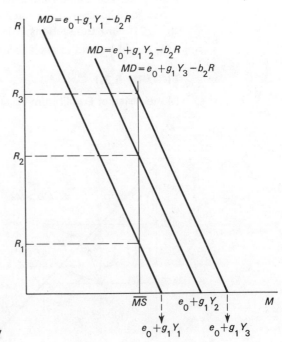

FIGURE 5.2.8

Total Demand for Money

Figure 5.2.8 is not added to the summary page. It is redundant. But it is an alternative picture of the money market which may clear up the questions raised by the above dichotomy of money demand.

5.3   MONEY MARKET EQUILIBRIUM

The money market is in equilibrium when the money stock equals money demand,

$$MS = MD \qquad (5.3.1)$$

or by Eq. (5.2.16)

$$MS = MT + MA \qquad (5.3.2)$$

We may derive the money market equilibrium curve by solving (5.3.2) for transactions balances in terms of asset balances and the money stock,

$$MT = MS - MA \qquad (5.3.3)$$

Given $MS = \overline{MS}$, we may vary asset balances and calculate the corresponding values of transactions balances. Figure 5.3.1 shows a picture of a money market equilibrium curve. As indicated by Eq. (5.3.3), both the vertical and horizontal axis intercepts of the curve are the values of the money stock. If zero transactions balances were held, the total stock of money, $\overline{MS}$, would be held in asset balances. Or at the other extreme, if zero asset

FIGURE 5.3.1

Money Market Equilibrium

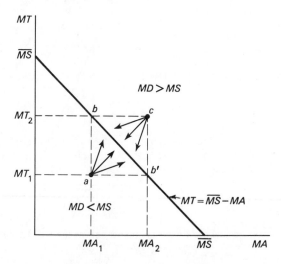

balances were held, the total stock of money, $\overline{MS}$, would be held for transaction purposes. The slope of the curve, $\partial MT/\partial MA = -1$, implies that any combination of asset and transactions money balances along the curve will just equal the money stock.

Given the stock of money, equilibrium is established only on the money market equilibrium curve. At all points below the curve the stock of money exceeds demand. At all points above the curve money demand exceeds the money stock. If equilibrium is temporarily displaced, there are two types of adjustments which take place. These are interest rate and income adjustments, since they are the endogenous explanatory variables in the model.

Assume that the money market is not in equilibrium. For example, suppose that $MD = MT_1 + MA_1$, as shown in Fig. 5.3.1 by point a. This implies that the money stock is greater than money demand, $\overline{MS} > MT_1 + MA_1$. That is, individuals are holding more money than they desire to hold. Correspondingly, it means that they are demanding more bonds and income to realized intended expenditures on goods than is being supplied at the current interest rate. As a result, the interest rate on bonds will fall as the quantity of bonds supplied increases to eliminate the excess demand in the bond market. Moreover, producers of goods and services will accommodate the excess demand for income by increasing production and thereby income. The increase in income increases the quantity demanded of transactions balances and the decrease in the interest rate increases the quantity demanded of asset money balances. The adjustment is complete when the income expenditures, bonds, and money markets are in equilibrium.

Since money demand is considered responsive to both the interest rate and income, movement will take place from point a to a point on the money market equilibrium curve between points b and b'. These boundaries define the set of points which represent increases in both asset and transactions balances. The precise point between b and b' toward which the money market is inclined depends on the relative influence of the change in income and the interest rate.[13]

Now assume that individuals demand more money than is supplied, as shown by point c in Fig. 5.3.1, where $MD = MT_2 + MA_2 > \overline{MS}$. Suppliers reduce the quantity supplied of bonds and intended expenditures fall. Thus, the interest rate rises and income falls. The decrease in income and the rise in the interest rate cause the quantity demanded of transactions and asset balances to fall from point c toward the money market equilibrium curve to a point between the boundaries of b and b'. Again the precise point between b and b' toward which the money market is inclined depends on the relative influence of the change in income and the change in the interest rate.

Changes in the stock of money displace equilibrium in the money market. These changes precipitate the adjustments discussed above. If, for example,

---

[13] As will become evident in Chapter 6, points outside the b and b' limits are excluded as *final* equilibrium points by the logic of the complete model.

the stock of money were to be increased to $\overline{\overline{MS}} > \overline{MS}$, then the money market equilibrium curve would shift rightward as shown in Fig. 5.3.2. The vertical and horizontal axis intercepts of the new money market equilibrium curve would be $\overline{\overline{MS}}$. Stated differently, the difference between the intercepts of the old and new money market equilibrium curve would be the change in the money stock, $\Delta MS = \overline{\overline{MS}} - \overline{MS}$. Conversely, decreases in the money stock shift the money market equilibrium curve leftward. In Fig. 5.3.2 assume that equilibrium in the money market is at point a where $MS = \overline{MS}$ and $MD = MA_1 + MT_1$. Now suppose that the Fed increases the money stock to $MS = \overline{\overline{MS}}$. Equilibrium is displaced. Now at point a the money stock is greater than money demand. Individuals hold more money than they desire to hold. Correspondingly, individuals demand more income to realize intended expenditures and bonds than are being supplied. Income rises and the interest rate falls as the quantity supplied of income generated by output supplied and bonds increases. The increase in income and the decrease in the interest rate increases the quantities demanded of transactions and asset balances toward some point on the money market equilibrium curve, $\overline{\overline{MS}}$, between the boundaries b and b' where both the quantities demanded of transactions and asset balances increase.

Thus, the impact of Fed policy on the economy is initiated by changes in the stock of money. We may now add the money market equilibrium curve in both equation and graphical forms to the summary page and proceed to the next section of this chapter where a condensed version of the money sector is illustrated.

FIGURE 5.3.2

Increase in the Money Stock

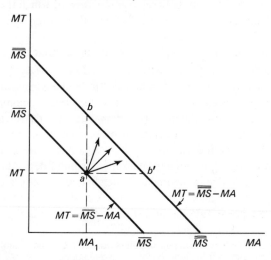

SUMMARY PAGE

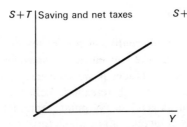

$S+T$ | Saving and net taxes

Y

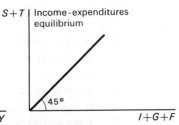

$S+T$ | Income-expenditures equilibrium

45°

$I+G+F$

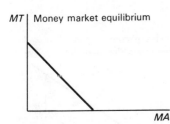

R | Asset money demand

MA

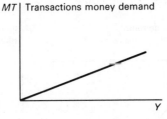

R | IS schedule

IS

Y

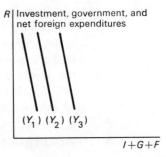

R | Investment, government, and net foreign expenditures

$(Y_1)\ (Y_2)\ (Y_3)$

$I+G+F$

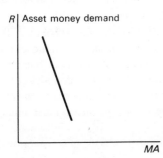

MT | Money market equilibrium

MA

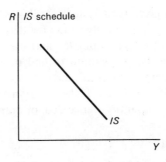

MT | Transactions money demand

Y

Equations

1. $S+T = -a_0 + a_1 t_0 + (1 - a_1 + a_1 t_1)\,Y$

2. $I+G+F = b_0^d - a_0^f + a_1^f t_0 + G_d + X$
   $\quad + (b_1^d - a_1^f(1 - t_1))\,Y - b_2 R$

3. $S+T = I+G+F$

4. $MT = g_1 Y$

5. $MA = e_0 - e_1 R$

6. $MS = MT + MA$

95

5.4 THE *LM* SCHEDULE

We may derive an alternative picture of the money market. The purpose is simple. It will be more convenient to interrelate the money sector with the other sectors of the model if we condense it into one equation and one diagram. The condensed version is called the *LM* schedule. The *LM* schedule is defined as a locus of points representing combinations of interest rates and levels of income, all of which satisfy the money market equilibrium condition for a given money stock, $MT + MA = \overline{MS}$.

Figure 5.4.1 graphically shows the derivation of the *LM* schedule. To begin, choose an interest rate, R_1, and use the asset money demand curve in the upper left-hand quadrant to find out the quantity of asset balances that would be demanded at this interest rate; the asset money demand curve indicates that $MA = MA_2$. If the money market equilibrium condition is to be satisfied, the quantity demanded of transactions balances must equal

FIGURE 5.4.1

Derivation of the *LM* Schedule

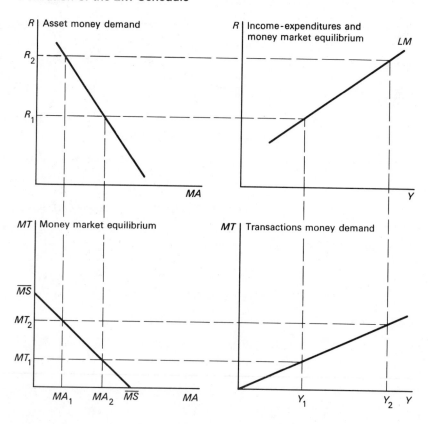

$\overline{MS} - MA_2 = MT_1$. According to the transactions demand curve, in order for transactions balances to be MT_1, income must be Y_1, as shown in the lower right-hand quadrant. Hence, (Y_1, R_1) is a combination of an interest rate and income level which satisfies the money market equilibrium condition. The combination is mapped into the upper right-hand quadrant. Similarly, we can determine another combination of an interest rate and income level, (Y_2, R_2). Moreover, for any given interest rate we can derive the corresponding level of income; the locus of points representing those combinations is the *LM* schedule, as shown in the upper right-hand quadrant.

Alternatively, the *LM* schedule can be derived algebraically. Equating the money stock to the money demand equation (5.2.16) gives

$$MS = e_0 - e_1 R + g_1 Y$$

and solving for income in terms of the interest rate gives

$$Y = \frac{-e_0}{g_1} + \frac{1}{g_1} MS + \frac{e_1}{g_1} R \qquad (5.4.1)$$

the equation for the *LM* curve which was graphically derived in Fig. 5.4.1. Given $MS = \overline{MS}$, the horizontal intercept of the *LM* schedule is $-e_0/g_1 + (1/g_1)\overline{MS}$ and the slope is $\partial Y/\partial R = e_1/g_1 > 0$.

For any given interest rate, changes in the money stock positively affects income,

$$\frac{\partial Y}{\partial MS} = \frac{1}{g_1} > 0$$

This means that increases (decreases) in the money stock shift the *LM* schedule rightward (leftward). Figure 5.4.2 illustrates graphically, for example, the impact of an increase in the stock of money from $\overline{MS}$ to $\overline{\overline{MS}}$ on the *LM* schedule. To begin, the *LM* schedule corresponds to the money market equilibrium curve $\overline{MS}$. Two combinations of interest rate and income levels on *LM* are identified by (Y_1, R_1) and (Y_3, R_2). The increase in the stock of money is shown by the rightward shift in the money market equilibrium curve to $\overline{\overline{MS}}$ and the *LM* schedule to LM'. For any given interest rate, say, $R = R_1$, income increases from Y_1 to Y_2, or if $R = R_2$, income increases from Y_3 to Y_4. Conversely, decreases in the stock have the opposite results.

Now that we have some understanding of the *LM* schedule, we may superimpose the *LM* curve into the quadrant of the summary page showing the *IS* schedule. Like the *IS* schedule, the *LM* schedule does not represent additional information. It is merely a condensed version of the structural equations of the money sector of the model. It is an alternative picture of the money sector of the model.

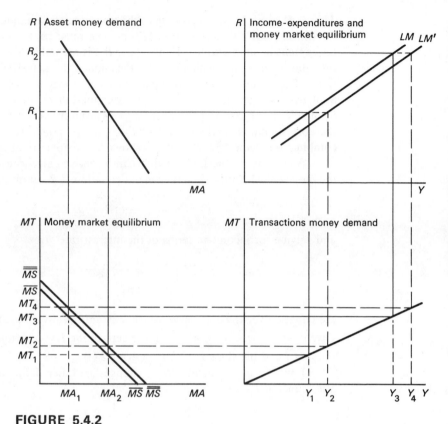

FIGURE 5.4.2

Impact of an Increase in the Money Stock on the *LM* Schedule

5.5   SUMMARY

The money sector of our skeleton model is now complete in terms of words, diagrams, and equations. The sector is interrelated as well. We discussed a naive version of the money creation process which shows the way in which the Fed precipitates changes in the money stock through changes in reserve requirements, open market operations, and discount policy. In our naive version where public preference for currency and time deposits is constant and banks' net free reserve ratio is zero, the Fed controls the money stock by changes in base money and reserve requirements. We also developed a theory of money demand where income determines transactions money demand and the interest rate determines asset money demand. The sector is in equilibrium when the money stock equals money demand. We can derive a locus of points representing combinations of interest rates and income levels which

SUMMARY PAGE

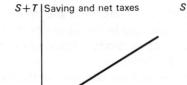

$S+T$ | Saving and net taxes

$S+T$ | Income-expenditures equilibrium

45°

$I+G+F$

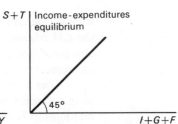

R | Asset money demand

MA

R | Income-expenditures and money market equilibrium

LM

IS

Y

R | Investment, government, and net foreign expenditures

$(Y_1) (Y_2) (Y_3)$

$I+G+F$

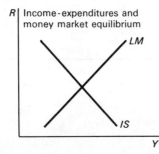

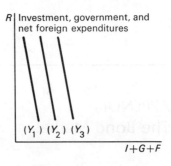

MT | Money market equilibrium

MA

MT | Transactions money demand

Y

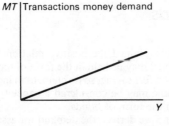

Equations

1. $S+T = -a_0 + a_1 t_0 + (1 - a_1 + a_1 t_1) \, Y$

2. $I+G+F = b_0^d - a_0^f + a_1^f t_0 + G_d + X$
    $+ (b_1^d - a_1^f (1 - t_1)) \; Y - b_2 R$

3. $S+T = I+G+F$

4. $MT = g_1 Y$

5. $MA = e_0 - e_1 R$

6. $MS = MT + MA$

99

satisfies the equilibrium condition in the money sector; the locus is called the *LM* schedule. Changes in the money stock shift the *LM* schedule. For any given interest rate an increase (decrease) in the money stock increases (decreases) the *LM* schedule.

After a brief explicit consideration of the bond market in the appendix to this chapter, we shall proceed to the next chapter and consider the inter-relationship between the money and the income-expenditures sectors.

APPENDIX
The Bond Market

THE DEMAND FOR BONDS

In Chapter 4 we explained the positive relationship between saving and income. Saving in our model may be held in the form of money or bonds. Just as changes in income positively affect saving, so do changes in income positively affect the demand for bonds. Income may be considered a capacity variable, indicating individuals' ability to save in the form of bonds.

In Chapter 5 we derived the demand for asset money balances where holding bonds were the alternative to holding asset money balances. Changes in the proportion of asset portfolio held in money or bonds depended on changes in the interest rate. The interest rate is an allocative variable which determines the proportions of money and bonds held in asset portfolio. It was shown that based on the assumption of risk aversion (see Fig. 5.2.6) changes in the interest rate are positively related to the demand for bond holdings or inversely related to the price of bonds, $1/R$.

The foregoing implies the following relationship for the demand for bonds, *BD*:

$$BD = BD\left(\frac{1}{R}, Y\right) \tag{5.A.1}$$

Let us assume that the relationship takes the linear form,

$$BD = h_0 - h_1 \frac{1}{R} + h_2 Y \tag{5.A.2}$$

Figure 5.A.1 shows a picture of the demand curve for bonds BD''. The curve is downward sloping because $\partial BD/\partial(1/R) = -h_1 < 0$. If $Y = Y_2$, the horizontal axis intercept is $h_0 + h_2 Y_2$.

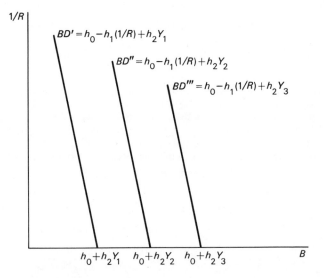

FIGURE 5.A.1

Demand for Bonds

Changes in income positively affect the demand for bonds because $\partial BD/\partial Y = h_2 > 0$. For example, an increase in income from Y_2 to Y_3 will increase saving and induce individuals to increase their demand for bonds to BD'''. Conversely, a decrease in income from Y_2 to Y_1 will decrease saving and induce individuals to decrease bond holdings such that the demand curve for bonds will shift leftward to BD'.

THE SUPPLY OF BONDS

When the government and/or firms supply bonds, they are borrowing. In Chapter 4 we saw that planned investment is positively related to the level of income. When income changes, investment plans change in the same direction. This induces a similar change in the investor's borrowing requirements. Thus, the change in income induces a parallel change in the supply of bonds.

Also in Chapter 4 we saw that planned investment is inversely related to the interest rate. For example, a decrease in the interest rate (increase in the price of bonds) means that planned investment increases. The higher bond price induces increased borrowing and thereby an increase in the supply of bonds. Conversely, an increase in the interest rate (decrease in the price of bonds) means that planned investment decreases. The lower bond price retards borrowing, and the supply of bonds decreases.

The foregoing implies the following relationship for the supply of bonds, BS:

$$BS = BS\left(\frac{1}{R}, Y\right) \qquad (5.A.3)$$

Let us assume that the supply relationship is linear,

$$BS = j_0 + j_1 \frac{1}{R} + j_2 Y \qquad (5.A.4)$$

Figure 5.A.2 shows a picture of the supply curve for bonds BS''. The curve is upward sloping because $\partial BS/\partial(1/R) = j_1 > 0$. If $Y = Y_2$, the horizontal axis intercept is $j_0 + j_2 Y_2$. Changes in income induce direct changes in the supply of bonds because $\partial BS/\partial Y = j_2 > 0$. For example, an increase in income from Y_2 to Y_3 shifts the bond supply curve rightward to BS'''. For every bond price, more bonds will be supplied if income increases. Conversely, a decrease in income from Y_2 to Y_1 shifts the bond supply curve leftward to BS'.

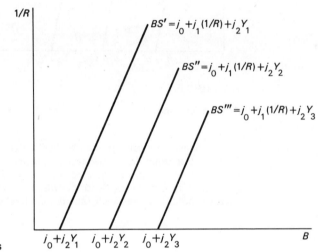

FIGURE 5.A.2

Supply of Bonds

BOND MARKET EQUILIBRIUM

The bonds market is in equilibrium when bonds supplied just equals the bonds demanded,

$$BS = BD \qquad (5.A.5)$$

Figure 5.A.3 superimposes Fig. 5.A.1 onto Fig. 5.A.2. Agreement between buyers and sellers yields an equilibrium price of bonds, $(1/R_1)$, and an equilibrium quantity, B_1, when bond supply is BS' and bond demand is BD'. A change in income shifts the supply and demand curves for bonds in the same direction. If income increases, for example, the supply and demand curves for bonds would shift to BS'' and BD'', respectively. Although it is strictly an empirical question, assume as shown in Fig. 5.A.3 that the supply and demand curves change by the same amount such that the bond price level does not change. The result is that the equilibrium bond price level, and therefore the interest rate, is invariant with respect to income changes as the quantity of bonds in our example increases from B_1 to B_2. Conversely, decreases in income, given our heroic assumption that the bond price level is invariant with income changes, decrease the equilibrium number of bonds exchanged in the bond market.

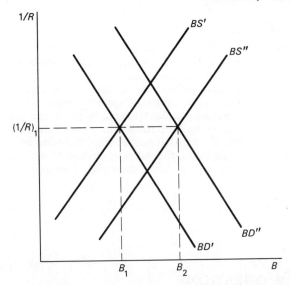

FIGURE 5.A.3

Bond Market

Figure 5.A.4 illustrates the character of the bond market when the market is not in equilibrium. Suppose that the bond market would be in equilibrium if $(B_3, (1/R)_2)$ prevailed. But the actual bond price level is $(1/R)_3$ where bonds supplied are B_5 greater than bonds demanded, B_2. The excess supply of bonds would not be sold in the market, since demanders are not willing to pay the price $(1/R)_3$. The price would fall toward $(1/R)_2$ until the excess was eliminated. Similarly, if the bond price level were $(1/R)_1$, bonds demanded, B_4, would be greater than the bonds supplied, B_1. Consequently, demand pressures would cause the bond price level to rise toward $(1/R)_2$ as suppliers responded by increasing the quantity supplied. Adjustment would continue until the excess demand was eliminated.

FIGURE 5.A.4

Disequilibrium Adjustment
in the Bond Market

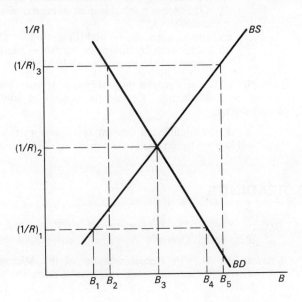

SUMMARY

As you can tell, the theoretical properties of the bond market follow from our previous analysis of the income-expenditure and money markets. In fact, you may wonder why the bond market is treated explicitly in the development of our model. The reason is simple. Experience has shown that for certain pedagogical reasons it is useful to include the bond market in our discussions. As we shall see in the next chapter the bond market analysis is technically redundant. For this reason we do not add the bond market diagram and equations to the summary page. However, in discussing the interrelationships of the model we shall make reference to the bond market. Thus, the explanations in this appendix will serve a useful purpose.

REVIEW QUESTIONS

1. Given the assumptions of our naive money creation process and that the legal reserve requirement ratio on demand deposits equals .20, what would the Fed do if it wanted to increase the money supply by $50 via open market operations?

2. Given

$$MT = g_1 Y \qquad MA = e_0 - e_1 R$$

where $g_1 = .25$, $e_0 = \$100$, $e_1 = \$500$, $R = .09$, $Y = \$1000$

(a) What are the quantities demanded of transactions and asset monies?
(b) If the money market is in equilibrium, what is the dollar value of the money stock?
(c) Answer questions (a) and (b) given $Y = \$1100$ $\qquad R = .10$.
(d) Under what conditions in the money market will an increase in the interest rate leave income unchanged?

3. If MS were greater than $MT + MA$, would the system be to the right or left of the LM schedule? Explain the process of adjustment to money market equilibrium.

4. If the equilibrium interest rate increases from 5 percent to 7 percent what will happen to the equilibrium price of a $100 bond held in perpetuity?

SELECTED READINGS

BAUMOL, W. J., "The Transactions Demand for Cash: An Inventory Theoretic Approach," *Quarterly Journal of Economics*, 66 (Nov. 1952), 545–56.

CLOWER, R. W., "A Reconsideration of the Microfoundations of Monetary Theory," *Western Economic Journal*, 6 (Dec. 1967), 1–8.

CROUCH, R. L., *Macroeconomics*, New York: Harcourt Brace, 1972.

CULBERTSON, J. M., *Money and Banking*, New York: McGraw-Hill, 1972, Part II.

HAMBURGER, M. J., *The Impact of Monetary Variables: A Selected Survey of the Recent Literature*, Staff Economic Study 34, Washington D.C.: Board of Governors of the Federal Reserve System, 1967.

KEYNES, J. M., *The General Theory of Employment, Interest, and Money*, London: Macmillan, 1936, Chaps. 13 and 15.

LEIJONHUFVED, A., *On Keynesian Economics and the Economics of Keynes*, New York: Oxford University Press, 1968, Chap. 5.3.

TEIGEN, R. L., "The Demand for and Supply of Money," in W. L. Smith and R. L. Teigen (eds.), *Readings in Money, National Income and Stabilization Policy*, Homewood, Ill.: Irwin, 1974, pp. 68–103.

TOBIN, J., "The Interest-Elasticity of the Transaction Demand for Cash," *Review of Economics and Statistics*, 38 (Sept. 1956), 241–47.

———, "Liquidity Preference as Behavior Towards Risk," *Review of Economic Studies*, 25 (Feb. 1958), 65–86.

Also see Chapter 13 of this book.

CHAPTER 6

The Determination of Output Demand

6.1 THE INTERRELATIONSHIP BETWEEN THE MONEY, BONDS AND INCOME EXPENDITURES SECTORS

IS-LM Equilibrium

Up to now we have considered the money, income-expenditures, and bonds sectors of the model that we are developing. In this chapter we shall show more clearly that these parts are interrelated and form the basis for a theory of aggregate output demand. Although we have included in their development the assumption that producers generate the income from output supply that is necessary to realize intended expenditures, we do not as yet have a theory of output and price determination. As we shall see in this chapter, we have merely used the concept of income generated from output supply to identify the income that is necessary to realize various levels of intended expenditures in such a way that the money, bonds, and income-expenditures equilibrium conditions are simultaneously satisfied. Once we have developed a theory of output supply in Chapter 7, aggregate output supply and demand will determine simultaneously the equilibrium values of income, output, and the price level consistent with all the equilibrium conditions in the complete model.

The *IS* schedule shows combinations of income levels and interest rates which are consistent with the equality of intended expenditures and income. The *LM* schedule shows combinations of income levels and interest rates consistent with the equality of money supply and demand. On the last summary page you will notice that the *IS-LM* quadrant brought together the income-expenditures and the money sectors. Both sectors are in agreement or mutual equilibrium where the *LM* and *IS* schedules intersect.

Figure 6.1.1 is a duplicate of the summary page which shows the equilibrium values of the endogenous variables of the two sectors of the model. The broken line connecting the equilibrium values of the endogenous variables represents a static state of the model. That is, it answers the question, what is the state (the equilibrium values) of the endogenous variables given a set of values for the exogenous variables and parameters of the model?

Mutual equilibrium values of income, Y_e, and the interest rate, R_e, are those which satisfy both the income-expenditures and money sector equilibrium conditions. Since income and the interest rate are the endogenous

FIGURE 6.1.1

Graphical Determination of the Equilibrium Values of the Endogenous Variables in the *IS-LM* Model

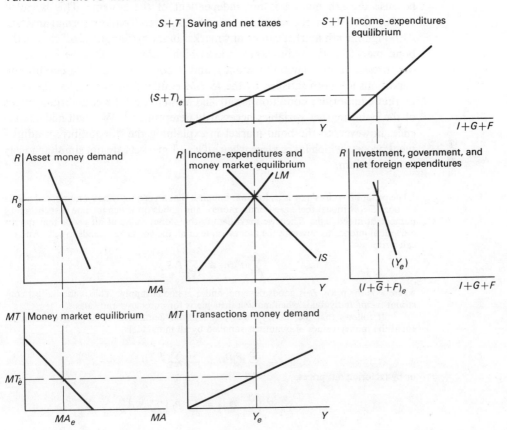

explanatory variables of the model, their equilibrium values, along with a given set of values of the exogenous variables, determine the other endogenous variables of the model. Since equilibrium income is Y_e, equilibrium saving plus net taxes are $(S + T)_e$ and equilibrium transactions money balances are MT_e. Since the equilibrium interest rate is R_e, equilibrium asset money balances are MA_e. Income explains import expenditures, and both income and the interest rate explain investment such that investment plus government plus net foreign expenditures are $(I + \bar{G} + F)_e$.

Walras' Law

The *IS-LM* equilibrium is one by which the equilibrium conditions of the money and income-expenditures sectors are simultaneously satisfied. But what about equilibrium in the bond market? In Chapter 5 we said that the bond market is technically redundant. What does this mean? It simply means that in a system when $n - 1$ market equilibrium conditions are satisfied, the remaining nth market equilibrium condition is satisfied as well because the nth market is not independent of the system. This is called *Walras' law*. Thus, the nth market may be excluded from our formal analysis. Although the nth market can be any market in the system, we shall choose the bond market as the redundant market which technically may be left out of our presentation. That the money and income-expenditures equilibrium conditions are both satisfied by the *IS-LM* equilibrium means that the bond market equilibrium condition is satisfied as well, and the equilibrium values of the bond market variables necessarily determined.[1] We shall make reference, however, to the bond market in explaining the disequilibrium adjustment process which takes place when all $n - 1$ markets are not simultaneously in equilibrium.

---

[1] The proof of Walras' law is as follows: Suppose that an economy has n number of goods (in our *IS-LM* model there are bonds, money, and goods on which income is spent) and j number of individuals. Then we may identify the money value of all goods that the jth individual intends to buy with the money value of all the goods he intends to sell. And we can write

$$\sum_{i=1}^{n} P_i D_{ij} \equiv \sum_{i=1}^{n} P_i S_{ij}$$

where P is the price, D is goods demand, and S is goods supply. This is the budget constraint facing individuals when making their plans for purchases and sales.

It follows that the money value of quantities demanded by all individuals must equal the money values of quantities supplied by all individuals,

$$\sum_{j=1}^{k} \sum_{i=1}^{n} P_i D_{ij} \equiv \sum_{j=1}^{k} \sum_{i=1}^{n} P_i S_{ij}$$

or by factoring out prices,

$$\sum_{i=1}^{n} P_i \left(\sum_{j=1}^{k} D_{ij} \right) \equiv \sum_{i=1}^{n} P_i \left(\sum_{j=1}^{k} S_{ij} \right)$$

IS-LM Disequilibrium Adjustments

In Fig. 6.1.1, combinations of interest rates and income levels other than (Y_e, R_e) are disequilibrium positions. Just as *IS-LM* equilibrium means that the money, bond, and income-expenditures sectors are in equilibrium simultaneously, disequilibrium means that all of them are not. Excess demand in at least one sector implies excess supply in at least one other sector. Income, and the interest rate adjust to reduce excesses, and adjustments continue until *IS-LM* equilibrium is established.

We shall not consider here all possible types of disequilibrium adjustments. But three good examples are given in order to selectively illustrate that related sectors will continue to adjust until the *IS-LM* equilibrium shown in Fig 6.1.1 is established.

Example 1: Figure 6.1.2 is a duplicate of the summary page modified to include the bond market that was developed in the appendix to Chapter 5. The bond market is the lower left-hand quadrant interrelated to the rest of the model through the operational quadrant directly above it. The equilibrium values of the endogenous variables are labeled by the subscript e. A disequilibrium set of values of the endogenous variables is labeled by the subscript d.

Since (Y_d, R_d) is a disequilibrium combination of income and interest rate which lies on the *LM* schedule, it is one that is consistent with money market equilibrium, $MS = MD$. But it is not consistent with equilibrium in the income-expenditures sector; income is insufficient to realize intended expenditures, $S + T < I + G + F$. Note also that the interest rate, R_d, is too low (the price of bonds, $1/R_d$, too high) to equilibrate the bond market. Since initially the money market is in equilibrium, initial adjustment takes place between the income-expenditures and the bond sectors.

The expressions in parentheses on the left- and right-hand sides are total market demand, D_i, and total market supply, S_i, respectively. Thus, we rewrite

$$\sum_{i=1}^{n} P_i D_i \equiv \sum_{i=1}^{n} P_i S_i$$

which is Walras' identity. This identity is true whether or not market prices equate supply and demand for each good. Yet, if we assume that in $n - 1$ markets a set of equilibrium prices exists, then we are sure that supply equals demand in those markets. By summing over $n - 1$ markets, we obtain

$$\sum_{i=1}^{n-1} P_i D_i = \sum_{i=1}^{n-1} P_i S_i$$

If this is subtracted from Walras' identity, we obtain

$$P_n D_n = P_n S_n$$

or

$$D_n = S_n$$

which implies that the nth market is also in equilibrium. Thus, if all markets except one are in equilibrium, the other market must be in equilibrium as well.

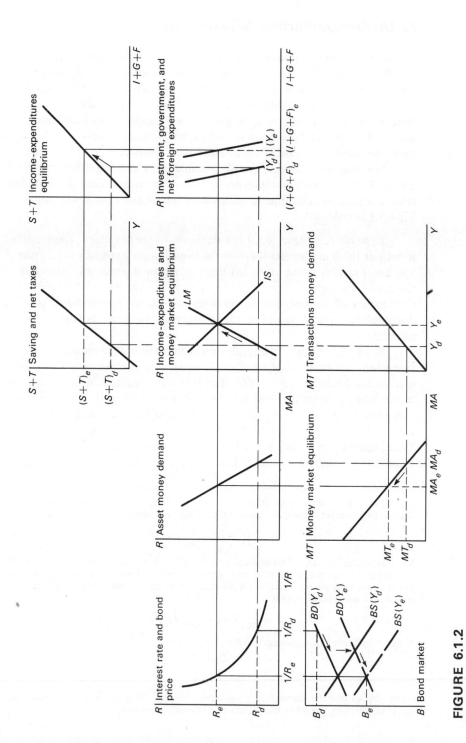

FIGURE 6.1.2
Disequilibrium Adjustment, Example 1

110

The income generated by output supply that is necessary to realize intended expenditures generated by output demand will increase as producers accommodate the excess demand. As income rises toward Y_e saving, net taxes, investment, import expenditures, transactions money balances, bond supply, and bond demand will increase to their corresponding equilibrium values because they are positively related to income.[2]

The price of bonds will fall toward $1/R_e$ to eliminate excess supply in the bond market and thereby the interest rate will rise to R_e as asset money balances and investment are reduced. Whether investment increases or decreases depends on the relative impacts of changes in income and the interest rate.

The arrows in Fig. 6.1.2 indicate the direction of net changes in the endogenous variables as income and interest rate adjustments take place.[3] Note that there is no net change in total money demand. The money stock is merely redistributed so that more is held in transactions balances and less is held in asset balances. Both the interest rate and income will continue to adjust until all sectors are in *IS-LM* equilibrium.

Example 2: In Fig. 6.1.3, (Y_d, R_d) lies on the *IS* schedule. Therefore, it is consistent with income-expenditures equilibrium, $S + T = I + G + F$. But (Y_d, R_d) does not lie on the *LM* schedule. Therefore, it is inconsistent with money market equilibrium. In fact, this combination shows that money supply exceeds money demand, $MS > MD$.

Since initially the income-expenditures sector is in equilibrium, excess supply in the money sector implies excess demand in the bond sector. Hence, initial adjustment will take place between the bond and money sectors.

With excess demand in the bond market, the price of bonds will rise toward $1/R_e$ and thereby the interest rate falls toward R_e. Asset balances increase because the yield on bonds is lower. Intended investment will rise as the interest rate falls, and thereby an excess of intended expenditures over income will occur. The income generated by output supply that is necessary to realize intended expenditures generated by output demand will increase as producers accommodate the excess demand. The increase in income toward Y_e increases saving, net taxes, investment, import expenditures, transactions balances, bond demand, and bond supply to their corresponding equilibrium values because they are positively stimulated by the increase in income.

---

[2] We again make the assumption that the income effect on both bond supply and bond demand is such that a change in income does not change the bond price. It only changes quantity. This assumption will be made in all our examples. This assumption is not necessary by Walras' law, but it simplifies our analysis. Regardless of the income effect on the bond price, adjustment will continue until *IS-LM* equilibrium is satisfied.

[3] We do not show the specific forms that the disequilibrium adjustment paths take. Here we show only the net changes in the endogenous variables as they adjust from a disequilibrium position to the equilibrium position.

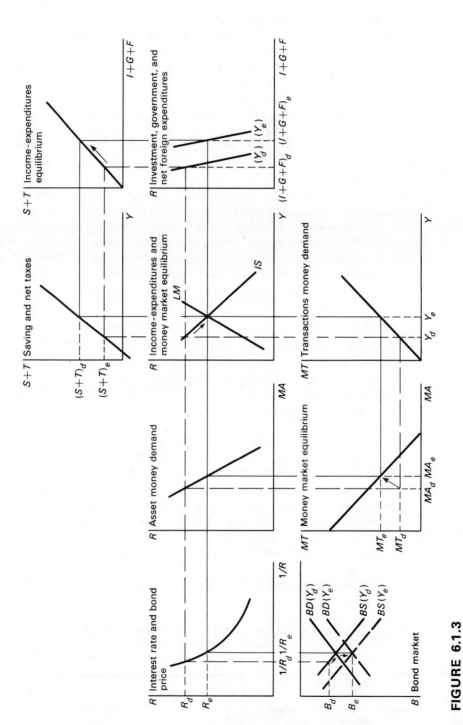

FIGURE 6.1.3

Disequilibrium Adjustment, Example 2

112

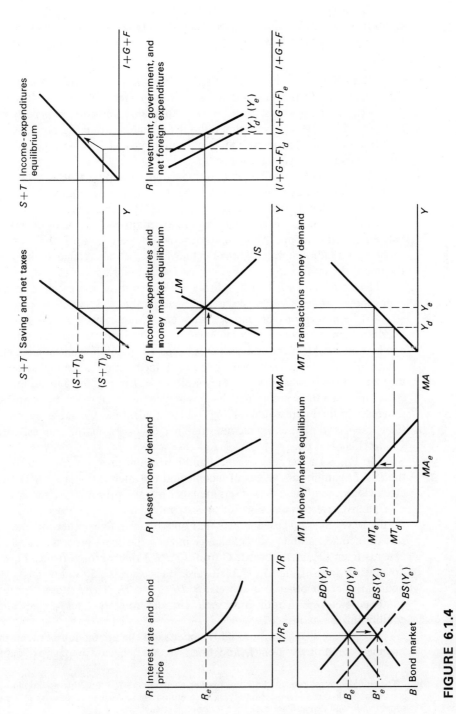

FIGURE 6.1.4

Disequilibrium Adjustment, Example 3

The arrows in Fig. 6.1.3 indicate the directions of net changes in the endogenous variables as income rises and the interest rate falls. Income and interest rate adjustments will continue until all sectors are in *IS-LM* equilibrium.

Example 3: In Fig. 6.1.4, (Y_d, R_e) does not lie on either the *IS* or *LM* schedules. In this case money supply is greater than money demand, $MS > MD$, and income is insufficient to realize intended expenditures, $S + T < I + F + G$. Note that although the interest rate, R_e, is consistent with mutual equilibrium in the bonds, money, and income-expenditures sectors, income, Y_d, is inconsistent.[4]

The income generated by additional output supply that is necessary to realize intended expenditures generated from output demand will increase as producers accommodate the excess demand. As income increases toward Y_e, saving, net taxes, investment, import expenditures, transactions money balances, bond supply, and bond demand increase toward their corresponding equilibrium values because they are positively related to income. Income will continue to increase until *IS-LM* equilibrium is satisfied.

The arrows in Fig. 6.1.4 indicate the direction of net changes in the endogenous variables as income rises. The interest rate shows no net change.

All combinations of interest rates and income levels in the *IS-LM* quadrant can be divided into eight subsets. Each subset represents those combinations which imply a particular type of disequilibrium adjustment. A type of adjustment is defined by the combined net directional changes in income and the interest rate. For example, type *A* in Fig. 6.1.5 identifies the subset in which there are no net changes in income but in which there are net decreases in the interest rate, $(\bar{Y}, R\downarrow)$. Type *B* identifies the subset in which there are net decreases in income and net decreases in the interest rate, $(Y\downarrow, R\downarrow)$, and so on.

In Fig. 6.1.5 the heavy vertical and horizontal lines are drawn through the *IS-LM* equilibrium values of income and the interest rate, (Y_e, R_e). In a clockwise manner the eight subsets are labeled from *A* through *H*. Subsets *A*, *C*, *E*, and *G* are combinations of interest rates and income levels which lie on the heavy lines. These indicate that only one variable, either the interest rate or income, exhibits any net change in the adjustment process. Subset *A* extends from (Y_e, R_e) upward, *C* from (Y_e, R_e) rightward, *E* from (Y_e, R_e) downward, and *G* from (Y_e, R_e) leftward. Subsets *A*, *C*, *E*, and *G* define the boundaries of the other four subsets, *B*, *D*, *F*, and *H*. These subsets contain combinations where both income levels and interest rates adjust until equilibrium is established.

To ensure that you thoroughly understand the interaction between the income-expenditures, money, and bonds sectors, list on a page of paper

---

[4] The initial interest rate in the bond market need not be R_e. But this assumption is consistent with our previous simplifying assumption that the income effects on bond supply and bond demand are such that R does not change.

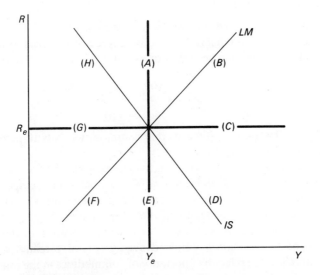

FIGURE 6.1.5

Types of Disequilibrium Adjustment

each type of disequilibrium adjustment and explain the appropriate inter-actions between the markets as they adjust toward mutual equilibrium. We have already explained a sample from subsets *F*, *G*, and *H*. You explain a sample from the others. You will find that the time has been well spent, particularly when we begin to consider the various impacts of monetary and fiscal policies on the economy.

6.2 THE OUTPUT DEMAND CURVE

The Transformation of the Model into Real Terms

Up to now we have cast both the income-expenditures and money sectors of our model in money or nominal units. For example, income, Y, is the sum of outputs, Q_i, produced and sold and valued at their market prices, P_i,

$$Y = \sum_{i=1}^{n} P_i Q_i \qquad (6.2.1)$$

The terms on the right are observable but so numerous that some system of aggregation is appropriate. We can substitute an average price or price level into (6.2.1) if we can find some reasonable way to calculate the average.

For a single commodity the price in a time period relative to the price in a base period is P_{it}/P_{io}, where P_{it} is the price of the commodity i in time period t and P_{io} is the price of the commodity i in the base period o. If we multiply the price relative by 100, we express it as a full number; the base year value would then be 100. For example, if $P_{it} = \$.22$ and $P_{io} = \$.20$,

$$\frac{P_{it}}{P_{io}} \times 100 = \frac{\$.22}{\$.20} \times 100$$

$$= 110$$

The price relative of 110 means that commodity i costs 10 percent more than it did in the base period.

If we average the price relatives over a number of commodities in a "market basket" and multiply by 100, we obtain an average of prices compared to their level in a base period. Such an average is a price index where equal weights are attached to all the price relatives.

A more appropriate means of reflecting changes in the cost of living would be to calculate a weighted average of price relatives. The weights should reflect the relative importance of commodities in the total expenditures on a market basket of goods and services. Price relatives associated with goods which account for a large share of expenditures, e.g., housing, food, and transportation, should be weighted more than prices associated with goods which account for a smaller share of expenditures, e.g., matches, pencils, and salaries to college professors. Changes in the prices of the more important goods will change the average more drastically than will changes in the less important goods. Thus, changes in the average will more closely approximate changes in the cost of living when prices are weighted by their importance in the share of expenditures.

Such an index,

$$PI_L = \sum_i \left(\frac{Q_{io}P_{io}}{\sum\limits_i Q_{io}P_{io}} \right) \frac{P_{it}}{P_{io}} \times 100$$

$$= \frac{\sum\limits_i Q_{io}P_{it}}{\sum\limits_i Q_{io}P_{io}} \times 100 \qquad (6.2.2)$$

is the base-weighted Laspeyres Index number, which is used to calculate the Consumer Price Index in the United States (1958 is currently the base year). Each price relative is weighted by its share in total expenditures in the base period. By canceling out, we derive the index number on the right.[5] This

---

[5] An alternative price index is the Paasche Index,

$$PI_P = \frac{\sum\limits_i Q_{it}P_{it}}{\sum\limits_i Q_{it}P_{io}}$$

The difference between the Paasche and Laspeyres indices is that the Paasche Index uses current outputs as weights and the Laspeyres Index uses base period outputs. Since consumers will probably reduce spending on those commodities which rise most in price, these commodities will have higher weights in a Laspeyres Index than in a Paasche Index. Hence, the Laspeyres Index will generally show more inflation than the Paasche Index.

price index measures the cost of buying the base period basket of commodities at current prices relative to the cost of buying the base period basket of commodities at base year prices. For example, if the Consumer Price Index is 130.0, consumer prices rose 30 percent since the base year period.

Although there are serious problems with the use of price indices as a measure of the price level,[6] we shall use the above index, PI_L, as an approximation of the price level, P.

Equation (6.2.1) can then be rewritten as

$$Y = P \sum_{i=1}^{n} Q_i \qquad (6.2.3)$$

If we divide through by P, we derive

$$\frac{Y}{P} = \sum_{i=1}^{n} Q_i \qquad (6.2.4)$$

which states that nominal income deflated by the price level (real income) is a workable measure of the sum of total physical output.

Changes in nominal income occur as both the price level and output change. Economic growth is best discussed in real terms because increases in nominal income may only mean higher prices with no growth in output (real income). Moreover, in preparation for deriving the aggregate demand for output, our model must explicitly include both the price level and output. It is for these reasons that we now convert our model to real terms. We shall not merely divide all equations by the price level because this presents a problem in both the investment and asset money demand equations. Since these equations include the rate of interest, dividing through by the price level would yield a complex term of the interest rate divided by the price level.[7] Thus, we convert the functional forms of the theoretical equations to real terms first and then assume that all equations are linear in real terms. The same parameter notations will be retained although the parameter values are now interpreted as relating the magnitudes of variables in real terms.

---

[6] One important problem is that quality changes tend to get mixed up with price changes. And improvements in quality should not be interpreted as inflationary. See M. L. Burnstein, "The Index Number Problem," in R. W. Clower (ed.), *Monetary Theory*, Baltimore: Penguin, Inc., 1969.

[7] We shall continue to use the nominal rate of interest without any adjustments for changes in the price level. The nominal interest rate is the nominal rate of return on an interest-bearing asset (bonds). An increase in the price level deflates the real value of that rate of return. If people anticipate the price increase, the decision to buy bonds and invest will depend on the real rate of interest, R_R; that is, the nominal rate, R, less the expected rate of change in prices $(dP/P)^*$, $R_R = R - (dP/P)^*$. If, for example, the nominal rate is 6 percent per year and if prices rise by 2 percent per year, then $R_R = 6$ percent $- 2$ percent $= 4$ percent. We shall not use the real rate of interest in our analysis. But if prices are rising rapidly over a period of time, the distinction between the real and nominal interest rates becomes important.

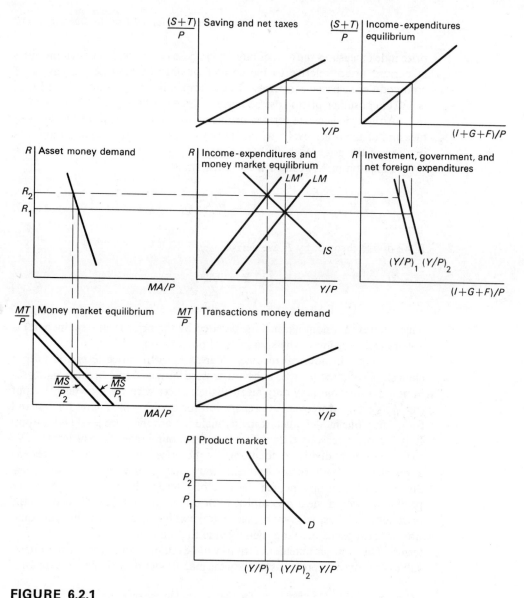

FIGURE 6.2.1

Derivation of the Aggregate Demand Curve

The Derivation of the Aggregate Demand Curve

Figure 6.2.1 uses the summary page of our model in real terms to illustrate the derivation of the aggregate demand curve. The demand curve is defined as a schedule which relates the quantities of real income (output) that will be demanded at various price levels.

118

Let us begin with a price level, P_1, which corresponds to the rate of interest, R_1, and real income, $(Y/P)_2$. The correspondence is indicated by the solid line which connects a set of static equilibrium values of the endogenous variables.

Assume now that the price level rises to P_2. This means that with the exogenous nominal money stock the economy's real stock of money is less, $\overline{MS}/P_2 < \overline{MS}/P_1$. It takes more nominal money units to facilitate the same level of transactions and asset money demands. The increase in price level shifts the money market equilibrium curve leftward to $\overline{MS}/P_2$. Correspondingly, the *LM* schedule shifts leftward to *LM'*. A new set of equilibrium values of the endogenous variables of the model are derived and shown by the broken line in Fig. 6.2.1. The new combination of real income and price level is mapped into the product market quadrant. If we continued to vary only the price level, either upward or downward, the changes in the real money stock would vary directly with real income, and the price level would vary inversely with real income. The combinations, $((Y/P)_1, P_2)$ and $((Y/P)_2, P_1)$, are but two points on the aggregate demand curve. A locus of all such combinations is the aggregate demand for real income (output) because it represents a schedule of real income (output) demanded at various price levels. The algebraic form of the aggregate output demand curve is derived in the appendix to this chapter by solving the *IS* schedule [Eq. (4.6.1)] and the *LM* schedule [Eq. (5.4.1)] simultaneously for the value of real income. Given any particular set of values for the exogenous variables and parameters, the output demand equation in the appendix, like the output demand curve in Fig. 6.2.1, indicates that real income (quantity of output) demanded varies inversely with the price level, $\partial(Y/P)/\partial P < 0$.

The aggregate demand curve has been derived by asking what happens to real income when the price level changes given a fixed set of values for the exogenous variables and parameters of the model. Simultaneous changes in the equilibrium values of real income and the other endogenous variables due to the price level changes are explained by movement along the demand curve. In the next section we shall explain changes or shifts in the output demand curve.

6.3 CHANGES IN OUTPUT DEMAND

In Chapters 4 and 5 we described how changes in the money stock shift the *LM* schedule, while changes in domestic government expenditures, export expenditures, exogenous net taxes, and the net tax rate shift the *IS* schedule. In the previous section of this chapter we examined the impact of changes in the price level on the quantity of real income (output) demanded and the other endogenous variables of the model for a given set of values of the exogenous variables and parameters. Movement along the aggregate output demand curve was thereby described.

We shall now graphically illustrate how changes in the exogenous variables and the tax parameters change (shift) the level of aggregate real income (output) demand. Shifts in the demand curve are derived by asking what happens to real income (output) demand at any given price level when the value(s) of one or more of the exogenous variables and/or parameters on the demand side of the model change.

The Impact of Changes in Government Expenditures

Figure 6.3.1 illustrates the impact of a change in domestic government expenditures for any given price level on the endogenous variables of the model. For example, suppose that an increase in domestic government expenditures and the resulting real income effect on real investment and real net foreign expenditures shift the real expenditure curve to Z'. Correspondingly, the increase in government expenditures shifts the *IS* schedule rightward to IS'. For any given price level, say P_1, equilibrium real income and the interest rate increase from $((Y/P)_1, R_1)$ to $((Y/P)_2, R_2)$. A higher real income at any given price level indicates that there is an increase (or rightward shift) in aggregate output demand from D to D'. Thus, the increase in domestic government expenditures displaces the initial *IS-LM* equilibrium. The type of disequilibrium adjustment which takes place until the new equilibrium is attained is *type F* (see Fig. 6.1.5). Although our model assumes that the values of the endogenous variables are determined simultaneously, we may explain the impact of a change in domestic government expenditures by relating the causal chain of activity which moves the system from one *IS-LM* equilibrium to another comparative static *IS-LM* equilibrium. The increase in domestic government expenditures initially creates an excess of intended real expenditures over real income $(I + G + F)/P > (S + T)/P$. Given the price level P_1, this means an excess of real income (output) demand over real income (output) supplied. Real income supplied will increase to eliminate the excess. The increase in real income increases real investment, real import expenditures (decreases real net foreign expenditures), and real transactions money balances.[8] The increase in real transaction money balances creates an excess of real money demand over real money supply, $MD/P > MS/P$. The interest rate rises to eliminate the excess. The increase in the interest rate reduces real asset money balances until the money market is in equilibrium. Real investment is retarded by the increase in the interest

---

[8] Since real import expenditures are positively related to real income, an increase in real income decreases the difference between exogenous real export expenditures and real import expenditures at any given price level. Hence, an increase in domestic government expenditures decreases real net foreign expenditures.

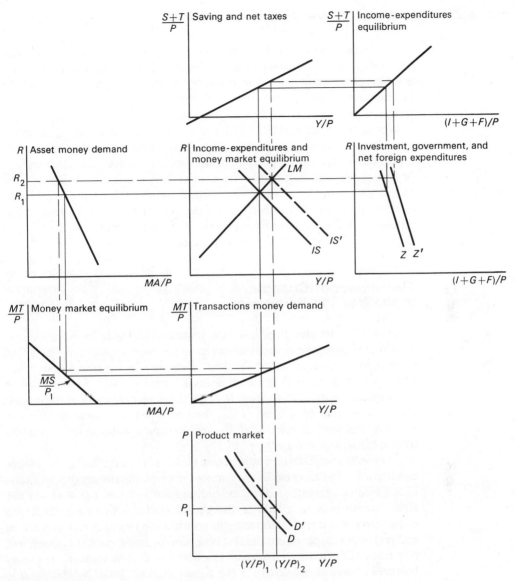

FIGURE 6.3.1

Increase in Government Expenditures

rate. The increase in real income increases real investment, while the increase in the interest rate decreases real investment. Whether or not there is a net increase in real investment depends on the influences of the change in real income relative to the change in the interest rate. After full adjustment the impact of the increase in government expenditures is shown in Fig. 6.3.1 by the difference between the solid and broken line values of the endogenous variables. Notice that with a fixed price level changes in the real values of the endogenous variables are the same as changes in their nominal values.

For any given price level changes in government import expenditures positively affect real import expenditures and thereby negatively affect real net foreign expenditures. For example, decreases in government import expenditures decrease real import expenditures. Thus, given real export expenditures, real net foreign expenditures increase, and the qualitative impact on the model is similar to that of an increase in domestic government expenditures. Of course, if the government changes the allocation of its expenditures by lowering (raising) its import expenditures and raising (lowering) its domestic expenditures, the impact on the values of the endogenous variables of the *IS-LM* model will depend on the real income increasing (decreasing) impact of lower (higher) real import government expenditures and the real income increasing (decreasing) impact of higher (lower) real domestic government expenditures.

The Impact of Changes in the Net Tax Parameters

Figure 6.3.2 illustrates graphically the impact of a change in exogenous net taxes on the endogenous variables of the model for any given price level. An increase in t_0, for example, shifts the real saving plus net taxes curve to X'. Correspondingly, the *IS* schedule shifts leftward to *IS'*. As indicated in the graphical analysis an increase in t_0 decreases real income and the interest rate for any given price level. Thus, the output demand curve decreases to D'. For example, at price level P_1, real income and the interest rate fall from $((Y/P)_2, R_2)$ to $((Y/P)_1, R_1)$.

Type B disequilibrium adjustment moves the system to its new *IS-LM* equilibrium. The increase in exogenous net taxes initially creates an excess of real income over intended real expenditures, $(S + T)/P > (I + G + F)/P$. Real income falls to eliminate the excess until the income-expenditures equilibrium is restored. Decreases in real income decrease real investment and real import expenditures, real saving, real-income-induced net taxes, and real transaction money balances. The decrease in real transaction money balances creates excess supply in the money market, $MS/P > MD/P$. And the interest rate falls to eliminate the excess. The decrease in the interest rate increases real asset money balances and gives stimulus to real investment. After full adjustment the impact of the increase in exogenous net taxes on the system is as shown by the difference between the solid and broken line values of the endogenous variables in Fig. 6.3.2. Notice that for a given price level, changes in the real values of the endogenous variables are the same as changes in their nominal values.

Figure 6.3.3 illustrates the impact of a change in the net tax rate for any given price level on the endogenous variables of the model. An increase in t_1, for example, pivots the real $S + T$ curve to X'. Correspondingly, the *IS* schedule pivots to *IS'*. The qualitative results are similar to those

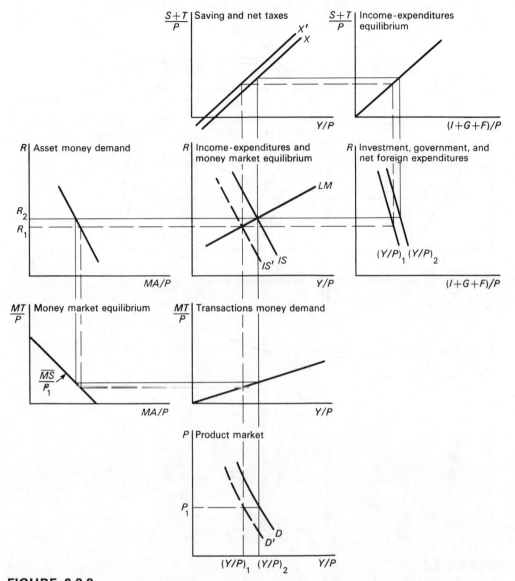

FIGURE 6.3.2

Increase in Exogenous Taxes

of an increase in exogenous net taxes. Type B disequilibrium adjustment moves the system to its new *IS-LM* equilibrium. However, the increase in the net tax rate decreases the slope of the demand curve; that is, in addition to an absolute decrease in real income at any given price level, the increase in the net tax rate makes real income less responsive to price changes. As individuals pay a higher percent of income in taxes relative to what they receive in transfer payments, they spend less, producers produce less, and real income is less for any given price level. Therefore, real income responds less

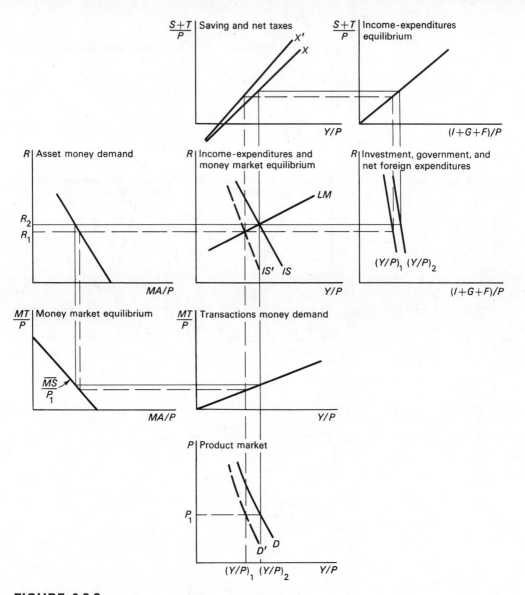

FIGURE 6.3.3

Increase in the Tax Rate

to price changes after the increase in the net tax rate, as shown by D'. Conversely, a decrease in the tax rate implies that real income becomes more responsive to price changes.

The Impact of Changes in Export Expenditures

Although the foreign sector represents but a small fraction of gross national product in the United States, we are concerned about the problem of an

124

unfavorable balance of import expenditures over export expenditures. Moreover, the possibility of increases in export expenditures is a potential means of further economic growth.

Figure 6.3.4 illustrates the impact of an increase in export expenditures for any given price level on the endogenous variables of the model. Suppose that such an increase and the resulting real income effect on real investment and real import expenditures shift the real expenditure curve rightward to Z'. Correspondingly, the IS schedule shifts to IS'. For any given price level,

FIGURE 6.3.4

Increase in Net Export Expenditures

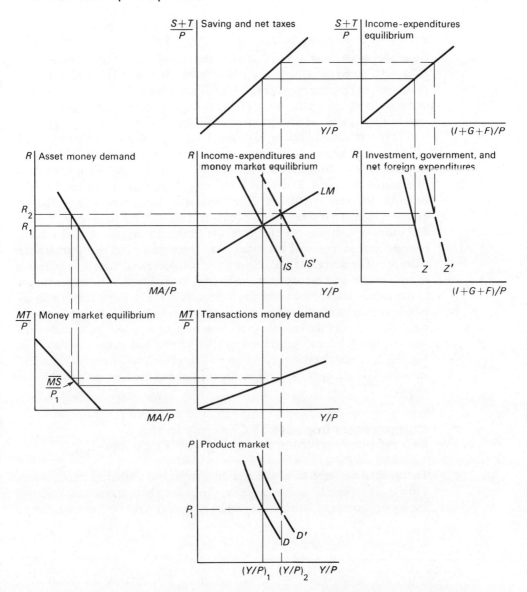

real income and the rate of interest rise. For example, at price level P_1, real income and the interest rate rise to $((Y/P)_2, R_2)$. Thus, the aggregate demand curve shifts from D to D'. Type F disequilibrium adjustment takes place until the new *IS-LM* equilibrium is attained. The qualitative description of the adjustment process is similar to that already explained for an increase in domestic government expenditures. Again notice the correspondence between changes in the nominal and real values of the endogenous variables when the price level is held fixed.

The Impact of Changes in the Money Stock

Figure 6.3.5 illustrates the impact of a change in the money stock for any given price level on the endogenous variables of the model. An increase in the money stock from $\overline{MS}$ to $\overline{\overline{MS}}$ shifts the money market equilibrium curve rightward. Correspondingly, the *LM* schedule shifts to *LM'*. For any given price level real income increases and the interest rate falls. Thus, the demand curve shifts rightward to D'. For example, at price level P_1, real income rises to $(Y/P)_2$ and the interest rate falls to R_1.

Type H disequilibrium adjustment takes place until the new *IS-LM* equilibrium is attained. The increase in the money stock initially creates excess supply in the money market, $MS/P > MD/P$. The interest rate falls to eliminate the excess. Decreases in the interest rate increase real asset money balances and real investment. The increase in real investment creates an excess of intended real expenditures over real income, $I + G + F > S + T$. Real income increases to eliminate the excess. Increases in real income increase real saving, real net taxes, real investment, and real transactions balances. The increase in real transactions balances means that both increases in real income and decreases in the interest rate eliminate the excess supply in the money market such that the increment in the money stock is split up into both real transactions and real asset money balances. After full adjustment the impact of the increase in the money stock is shown by the difference between the solid and broken line values of the endogenous variables in Fig. 6.3.5. Again notice that for any given price level changes in the real values of the endogenous variables are the same as changes in their nominal values.

Comparative Impacts of Changes in the Exogenous Variables for any given Price Level

The qualitative impacts of changes in domestic government expenditures and export expenditures are the same. Since they have the same qualitative impact on the rate of interest and real income, they have the same qualitative

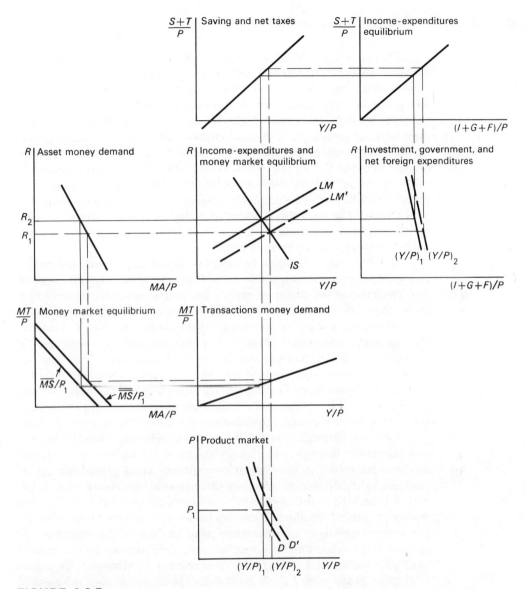

FIGURE 6.3.5

Increase in the Money Stock

impacts on the other endogenous variables of the model. Such changes positively affect real investment if changes in real income have a greater impact on real investment than do changes in the interest rate. An increase, for example, in either domestic government expenditures and/or export expenditures increases real income and raises the interest rate. Thus, there are both a positive influence and negative influence on real investment. The net effect will determine the actual impact on real investment.

127

There is a similarity in the impact of changes in the tax parameter and domestic government expenditures on the endogenous variables of the model. This is particularly true of changes in domestic government spending and exogenous net taxes. But there are major differences as well. For example, attempts to expand output by increases in government expenditures increases government's share of output. But attempts to expand output by decreases in exogenous net taxes increase the private sector's share of output. A cut in the net tax rate shifts the initial stimulus to an increase in consumption and thereby increases the share of output going to consumers; the extent of the increase in consumption depends on the marginal propensity to consume. The appropriate choice of policy on balance depends in part on the judgment of the relative social benefits of reallocating resources into public versus private goods production.

Another major difference between the impact of government expenditure policy versus net tax policy stems from the possibility that with an increase in the net tax rate or exogenous net taxes, consumers may perceive it to be temporary, decrease the propensity to save, and thereby partially offset the contractionary effect on real income of the net tax increase. Conversely, the response to a decrease in net tax rate or exogenous net taxes may cause the propensity to save to increase and thereby curb expansion. This does not occur with changes in government spending, since the government can make sure that its expenditures change by the desired amount. Thus, tax and transfer payment policy presents a more uncertain outcome than expenditure policy because the propensity to save may vary in response to net tax policies.

Increases (decreases) in the money stock indirectly stimulate (retard) real investment through decreases (increases) in the interest rate, whereas increases (decreases) in government expenditures retard (stimulate) real investment indirectly through increases (decreases) in the interest rate. However, it cannot be said that changes in government spending policy tend to replace investment spending. Even with higher interest rates due to increased government spending, real investment may increase if the impact of the increase in real income due to government spending increases real investment more than the increase in the interest rate reduces it. Moreover, the impact of changes in the money stock depends on the degree of responsiveness of investors to changes in the interest rate and real income. If this response is uncertain, then changes in the money stock offer a more uncertain outcome than changes in government expenditures.

6.4   SUMMARY

In this chapter we have brought together the money and income-expenditure sectors of the model as a basis for a theory of aggregate real income (output) demand. At any given price level, the determination of the quantity of output demanded can be described as a process which ensures that real income and the interest rate will adjust until the money market and income-expenditure equilibrium conditions are simultaneously satisfied, that is, until *IS-LM* equilibrium is attained. The adjustment process also involves the bond market, but by Walras' law when $n - 1$ sectors are in equilibrium, the nth market is automatically in equilibrium. That is, when *IS-LM* equilibrium exists, the bond market is in equilibrium as well.

We graphically derived an aggregate output demand curve for a set of values of the exogenous variables and parameters of the *IS-LM* model. Movement along the demand curve was explained by the response of the quantity of real income demanded to price changes. Shifts in the demand curve were explained by the response of real income demand to changes in at least one of the values of the exogenous variables or parameters of the *IS-LM* model. In the appendix to this chapter we shall derive the reduced-form equation for real income (output) and identify it as the output demand equation. The signs of the reduced-form multipliers verify the qualitative results of changes in the exogenous variables on real income which were obtained in our graphical analysis.

APPENDIX
Algebraic Derivation
of the Output Demand Curve

We can solve the *LM* schedule [Eq. (5.4.1)],

$$\frac{Y}{P} = \frac{-e_0}{g_1} + \frac{1}{g_1}\left(\frac{MS}{P}\right) + \frac{e_1}{g_1} R \qquad (6.A.1)$$

and the *IS* schedule [Eq. (4.6.1)],

$$\frac{Y}{P} = \frac{b_0^d + a_0^d - a_1^d t_0}{1 - a_1^d + a_1^d t_1 - b_1^d} + \frac{1}{1 - a_1^d + a_1^d t_1 - b_1^d}\left(\frac{X + G_d}{P}\right)$$

$$- \frac{b_2}{1 - a_1^d + a_1^d t_1 - b_1^d} R \qquad (6.A.2)$$

simultaneously for the two unknown endogenous variables on the demand side of the model: real income, Y/P, and the interest rate, R. If we set (6.A.1) equal to (6.A.2) and solve for the interest rate, we derive the equation for the equilibrium value of the interest rate, i.e., the reduced form for the interest rate given the temporary assumption that the price level is exogenous. Next, we can substitute the interest rate equation into either (6.A.1) or (6.A.2) and thereby derive the equation for the equilibrium value of real income, i.e., the reduced form for real income (output) given the temporary assumption that the price level is exogenous. The reduced form for real income,

$$\frac{Y}{P} = \frac{e_1(b_0^d + a_0^d - a_1^d t_0) - b_2 e_0}{e_1(1 - a_1^d + a_1^d t_1 - b_1^d) + b_2 g_1}$$

$$+ \left[\frac{e_1}{e_1(1 - a_1^d + a_1^d t_1 - b_1^d) + b_2 g_1} \right] \frac{X + G_d}{P}$$

$$+ \left[\frac{b_2}{e_1(1 - a_1^d + a_1^d t_1 - b_1^d) + b_2 g_1} \right] \frac{MS}{P} \qquad (6.A.3)$$

is the aggregate demand equation for real income. The composites of parameters inside the brackets are the reduced-form multipliers for the exogenous variables. The reduced-form multipliers can be interpreted in much the same way that the multipliers in Chapter 3 were interpreted.

Notice in (6.A.3) that the quantity of real income (output) varies inversely with the price level, $\partial(Y/P)/\partial P < 0$. The same qualitative relationship is indicated in our graphical analysis. For any given price level, the following qualitative results, which are indicated in the graphical analysis, are verified by inspection of (6.A.3): $\partial(Y/P)/\partial t_0 < 0$, $\partial(Y/P)/\partial t_1 < 0$, $\partial(Y/P)/\partial((X + G_d)/P) > 0$, and $\partial(Y/P)/\partial(MS/P) > 0$. Moreover, (6.A.3) indicates that the impact of changes in export and government expenditures in a crucial way depends on the value of the slope of the asset money demand function, $(\partial(MA/P)/\partial R) = -e_1$. The less (greater) the absolute value of e_1, i.e., the less (greater) the sensitivity of asset money balances to changes in the interest rate, the less (greater) the impact of changes in export and/or government expenditures on real income. Similarly, the impact of changes in the money stock depends on the value of the slope of the investment function $(\partial(I/P)/\partial R) = b_2$. More will be said in Chapter 8 about these crucial parameter values and how they govern the relative effectiveness of monetary and fiscal policies in changing aggregate demand.

By substituting the reduced-form equation for real income and/or the reduced-form equation for the interest rate into the structural equations of the model, we can derive the reduced-form equations for the other unknown endogenous variables of the *IS-LM* model. These reduced forms may be used to evaluate the effects of changes in the exogenous variables on the respective endogenous variables. Since the graphical analysis is sufficient to answer our qualitative questions and the additional reduced forms are rather complex, we shall not undertake their derivation here.

REVIEW QUESTIONS

1. Given:

	Q_{io}	Q_{it}	P_{io}	P_{it}
Bread	2	3	$ .15	$ .50
Wine	3	10	$ 1.00	$ 1.40
Radios	1	2	$10.00	$20.00

where Q_{io} are the quantities of goods purchased in the base period, P_{io} are the corresponding prices, Q_{it} are quantities of goods purchased in the current period, and P_{it} are the corresponding prices, calculate both the Laspeyres and Paasche price indices. If the values of the two indices are different, explain.

2. (a) On a separate piece of paper, copy the table given below. For increases in each of the exogenous variables, indicate the direction of change in the endogenous variables (+ for increases; − for decreases; 0 for no change) when all other exogenous variables remain unchanged. State any necessary qualifications to your answer. Examples are given.

EXO \ END	⇹	G	t_0	t_1	X	MS	P
Y/P	+						
R		−					
C/P							−
S/P							
T/P							
I/P							
IM/P							
MT/P							
MA/P							

(b) Changes in which of the exogenous variables listed in the table above explain movement along the aggregate output demand curve and which explain shifts in output demand?

3. Each of the types of *IS-LM* disequilibrium adjustment defined in the chapter imply an initial disequilibrium state of the system. State the inequalities for each of these disequilibrium states that describe the money and income-expenditure sectors.

SELECTED READINGS

BAUMOL, W. J., *Economic Theory and Operations Analysis*, Englewood Cliffs, N.J.: Prentice-Hall, 1961, Chap. 12.

CROUCH, R. L., *Macroeconomics*, New York: Harcourt Brace, 1972, Chaps. 13 and 14.

HANSEN, A. H., *Monetary Theory and Fiscal Policy*, New York: McGraw-Hill, 1949.

HICKS, J. R., "Mr. Keynes and the Classics," *Econometrica*, 5 (April 1937), 147–59.

PATINKIN, D., *Money, Interest, and Prices*, 2nd ed., New York: Harper & Row, 1965.

SAMUELSON, P. A., "The Simple Mathematics of Income Determination," in L. A. Metzler (ed.), *Essays in Honor of Alvin H. Hansen*, New York: Norton, 1948.

CHAPTER 7

The Determination of Output Supply

The amount of goods and services that an economy can produce (and that will be the real income of the economy's participants) depends largely on the amount of labor employed and the productivity of that labor. Firms will maximize profit in the short run by hiring only enough workers to produce the output which is salable in the market for at least enough to pay for labor's services and other variable costs of production.

As long as we are concerned with the economics of a depressed economy in which labor supply is almost unlimited, stimulus to aggregate demand will increase output and employment without incurring problems with rising prices. Thus, the perfectly elastic output supply curve implied by the exogenous price level assumption in the preceding chapters was quite reasonable. Empirical studies indicate that such an analysis was applicable in the U.S. in the 1930s when widespread unemployment prevailed and again between 1961 and 1965 when monetary and fiscal policies were used to decrease unemployment without excessive price increases.

But a model restricted to analysis of depressions and recessions is not general enough for our purposes. And the exogenous price level assumption is not acceptable when labor supply is not perfectly elastic. Thus, we shall develop the theory of aggregate output supply so that by equating supply and demand, we obtain an endogenously determined price level.

7.1 THE PRODUCTION PROCESS

The quantity of goods and services produced in the economy requires a host of factor inputs. These include labor, capital, technology, land, entrepreneurial and managerial talents, and raw materials. The aggregate production process may be specified by a production function. A production function is simply a technical relationship which specifies that the quantity of output produced depends on combinations of factor inputs.

Our production function,

$$\frac{Y}{P} = \frac{Y}{P}(L_d, K, \text{TEC}) \tag{7.1.1}$$

states that output depends on labor requirements, L_d, capital, K, and technical progress, TEC. All other input variables, like material inputs, not explicitly specified in (7.1.1) are assumed to vary in direct proportion to capital input and therefore need not be included.

In our analysis of aggregate output demand we defined net investment as an increase in the capital stock. In the long run the new capital is employed in the production process. But in the short run we shall assume that changes in the capital stock due to net investment are relatively small so that the capital stock is roughly fixed.

Technical progress will be considered exogenous as well. Technology is the economy's state of knowledge regarding the principles of physical and social phenomena that can be applied in the production process. Technical progress is the advance of technology and includes (1) advances which improve the productive quality of other input factors such as labor skills resulting from education and training; (2) advances which provide new products with important new characteristics; (3) advances which provide improved methods of producing products; (4) new techniques of organization, management, and marketing; and (5) public investment in social overhead capital, such as highways, that indirectly enhances the efficiency of private industry.[1]

Let us assume that the form that the aggregate production function takes is

$$\frac{Y}{P} = L_d^{\alpha} K^{\beta} \text{TEC}^{\gamma}, \qquad 0 < \alpha, \beta, \gamma < 1 \tag{7.1.2}$$

---

[1] For simplification purposes we assume that technical progress can be identified and quantified separately from units of capital, labor, and other factor inputs. Technical progress implies that an increase in output can occur over time given other input resources. It can take a variety of forms.

Technical progress can be *labor-using* if it raises the marginal product of labor relative to the marginal product of capital. It is *capital-using* if it raises the marginal product of capital relative to the marginal product of labor. If it raises both of the marginal products in the same proportion, technical progress is neutral. Another distinction that is made is whether technical progress is embodied or *disembodied*. The question here is whether technical progress must be embodied in, say, new investment in order to affect output, or whether it is disembodied in the sense that it can be considered as an independent factor which affects output without new investment to become operative. In our model we have assumed that the technical progress is disembodied.

This is a multiplicative function (linear in logs), and as such it will complicate our forthcoming algebraic analysis. But a linear production function is not only empirically questionable, it is theoretically implausible because it would say that on an either/or basis labor, capital, or technical progress can independently produce output. This is highly improbable in the aggregate production process.[2]

A picture of (7.1.2) is shown in Fig. 7.1.1. By varying the units of labor input with an exogenous capital stock, $\overline{K}$, and level of technical progress, $\overline{TEC}$, we may calculate the corresponding values of output. For any given level of output the production function tells us how many units of labor will be required to produce it. For example, if producers wish to produce $(Y/P)_1$, they must hire L_1 units of labor. If producers wish to increase output to $(Y/P)_2$, they must increase employment to L_2.

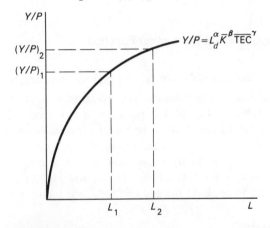

FIGURE 7.1.1

Aggregate Production Function

Increases (decreases) in both the capital stock and technical progress increase (decrease) output per unit of labor employed because $\partial(Y/P)/\partial K = \beta L_d^\alpha TEC^\gamma K^{\beta-1} > 0$ and $\partial(Y/P)/\partial TEC = \gamma L_d^\alpha K^\beta TEC^{\gamma-1} > 0$. For example, suppose that the stock of capital input were increased from $\overline{K}$ to $\overline{\overline{K}}$. In Fig. 7.1.2 for any given quantity of labor, for example, L_1, output would be greater as shown by $(Y/P)_3 > (Y/P)_2$. The additional units of capital input

---

[2] Firms in the economy may have various types of production functions: one like (7.1.2), a fixed coefficient production function where there is no possibility for substitution between factor inputs to take place; the C.E.S. production function, which assumes that the elasticity of substitution is constant (but not necessarily 1); and a variety of production functions exhibiting other theoretical properties and assumptions. Regardless of the mixture, the aggregate production function is likely to be approximated by (7.1.2).

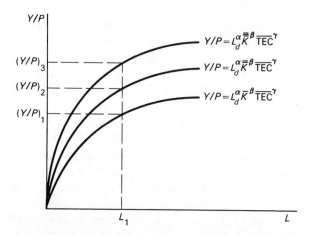

FIGURE 7.1.2

Shifts in the Aggregate Production Function

in the production process make labor input more productive. Conversely, if the stock of capital input were decreased from $\bar{\bar{K}}$ to $\bar{K}$, any given unit of labor, for example, L_1, would produce less output, $(Y/P)_1 < (Y/P)_2$. Similarly, increases (decreases) in technical progress increase (decrease) the output per unit of labor used in the production process.

The foregoing gives us some basic understanding of the aggregate production process. We may add Eq. (7.1.2) and Fig. 7.1.1 to our summary page and go on to consider the demand for labor input.

7.2 LABOR DEMAND

When making the decision about how many workers to hire, each producer will want to know the following: For a given capital stock and level of technical progress, how much will output change if an additional worker is hired? In symbols, producers want to know $\partial(Y/P)/\partial L_d$. The answer in the aggregate is derived by partially differentiating (7.1.2) with respect to labor input.

$$\frac{\partial(Y/P)}{\partial L_d} = \alpha K^{\beta} TEC^{\gamma} L_d^{\alpha-1} \tag{7.2.1}$$

This is the equation for labor's marginal product. It tells us what the increment in output will be when only additional units of labor are employed. We can draw a picture of this relationship for given values of the capital stock, technical progress, and the parameters by varying units of labor input, calculating corresponding marginal products, and plotting the data. Or graphically, we can derive the marginal product curve of labor as illustrated

SUMMARY PAGE

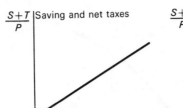

$\frac{S+T}{P}$ | Saving and net taxes

Y/P

$\frac{S+T}{P}$ | Income-expenditures equilibrium

45°

$I+G+F/P$

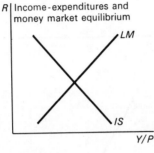

R | Asset money demand

MA/P

R | Income-expenditures and money market equilibrium

LM

IS

Y/P

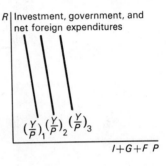

R | Investment, government, and net foreign expenditures

$\left(\frac{Y}{P}\right)_1 \left(\frac{Y}{P}\right)_2 \left(\frac{Y}{P}\right)_3$

$I+G+F \; P$

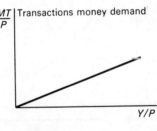

$\frac{MT}{P}$ | Money market equilibrium

MA/P

$\frac{MT}{P}$ | Transactions money demand

Y/P

P | Product market

D

Y/P

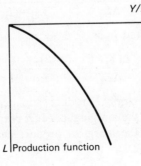

L | Production function

Equations

1. $\dfrac{S+T}{P} = -a_0 + a_1 t_0 + (1-a_1+a_1 t_1)\dfrac{Y}{P}$

2. $\dfrac{I+G+F}{P} = b_0^d - a_0^f + a_1^f t_0 + \dfrac{G_u}{P} + \dfrac{X}{P}$

   $+ (b_1^d - a_1^f(1-t_1))\dfrac{Y}{P} - b_2 R$

3. $\dfrac{S+T}{P} = \dfrac{I+G+F}{P}$

4. $\dfrac{MT}{P} = g_1 \dfrac{Y}{P}$

5. $\dfrac{MA}{P} = e_0 - e_1 R$

6. $\dfrac{MS}{P} = \dfrac{MT}{P} + \dfrac{MA}{P}$

7. $Y/P = L_d^\alpha K^\beta \mathrm{TEC}^\gamma$

137

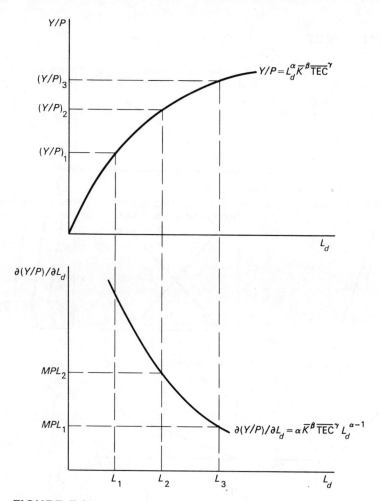

FIGURE 7.2.1

Graphical Derivation of Labor's Marginal Product Curve

in Fig. 7.2.1. Since we are working with decrete units in the diagram, the slope of the production function between L_1 and L_2 is approximately

$$\frac{\Delta(Y/P)}{\Delta L_d} = \frac{(Y/P)_2 - (Y/P)_1}{L_2 - L_1} = \text{MPL}_2$$

and between L_2 and L_3 is

$$\frac{\Delta(Y/P)}{\Delta L_d} = \frac{(Y/P)_3 - (Y/P)_2}{L_3 - L_2} = \text{MPL}_1$$

A locus of such marginal product estimates and the corresponding values of labor input form the marginal product curve of labor. For small changes in the labor input, the marginal product curve derived in Fig. 7.2.1 closely represents Eq. (7.2.1).

138

Notice that $\text{MPL}_2 > \text{MPL}_1$. As we move along the production function the marginal product of labor falls. Differentiating (7.2.1) with respect to labor gives

$$\frac{\partial[(\partial Y/P)/\partial L_d]}{\partial L_d} = \underbrace{(\alpha - 1)\alpha K^{\beta}\text{TEC}^{\gamma}L_d^{\alpha - 2}}_{\displaystyle \underset{+}{-}} < 0 \qquad (7.2.2)$$

That is, as additional units of labor are hired to produce additional units of output, the marginal product of labor falls. How do we know this? Because where $0 < \alpha < 1$, the slope of Eq. (7.2.1), as shown by Eq. (7.2.2), is negative. The marginal product of labor falls as units of labor are added to the fixed factors in the production process. As you may recall, this is the *law of diminishing return*.

In Fig. 7.1.2 we illustrated the effect of changes in the exogenous capital stock on the production function. Figure 7.2.2 shows the effect on

FIGURE 7.2.2

Shifts in the Marginal Product Curve of Labor

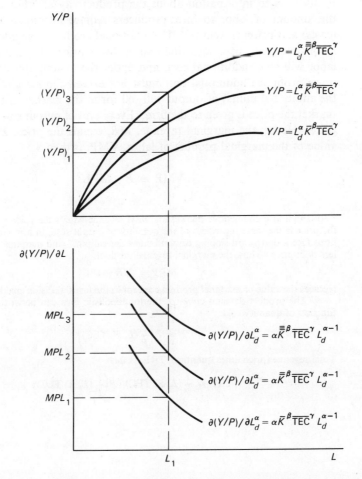

labor's marginal product curve. Suppose again that the capital stock increases from $\overline{K}$ to $\overline{\overline{K}}$. Since $\partial(Y/P)/\partial K = \beta\text{TEC}^\gamma L_d^\alpha K^{\beta-1} > 0$, for any given quantity of labor input, output increases, i.e., each unit of labor becomes more productive. Thus, labor's marginal product curve shifts upward such that for $L_d = L_1$, $\text{MPL}_3 > \text{MPL}_2$. Conversely, when the stock of capital falls from $\overline{K}$ to $\underline{K}$ labor's marginal product curve shifts downward such that for $L_d = L_1$, $\text{MPL}_2 > \text{MPL}_1$.

Similarly, since $\partial(Y/P)/\partial\text{TEC} = \gamma K^\beta L_d^\alpha \text{TEC}^{\gamma-1} > 0$, increases (decreases) in technical progress increase (decrease) labor's marginal product for any given quantity of labor input.

Since we have already added the upper diagram in Fig. 7.2.2 to the summary page we need add only the lower diagram. Since Eq. (7.2.1) is derived from the production function it is not included on the summary page as a separate equation.

Wages and Prices

In addition to information about the productivity of labor in determining the amount of labor to hire, producers require information about wages (costs) and prices (revenues). The additional product of an additional unit of labor input must be sold in the market for a price. The additional unit of labor will incur additional cost, and under the assumption that firms maximize profit the additional cost must not exceed the marginal revenue that the additional unit(s) of output will sell for in the market. In a competitive market the price is given to the firm. Every unit of output sold is sold at that price. Hence, the marginal revenue, MR, equals the price, P. The market value of the marginal product of labor, VMP, is then

$$\text{VMP} \equiv P \cdot \text{MPL}\,[3] \qquad (7.2.3)$$

---

[3] Although in a competitive market marginal revenue equals the price of output because the price is the same regardless of the quantity of output sold, in a monopolistic market, firms face a downward-sloping demand curve for output. And marginal revenue, MR, is less than price. Thus, the marginal revenue product,

$$\text{MRP} \equiv MR \cdot \text{MPL}$$

replaces the value of marginal product concept in the firms' decision-making process.

The product demand curve of the monopolistic firm can be written as an implicit function of quantity sold:

$$P = P\left(\frac{Y}{P}(L, K, \text{TEC})\right)$$

Total revenue (price times quantity), TRE, is then

$$\text{TRE} = \frac{Y}{P}(L, K, \text{TEC}) \cdot P\left(\frac{Y}{P}(L, K, \text{TEC})\right)$$

Firms will minimize cost (maximize profit) by hiring additional units of labor until the value of the marginal product equals the nominal wage rate, W,

$$W = P \cdot \text{MPL}^4 \tag{7.2.4}$$

If $W > P \cdot \text{MPL}$, the nominal wage rate exceeds the value of the product for which the additional unit of labor was hired to produce. Hence, firms will reduce employment. If $W < P \cdot \text{MPL}$, the nominal wage rate is less than the value of the product for which the additional unit of labor was hired to produce. Hence, firms will increase employment.

By dividing (7.2.4) through by the price level we derive

$$\frac{W}{P} = \text{MPL} \tag{7.2.5}$$

an alternative statement of the profit maximizing equilibrium condition in the labor market. When the real wage rate equals the marginal product of labor the equilibrium quantity of labor demanded to produce the profit maximizing quantity of output supplied is determined.

The change in revenue given a small change in employment can be shown by differentiating the TRE equation,

$$\frac{d\text{TRE}}{dL} = \frac{Y}{P} \frac{dP}{d(Y/P)} \frac{\partial(Y/P)}{\partial L} + P \frac{\partial(Y/P)}{\partial L}$$

$$= P \frac{\partial(Y/P)}{\partial L} \left(1 + \frac{Y/P}{P} \frac{dP}{d(Y/P)} \right)$$

The last term inside the parentheses is simply 1 over the elasticity of product demand, e_d, so that marginal revenue product is

$$\text{MRP} \equiv P \left(1 + \frac{1}{e_d} \right) \frac{\partial(Y/P)}{\partial L}$$

and since $P(1 + 1/e_d) = MR$ and $\partial(Y/P)/\partial L = \text{MPL}$,

$$\text{MRP} \equiv MR \cdot \text{MPL}$$

[4] The monopolistic firm will maximize profit by hiring additional labor inputs until marginal revenue product equals the nominal wage rate. In the competitive market, where $P = MR$,

$$W = P \cdot \text{MPL}$$

and in the monopolistic market

$$W = P \left(1 + \frac{1}{e_d} \right) \text{MPL}$$

In an economy with both competitive and monopolistic firms, the aggregate demand for labor will be the horizontal sum of the individual demand curves. If product demand changes do not alter substantially the output mix between the two types of firms or the elasticity of demand for monopolistic firms, the aggregate demand for labor can be written as

$$W = P \cdot F(L)$$

where $F'(L) < 0$.

SUMMARY PAGE

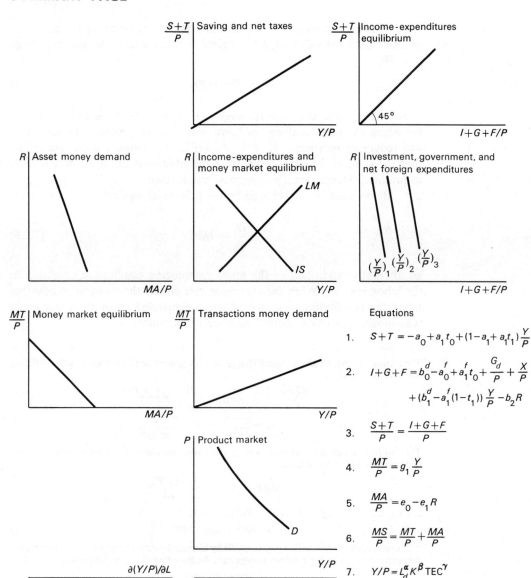

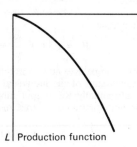

Saving and net taxes — $\frac{S+T}{P}$ vs Y/P

Income-expenditures equilibrium — $\frac{S+T}{P}$ vs $I+G+F/P$, 45°

Asset money demand — R vs MA/P

Income-expenditures and money market equilibrium — R vs Y/P, LM, IS

Investment, government, and net foreign expenditures — R vs $I+G+F/P$, $\left(\frac{Y}{P}\right)_1$, $\left(\frac{Y}{P}\right)_2$, $\left(\frac{Y}{P}\right)_3$

Money market equilibrium — $\frac{MT}{P}$ vs MA/P

Transactions money demand — $\frac{MT}{P}$ vs Y/P

Product market — P vs Y/P, D

Labor market — $\partial(Y/P)/\partial L$ vs L, MPL

Production function — Y/P vs L

Equations

1. $S+T = -a_0 + a_1 t_0 + (1-a_1+a_1 t_1)\frac{Y}{P}$

2. $I+G+F = b_0^d - a_0^f + a_1^f t_0 + \frac{G_d}{P} + \frac{X}{P}$
   $\qquad + (b_1^d - a_1^f(1-t_1))\frac{Y}{P} - b_2 R$

3. $\frac{S+T}{P} = \frac{I+G+F}{P}$

4. $\frac{MT}{P} = g_1 \frac{Y}{P}$

5. $\frac{MA}{P} = e_0 - e_1 R$

6. $\frac{MS}{P} = \frac{MT}{P} + \frac{MA}{P}$

7. $Y/P = L_d^\alpha K^\beta \mathrm{TEC}^\gamma$

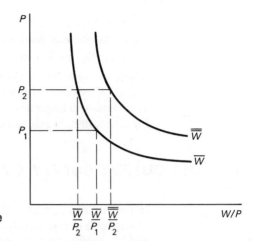

FIGURE 7.2.3

Relationship between the Price
Level and the Real Wage Rate

Let us assume that the aggregate demand for labor input is the horizontal sum of all of the firms' labor demand curves and that the nominal wage rate, W, is exogenous. That is, the nominal wage rate is determined by collective bargaining agreements in the short run and given to the model. Figure 7.2.3 shows the relationship between the price level and the real wage rate for given levels of the nominal wage rate. Given the nominal wage rate there is an inverse relationship between the price level and the real wage rate. In fact, there is a proportional relationship between price levels and real wage rates for given values of the nominal wage rate such that the curve relating them is a rectangular hyperbola.[5] A decrease, for example, in the price level from P_2 to P_1 when $W = \overline{W}$ means the real wage rate increases from $\overline{W}/P_2$ to $\overline{W}/P_1$. Shifts in the price-real wage rate curve occur when the

---

[5] The relationship between the price level and real wage rate can be specified as

$$P = \frac{W}{W/P}$$

Differentiating price with respect to the real wage rate where $W = \overline{W}$ gives

$$\frac{dP}{d(W/P)} = -\frac{\overline{W}}{(W/P)^2}$$

Hence, the relationship between price and the real wage rate is hyperbolic. Moreover, the relationship is a rectangular hyperbola because its elasticity e is minus unity throughout:

$$e = \frac{dP}{d(W/P)} \cdot \frac{W/P}{P}$$

$$= -\frac{W}{(W/P)^2} \cdot \frac{W/P}{P}$$

$$= -W \cdot \frac{P}{W} \cdot \frac{1}{P}$$

$$= -1$$

nominal wage rate changes. Increases (decreases) in the nominal wage rate mean that for any given price level the real wage rate increases (decreases). For example, an increase in the nominal wage rate from $\overline{W}$ to $\overline{\overline{W}}$ shifts the price-real wage curve rightward such that for $P = P_2$, $W/P = \overline{\overline{W}}/P_2 > \overline{W}/P_2$. Conversely, leftward shifts in the price-real wage rate curve are associated with lower nominal wage rates. The price-real wage rate quadrant, Fig. 7.2.3, may be added to the summary page along with Eq. (7.2.5).

7.3 THE OUTPUT SUPPLY CURVE

In the last two sections of this chapter we developed the basis for a theory of aggregate output supply. Given a set of values for the exogenous variables and parameters on the supply side of our model, the output supply curve is a schedule of quantities of output producers are willing to make available in the market at various price levels. In Fig. 7.3.1 if the price level is P_2, firms

FIGURE 7.3.1

Graphical Derivation of the Aggregate Supply Curve

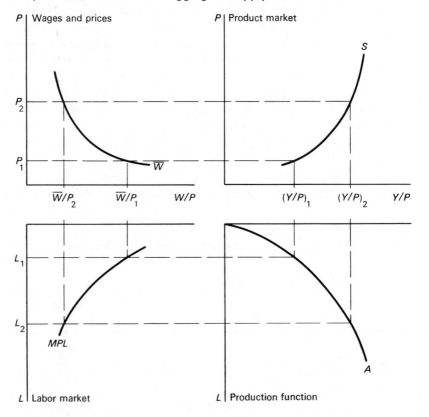

SUMMARY PAGE

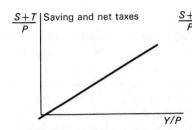

$\frac{S+T}{P}$ | Saving and net taxes

(x-axis: Y/P)

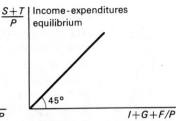

$\frac{S+T}{P}$ | Income-expenditures equilibrium

45°

(x-axis: $I+G+F/P$)

R | Asset money demand

(x-axis: MA/P)

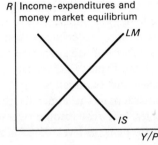

R | Income-expenditures and money market equilibrium

LM

IS

(x-axis: Y/P)

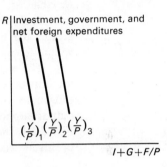

R | Investment, government, and net foreign expenditures

$\left(\frac{Y}{P}\right)_1 \left(\frac{Y}{P}\right)_2 \left(\frac{Y}{P}\right)_3$

(x-axis: $I+G+F/P$)

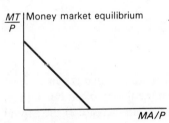

$\frac{MT}{P}$ | Money market equilibrium

(x-axis: MA/P)

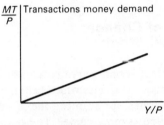

$\frac{MT}{P}$ | Transactions money demand

(x-axis: Y/P)

Equations

1. $\quad \frac{S+T}{P} = -a_0 + a_1 t_0 + (1 - a_1 + a_1 t_1)\frac{Y}{P}$

2. $\quad \frac{I+G+F}{P} = b_0^d - a_0^f + a_1^f t_0 + \frac{G_d}{P} + \frac{X}{P}$
   $\qquad + (b_1^d - a_1^f(1 - t_1))\frac{Y}{P} - b_2 R$

3. $\quad \frac{S+T}{P} = \frac{I+G+F}{P}$

4. $\quad \frac{MT}{P} = g_1 \frac{Y}{P}$

5. $\quad \frac{MA}{P} = e_0 - e_1 R$

6. $\quad \frac{MS}{P} = \frac{MT}{P} + \frac{MA}{P}$

7. $\quad Y/P = L_d^\alpha K^\beta \mathrm{TEC}^\gamma$

8. $\quad W/P = \partial(Y/P)/\partial L_d$

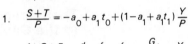

P | Wages and prices

$\overline{W}$

(x-axis: W/P)

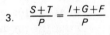

P | Product market

D

(x-axis: Y/P)

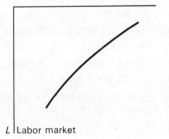

(y-axis: L) Labor market

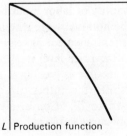

(y-axis: L) Production function

145

will hire L_2 units of labor where MPL $= \overline{W}/P_2$ and produce $(Y/P)_2$ units of profit-maximizing output. Similarly, given the same values of the exogenous variables and parameters, if the price level is $P_1 < P_2$, firms will hire L_1 units of labor where MPL $= \overline{W}/P_1$ and produce $(Y/P)_1$ units of profit-maximizing output. A locus of such combinations of the price levels and quantities of output supplied form the aggregate output supply curve shown in the upper right-hand quadrant. Given a set of values for the exogenous variables and parameters on the supply side of the model, changes in the price level indicate movement along the aggregate output supply curve. The greater the price level, the greater the quantity of output producers are willing to supply and the greater the quantity of labor employed.

The algebraic form of the aggregate output supply curve is derived in the appendix to this chapter. Given any particular set of values for the exogenous variables and parameters on the supply side of the model, the output supply equation in the appendix, like the output supply curve in Fig. 7.3.1, indicates that real income (the quantity of output) supplied is positively related to the price level, $\partial(Y/P)/\partial P > 0$.

The Impact of Changes in the Capital Stock

Shifts in the output supply curve occur when there are changes in at least one of the exogenous variables which help form the theory of output supply. Figure 7.3.2 illustrates, for example, the impact of an increase in the capital stock on the output supply curve. The output supply curve, S, is derived from the production function, A; the labor demand curve, MPL; and the price-real wage rate curve, $\overline{W}$. If the price level is P_1, firms will hire L_1 units of labor (where MPL $= \overline{W}/P_1$) and produce $(Y/P)_1$ units of profit-maximizing output.

Suppose, for example, that the stock of capital increases such that the production function shifts to A'; for any given quantity of labor input, more output can be produced. Correspondingly, the labor demand curve shifts to MPL'; for any given quantity of labor input labor's marginal product is higher and profit-maximizing producers are willing to pay a higher real wage rate for any given quantity of labor input because labor is more productive. With no change in the nominal wage rate and technical progress, firms will hire L_2 units of labor (employment increases) and produce $(Y/P)_2 > (Y/P)_1$ units of output when the price level is P_1. Moreover, given an increase in the capital stock real income is greater at any given price level. Thus, the output supply curve shifts (the output supply curve becomes relatively more price elastic) rightward to S'. Conversely, decreases in the capital stock shift the output supply curve leftward.

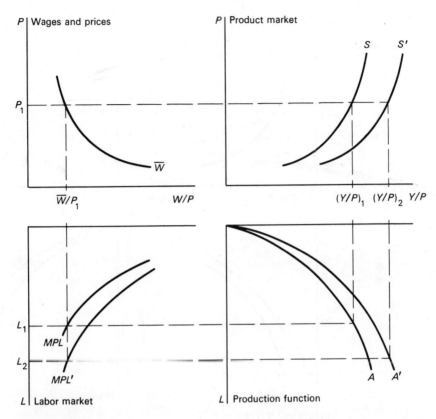

FIGURE 7.3.2

Effect of an Increase in the Capital Stock on the Aggregate Supply Curve

The Impact of Changes in Technical Progress

Figure 7.3.3 illustrates the impact of a change in technical progress on the output supply curve. The output supply curve, S, is derived from the production function, A; the labor demand curve, MPL; and the price-real wage rate curve, $\overline{W}$. If the price level is P_1, firms will hire L_1 units of labor (where MPL $= \overline{W}/P_1$) to produce $(Y/P)_1$ units of profit-maximizing output.

Suppose, for example, that the level of technical progress increases such that the production function shifts to A'; for any given unit of labor input more output can be produced. Correspondingly, the labor demand curve shifts to MPL', where the marginal product and thereby the real wage rate is higher for any given quantity of labor input. With no change in the nominal wage rate and the capital stock at the price level P_1, firms will hire L_2

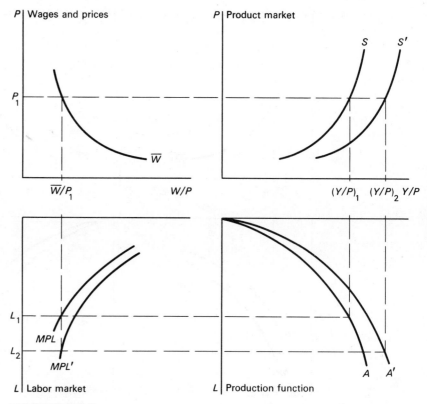

FIGURE 7.3.3

Effect of an Increase in Technical Progress on the Aggregate Supply Curve

units of labor (employment increases) to produce $(Y/P)_2 > (Y/P)_1$ units of output. Moreover, an increase in technical progress means that real income is greater at any given price level. Thus, the output supply curve shifts (the output supply curve becomes relatively more price elastic) rightward to S'. Conversely, decreases in technical progress shift the output supply curve leftward.

The Impact of Changes in the Nominal Wage Rate

Figure 7.3.4 illustrates the impact of changes in the nominal wage rate on the output supply curve. Initially, the output supply curve, S, reflects the production function, A; the labor demand curve, MPL; and the price-real wage rate curve, $\overline{W}$. If the price level is P_1, firms will hire L_1 units of labor (where MPL $= \overline{W}/P_1$) to produce $(Y/P)_2$ units of profit-maximizing output.

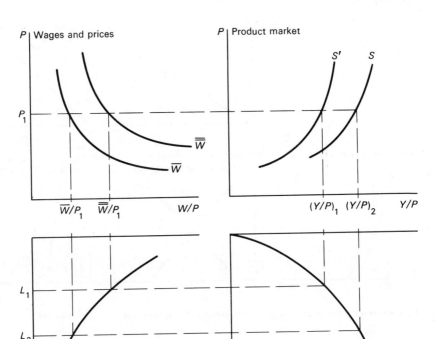

FIGURE 7.3.4

Effect of an Increase in the Nominal Wage on the Aggregate Supply Curve

Suppose, for example, that the nominal wage rate increases to $\overline{\overline{W}}$. The price-real wage rate curve shifts rightward, as shown in the upper left-hand quadrant of Fig. 7.3.4. At any given price level, output supplied is less (the output supply curve becomes relatively more price inelastic). For example, if the price level is P_1, firms will hire L_1 units of labor (employment decreases) because at the higher real wage rate $\overline{\overline{W}}/P_2 > \overline{W}/P_1$, firms must cut back production to $(Y/P)_1 < (Y/P)_2$ units of output in order to maximize profit (MPL $= \overline{\overline{W}}/P_1$).

Now that we have some preliminary understanding of a theory of aggregate output supply, we may add the aggregate output supply curve to the product market quadrant on the summary page and proceed to the next section where we shall discuss the supply of labor and concepts of unemployment.

SUMMARY PAGE

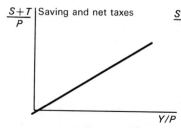

$\frac{S+T}{P}$ | Saving and net taxes

Y/P

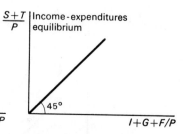

$\frac{S+T}{P}$ | Income-expenditures equilibrium

45°

$I+G+F/P$

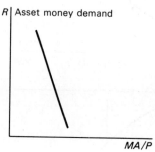

R | Asset money demand

MA/P

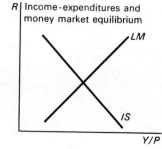

R | Income-expenditures and money market equilibrium

LM

IS

Y/P

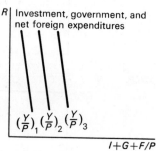

R | Investment, government, and net foreign expenditures

$(\frac{Y}{P})_1 \ (\frac{Y}{P})_2 \ (\frac{Y}{P})_3$

$I+G+F/P$

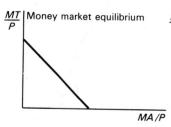

$\frac{MT}{P}$ | Money market equilibrium

MA/P

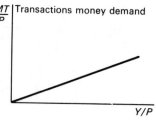

$\frac{MT}{P}$ | Transactions money demand

Y/P

Equations

1. $\dfrac{S+T}{P} = -a_0 + a_1 t_0 + (1 - a_1 + a_1 t_1)\dfrac{Y}{P}$

2. $\dfrac{I+G+F}{P} = b_0^d - a_0^f + a_1^f t_0 + \dfrac{G_d}{P} + \dfrac{X}{P}$
   $\qquad + (b_1^d - a_1^f(1 - t_1))\dfrac{Y}{P} - b_2 R$

3. $\dfrac{S+T}{P} = \dfrac{I+G+F}{P}$

4. $\dfrac{MT}{P} = g_1 \dfrac{Y}{P}$

5. $\dfrac{MA}{P} = e_0 - e_1 R$

6. $\dfrac{MS}{P} = \dfrac{MT}{P} + \dfrac{MA}{P}$

7. $Y/P = L_d^\alpha K^\beta TEC^\gamma$

8. $W/P = \partial(Y/P)/\partial L_d$

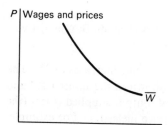

P | Wages and prices

$\overline{W}$

W/P

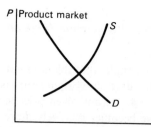

P | Product market

S

D

Y/P

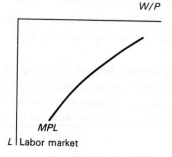

MPL

L | Labor market

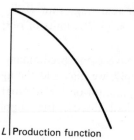

L | Production function

150

7.4 LABOR SUPPLY

The Work-Leisure Decision

The decision to offer labor services measured in hours per time period necessarily involves the decision to take a residual number of hours per time period in leisure. Workers are becoming increasingly too sophisticated to consider only nominal wages when making work-leisure decisions. Rather, they will be guided by real wages, or nominal wages relative to the price level that they expect to pay for goods and services.

There are two sides to the decision-making process, the subjective and the objective sides. On the subjective side a worker derives utility or satisfaction from real wages. He knows what his nominal wages will be when he accepts employment, but he can only predict what the price level will be. Thus, expected utility will depend on expected real wages. Moreover, the hours worked will incur disutility or dissatisfaction because the worker must give up hours of leisure to work. Thus, the worker's utility function may be specified as

$$E(U) = U\left(E\left(\frac{TW}{P}\right), H\right) \tag{7.4.1}$$

where expected utility, $E(U)$, is expressed as a function of expected total real wages, $E(TW/P)$, and hours of work, H. $\partial E(U)/\partial E(TW/P) > 0$ because increases in expected real wages increase expected satisfaction for every hour worked. $\partial E(U)/\partial H < 0$ because increases in hours worked decrease expected satisfaction for any given level of expected real wages.

Solving (7.4.1) for expected real wages in terms of expected satisfaction and hours of work given

$$E\left(\frac{TW}{P}\right) = U^{-1}(E(U), H)^6 \tag{7.4.2}$$

and draw a picture of a worker's indifference curves between expected real wages and hours worked for varying levels of expected satisfaction. Figure 7.4.1 shows three such indifference curves for levels of expected satisfaction, $E(U)_3 > E(U)_2 > E(U)_1$. For any given level of expected satisfaction, (7.4.2) implies an indifference curve along which workers are willing to work additional hours if they are compensated with additional expected real wages.

Each indifference curve in Fig. 7.4.1 shows that the marginal rate of

---

[6] Again we assume that the hypothesis of the implicit function therein is satisfied so that we may solve (7.4.1) for $E(TW/P)$ as a function of $E(U)$ and H.

substitution between hours of work and expected real wages (the slope of the indifference curve) is positive. Hence, we are making an assumption similar to the one of *risk aversion* that was made in our analysis of asset money demand. That is, the worker exhibits *work aversion* behavior in specifying his work-leisure preferences. There are two kinds of work averters: Along the worker's indifference curves in Fig. 7.4.1 the marginal rate of substitution is increasing. This worker requires larger and larger expected real wages if he is to work additional hours; he is a *work-leisure diversifier*. If the indifference curves were concave from below, the marginal rate of substitution would be decreasing. This worker would be a *work plunger* because he is willing to accept smaller and smaller units of expected real wages for additional units of hours worked. Of course, if the worker were a *work lover*,

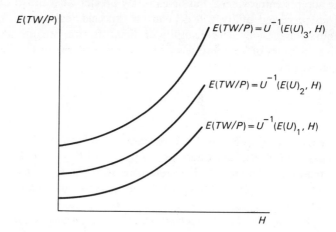

FIGURE 7.4.1

Indifference Curves Relating Expected Real Wages and Hours Worked

he would have a negative marginal rate of substitution. That is, he would derive positive expected satisfaction from the work itself and he would be willing to accept less expected real wages with additional hours of work. Although the cases of work plunger and work lover are interesting, we shall assume in the rest of our analysis that on balance workers are work-leisure diversifiers.

The objective side of the work-leisure decision involves primarily two constraints, the expected real wage per hour (or expected real wage rate) constraint and the capacity constraint.

The capacity constraint is simply the maximum number of hours the worker has to allocate between work and leisure per time period. The maximum is both physically and culturally determined. A worker must have a minimum number of hours of leisure to take care of his physical needs, e.g., to sleep and eat food. A worker must also have a minimum amount of leisure to cultivate the status associated with leisure activities. The minimum leisure requirements imply a maximum number of hours available for work, $\bar{H}$.

The expected real wage rate constraint is an expression of the total expected real wages as the number of hours worked multiplied by the expected real wage rate, $E(W/P)/H$,

$$E\left(\frac{TW}{P}\right) = \frac{E(TW/P)}{H} \cdot H \qquad (7.4.3)$$

$\partial E(TW/P)/\partial H = E(TW/P)/H > 0$ because for any given expected real wage rate, expected real wages will increase when hours worked increase. For example, in Figure 7.4.2 the slope of each of the lines from the origin represents a particular expected real wage rate. The higher the expected real wage rate, the greater the slope of the real wage rate constraint as shown by

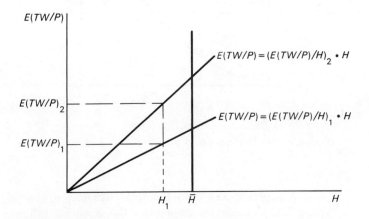

FIGURE 7.4.2

Real Wage Rate and Capacity Constraints

$(E(TW/P)/H)_2 > (E(TW/P)/H)_1$. For every hour worked the greater the expected real wage rate, the higher the expected real wages. For example, given $H = H_1$, as the expected real wage rate increases from $(E(TW/P)/H)_1$ to $(E(TW/P)/H)_2$ expected total real wage rise from $E(TW/P)_1$ to $E(TW/P)_2$.

The upper half of Figure 7.4.3, the workers' indifference map (Figure

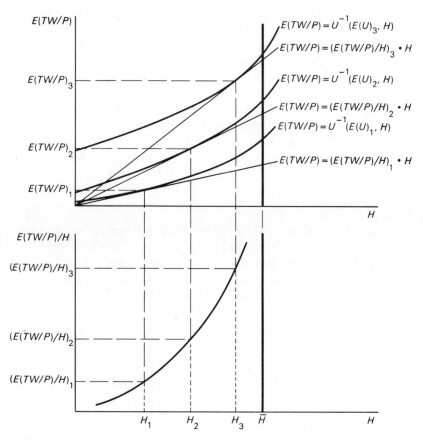

FIGURE 7.4.3

Work-Leisure Decision and the Workers' Supply Curve

7.4.1), is superimposed onto the real wage rate and capacity constraints (Figure 7.4.2). Under the assumption that a worker will maximize expected satisfaction, he will choose that combination of expected total real wages and hours to work which he is able to choose (given the expected real wage rate) so as to reach the highest possible level of expected satisfaction. The expected satisfaction-maximizing combination is the one where the expected real wage rate constraint is just tangent to the highest achievable indifference curve and to the left of $\bar{H}$. At this point the slope of the constraint (the expected real wage rate) just equals the slope of the highest indifference curve attainable [the marginal rate of substitution of hours he is willing to work (leisure foregone) for expected real wages]. For example, if the expected real wage rate is

$(E(TW/P)/H)_1$, the worker is willing to accept H_1 hours of work and receive $E(TW/P)_1$ expected real wages because $E(U)_1$ is the highest level of expected satisfaction he can reach. If the expected real wage rate rises to $(E(W/P)/H)_2$, he is willing to accept $(E(TW/P)_2, H_2)$ because $E(U)_2$ is the highest level of expected satisfaction he can achieve. If the real wage rises to $(E(TW/P)/H)_3$, then he is willing to accept $(E(TW/P)_3, H_3)$ because $E(U)_3$ is the highest level of expected satisfaction he can reach. As the expected real wage rate rises, the worker approaches his capacity constraint.[7]

In the lower half of Fig. 7.4.3 we may map the expected utility-maximizing combinations of expected real wage rates and hours of work the worker is willing to accept. A locus of such combinations is the worker's expected or perceived supply curve for labor because it tells how many hours of work a worker is willing to accept at various expected real wage rates. The curve is positively sloped under the assumption of work-leisure diversification and approaches the capacity constraint, $\bar{H}$. The aggregate perceived labor market supply curve is derived by horizontally summing all individual supply curves. The properties of the aggregate supply curve are similar to that of the worker's supply curve shown in Fig. 7.4.3.

We could continue to discuss our theory of labor supply in terms of hours of labor units or man-hours (workers times hours). However, since we shall be discussing the concept of unemployment in terms of the number of workers unemployed in the forthcoming sections of the book, we shall convert the labor supply curve from hour units to man units.

Assume that the aggregate labor supply curve in Fig. 7.4.3 can be expressed as an exponential relationship between the expected real wage rate and hours,

$$\frac{E(TW/P)}{H} = H^\lambda, \qquad \lambda > 0 \qquad\qquad (7.4.4)$$

Moreover, let us assume that the ratio of hours per man is constant. As the number of workers increases there is a proportional increase in hours offered for sale in the labor market. The assumption is reasonable in the short run where the composition of the labor force is relatively fixed and where the hours worked in each occupation are predetermined by relatively fixed preferences and institutional arrangements. Given a constant ratio of hours to

---

[7] At higher expected real wage rate levels, a worker's expected satisfaction-maximizing position may be such that the number of hours he is willing to work decreases as the expected real wage rate increases. This is the case of the backward-bending supply curve for labor. Or if the real wage rate rises such that the tangency of the highest level of satisfaction and the real wage rate constraint lies to the right of $\bar{H}$, the worker will only be able to achieve the level of satisfaction where the real wage rate and capacity constraints intersect. In this case the labor supply curve will have a vertical segment at $\bar{H}$ for higher real wage rates.

men in the short run, it can be shown that the labor supply curve in hour units can be converted to man units, L_s.[8] The conversion yields

$$\frac{E(TW/P)}{L_s} = \theta L_s^{\lambda}, \qquad \lambda > 0 \qquad (7.4.5)$$

As the expected real wage rate rises the number of workers *willing to accept* employment will increase.

Similar to the way in which the supply curve in hour units approaches the maximum number of available hours, the supply curve in labor units approaches the maximum feasible level of employment, L_f. This maximum is the total number of workers *willing to work*, and we shall call it the *labor force*.[9] Figure 7.4.4 is a picture of the labor supply and labor force curves.

[8] Hours can be defined in terms of the number of workers by

$$H \equiv L_s \cdot \frac{H}{L_s}$$

and their expected real wage per hour,

$$\frac{E(TW/P)}{H} = \left(E\left(\frac{TW}{P}\right) L_s \right) \cdot \frac{L_s}{H}$$

If we substitute these two expressions into (7.4.4), we get

$$\left(\frac{E(TW/P)}{L_s} \right) \cdot \frac{L_s}{H} = \left(L_s \cdot \frac{H}{L_s} \right)^{\lambda}$$

and rearranging terms gives

$$\frac{E(TW/P)}{L_s} = \left(\frac{H}{L_s} \right)^{\lambda+1} L_s^{\lambda}$$

If we assume that hours per man, H/L_s, is some constant such that $(H/L_s)^{\lambda+1} = \theta$, then we can rewrite,

$$\frac{E(TW/P)}{L_s} = \theta L_s^{\lambda}$$

where the expected real wage per worker is positively related to number of workers, $\partial(E(TW/P)/L_s)/\partial L_s = \lambda\theta L_s^{\lambda-1} > 0$. Moreover, if we assume that $\lambda > 1$, the slope is not only positive, but increasing, $\partial(\partial(E(TW/P)/L_s))/\partial L_s = (\lambda - 1)\lambda\theta L_s^{\lambda-2} > 0$. Thus, as the expected real wage per worker rises, fewer and fewer units of labor will be offered for sale in the market.

[9] One might expect that there is a positive relationship between the labor force and the real wage. As the real wage increases (decreases) the quantity of labor willing to work increases (decreases). But heads of families are not free to enter or leave the labor force as the real wage rate varies. They may choose unemployment in order to look for a better job, but they do not leave the labor force.

Variations in the labor force due to changes to the real wage rate occur primarily due to the variations in the number of secondary workers, primarily wives, willing to work. As the real wage rate rises one of two things may occur: Either nonworking wives may enter the labor force because they are attracted by the higher real wage rate, or since heads of families enjoy more real income with the rise in the real wage rate, working wives may leave the labor force and stay at home. For simplification purposes, we shall assume that the number of secondary workers leaving the labor force in any period just offsets those entering the labor force. Hence, we assume that the labor force is invariant with respect to the real wage rate. Changes in the labor force are caused primarily by changes in the working age population.

We have derived the aggregate labor supply curve where the decision to accept employment is based on labor's expectations of the real wage rate. Remember that the nominal wage rate is exogenous. However, labor's forecasts of the price level that will prevail once labor services are employed may be erroneous. The price level forecast error, PE, is defined by the difference between the actual price level, P, and the expected price level, $E(P)$,

$$PE = E(P) - P \qquad (7.4.6)$$

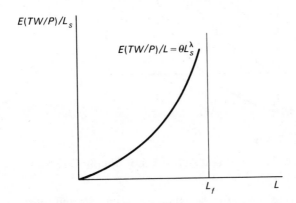

FIGURE 7.4.4

Expected or Perceived Aggregate Labor Supply Curve

And for a fixed nominal wage, the real wage rate forecast error, FE, is defined by the difference between the expected and actual real wage rates,

$$FE = \frac{E(TW/P)}{L_s} - \frac{TW/P}{L_s} \qquad (7.4.7)$$

Forecast errors can be either zero, positive, or negative.[10] If forecast error is zero, it means that $E(P) = P$ and that $E(TW/P)/L_s = (TW/P)/L_s$. Thus, labor has perceived correctly. When $E(P) > P$, $PE > 0$ and labor has overestimated the actual price level. Hence, $E(TW/P)/L_s < (TW/P)/L_s$ and $FE < 0$ because labor has underestimated the actual real wage rate. When $E(P) < P$, $PE < 0$ and labor has underestimated the actual price level. Hence, $E(TW/P)/L_s > (TW/P)/L_s$ and $FE > 0$ because labor has overestimated the actual real wage rate.

---

[10] Normally reference is made to the absolute value of forecast error such that only two cases exist, zero and positive, with two kinds of positive forecast errors, overestimates and underestimates. But we shall use three sets of value ranges for reasons that will soon become apparent.

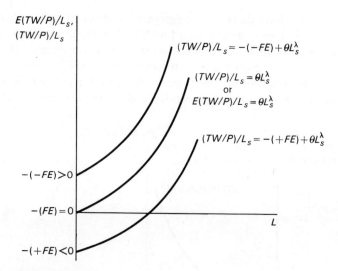

FIGURE 7.4.5

Aggregate Perceived and Actual Labor Supply Curves

Solving (7.4.7) for the actual real wage rate and substituting the results into (7.4.5) give

$$\frac{TW/P}{L_s} = -FE + \theta L_s^\lambda \qquad (7.4.8)$$

an expression of the actual real wage rate in terms of the number of workers and the real wage rate forecast error term. If $FE = 0$, the actual labor supply curve, (7.4.8), is the same as the perceived supply curve of labor, (7.4.5), as shown in Fig. 7.4.5. If $FE > 0$, $-(+FE) < 0$, and the actual labor curve lies to the right of the perceived supply curve. For any given worker, the expected real wage rate is greater than the actual real wage rate because labor overestimated the real wage rate. If $FE < 0$, $-(-FE) > 0$, and the actual labor supply curve lies to the left of the perceived supply curve for labor. For any given worker the expected real wage rate is less than the actual real wage rate because labor underestimated the real wage rate.

In Chapter 9 we shall consider the cases of positive forecast error when labor underestimates and overestimates the price level that will prevail after the jobs are accepted. These cases have particular relevance when discussing the theory of the inflation process. But for now we shall assume zero forecast error, $-FE = 0$, such that there is no difference between the actual and perceived labor supply curves.

We may now add Eq. (7.4.8) (under the zero forecast error assumption), the corresponding labor supply curve in Fig. 7.4.5, and the labor force curve to the labor market quadrant to the summary page. For simplification purposes we shall use W/P to denote the actual real wage rate, $(TW/P)L_s = W/P$.

Unemployment

Figure 7.4.6 is a duplicate of the labor market quadrant from the summary section where the actual labor supply and labor force curves are superimposed onto the labor demand curve. Suppose that the price level and the nominal wage are such that the real wage is $(W/P)_l$. Firms will maximize profit by hiring L_l units of labor so that $W/P = $ MPL. Total unemployment is the difference between the number of workers willing to work and employment,

$$U = L_f - L_d \tag{7.4.9}$$

For $W/P = (W/P)_l$, $L_d = L_l$ and $U = L_f - L_l$. Unemployment in our model can be involuntary. That is, for any real wage rate if there exists an excess supply of labor, then the excess represents the workers willing to accept employment but unable to find jobs at the prevailing real wage rate. Involuntary unemployment, IU, is determined by

$$IU - L_s - L_d \tag{7.4.10}$$

FIGURE 7.4.6

Less-Than-Full Employment Equilibrium in the Labor Market with Both Voluntary and Involuntary Unemployment

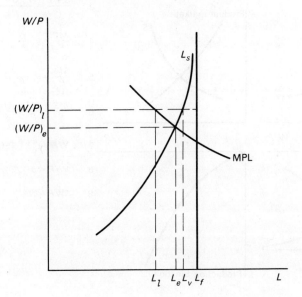

SUMMARY PAGE

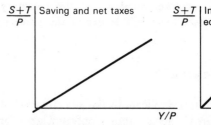

$\frac{S+T}{P}$ | Saving and net taxes

$\frac{S+T}{P}$ | Income-expenditures equilibrium

45°

$I+G+F/P$

Y/P

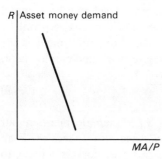

R | Asset money demand

MA/P

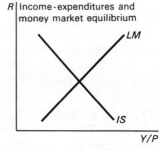

R | Income-expenditures and money market equilibrium

LM

IS

Y/P

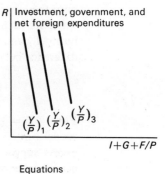

R | Investment, government, and net foreign expenditures

$\left(\frac{Y}{P}\right)_1 \left(\frac{Y}{P}\right)_2 \left(\frac{Y}{P}\right)_3$

$I+G+F/P$

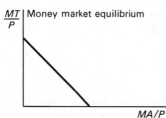

$\frac{MT}{P}$ | Money market equilibrium

MA/P

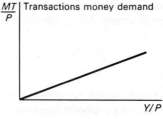

$\frac{MT}{P}$ | Transactions money demand

Y/P

Equations

1. $\dfrac{S+T}{P} = -a_0 + a_1 t_0 + (1 - a_1 + a_1 t_1)\dfrac{Y}{P}$

2. $\dfrac{I+G+F}{P} = b_0^d - a_0^f + a_1^f t_0 + \dfrac{G_d}{P} + \dfrac{X}{P}$
$\qquad + (b_1^d - a_1^f(1-t_1))\dfrac{Y}{P} - b_2 R$

3. $\dfrac{S+T}{P} = \dfrac{I+G+F}{P}$

4. $\dfrac{MT}{P} = g_1 \dfrac{Y}{P}$

5. $\dfrac{MA}{P} = e_0 - e_1 R$

6. $\dfrac{MS}{P} = \dfrac{MT}{P} + \dfrac{MA}{P}$

7. $Y/P = L_d^{\alpha} K^{\beta} TEC^{\gamma}$

8. $W/P = \partial(Y/P)/\partial L_d$

9. $W/P = \theta L_s^{\lambda}$

P | Wages and prices

$\overline{W}$

W/P

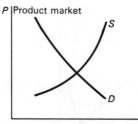

P | Product market

S

D

Y/P

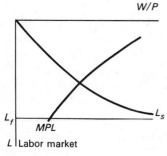

L_f

MPL

L_s

L | Labor market

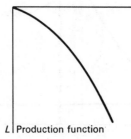

L | Production function

For $W/P = (W/P)_l$, $L_d = L_l$ and $L_s = L_v$ such that $IU = L_v - L_l$. The remainder of the unemployment is those workers who are willing to work, but are voluntarily unemployed because they are unwilling to accept employment at the prevailing real wage rate. Voluntary unemployment, VU, is determined by

$$VU = L_f - L_s \tag{7.4.11}$$

For $W/P = (W/P)_l$, $L_s = L_v$ and $VU = L_f - L_v$.

The concept of voluntary unemployment suggests that workers may be willing to accept the cost of unemployment and devote full time to seeking a better job without leaving the labor force. These workers are considered voluntarily or frictionally unemployed. They choose to accept unemployment and incur a cost necessary to acquire information about better job opportunities in a real world of imperfect knowledge. The cost takes the form of real wages foregone by choosing the unemployment. The unemployment is rational only if a worker expects to increase his lifetime earnings over the costs of unemployment by finding another job that pays a higher real wage. This phenomenon distinguishes the number of workers "willing to accept employment" at various real wage rates (labor supply) from the total labor force. As the equilibrium real wage rate rises, the number of frictionally unemployed workers falls (total employment increases).

Of course, if the nominal wage rate and the price level were flexible downward, then the excess labor supply at $(W/P)_l$ would cause the real wage rates to fall to $(W/P)_e$, and the quantity of labor demanded would increase to L_e where involuntary unemployment falls to zero and $L_f - L_e$ workers would be voluntarily unemployed. But the nominal wage rate tends to be sticky downward such that less than full employment, L_l, can exist. If the real wage rate were below full involuntary employment equilibrium, the nominal wage rate would probably rise because it is not generally considered inflexible upward. Then full employment would be restored. We shall assume that the nominal wage rate is exogenous and concern ourselves with only the results of possible downward wage rate inflexibility when the real wage rate is above the full involuntary employment equilibrium real wage rate.

Temporary shifts in the labor supply and demand curves will change both voluntary and involuntary unemployment. Permanent changes, such as sustained advances in the level of productivity, shift the labor demand curve and permanently change voluntary and involuntary unemployment. If, for example, as shown in Fig. 7.4.7, an increase in technical progress or the capital stock shifts the demand for labor rightward to MPL', involuntary unemployment, $L_v - L_l$, at $(W/P)_l$ would be eliminated.

We may now add the unemployment equations (7.4.10) and (7.4.11) to the summary page.

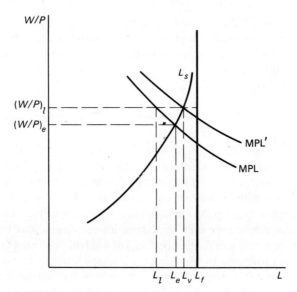

FIGURE 7.4.7

Impact of Changes in Labor Productivity
on the Real Wage Rate and Employment

Nominal Wage (In)flexibility and Output Supply

In Section 7.3 we derived an output supply curve based on the short-run assumption that the nominal wage rate is exogenous. Given the nominal wage rate, changes in the price level change the real wage rate, employment, and the quantity of output supplied. As long as we had no theory of labor supply (except the implicit assumption that labor supply is unlimited) the labor supply curve has no influence on the shape of the output supply curve. However, the introduction of a theory of labor supply in this section brings up the question of nominal wage rate (in)flexibility whenever there is either a surplus (excess supply) or shortage (excess demand) of labor. The shape of the output supply curve depends on the assumption(s) made.

A nominal wage rate that neither rises nor falls in response to labor shortages or surpluses can be explained by (1) legal restrictions which are imposed to prevent changes in the nominal wage rate; (2) collusion by employers to eliminate the competition for labor, which leads to increases in the nominal wage rate; and (3) collusion by labor to prevent competition for jobs, which leads to decreases in the nominal wage rate.

When there is surplus labor (labor supply exceeds labor demand) and the nominal wage rate is strictly inflexible, increases in the price level increase

SUMMARY PAGE

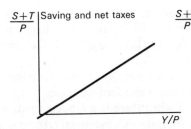

$\dfrac{S+T}{P}$ | Saving and net taxes

$\dfrac{S+T}{P}$ | Income-expenditures equilibrium

45°

$I+G+F/P$

Y/P

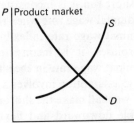

R | Asset money demand

MA/P

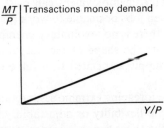

R | Income-expenditures and money market equilibrium

LM

IS

Y/P

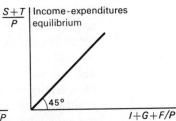

R | Investment, government, and net foreign expenditures

$\left(\dfrac{Y}{P}\right)_1 \left(\dfrac{Y}{P}\right)_2 \left(\dfrac{Y}{P}\right)_3$

$I+G+F/P$

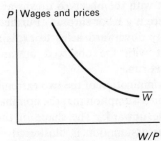

$\dfrac{MT}{P}$ | Money market equilibrium

MA/P

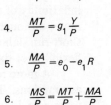

$\dfrac{MT}{P}$ | Transactions money demand

Y/P

Equations

1. $\dfrac{S+T}{P} = -a_0 + a_1 t_0 + (1 - a_1 + a_1 t_1)\dfrac{Y}{P}$

2. $\dfrac{I|G|F}{P} = b_0^d - a_0^f + a_1^f t_0 + \dfrac{G_d}{P} + \dfrac{X}{P}$
   $+ (b_1^d - a_1^f(1 - t_1))\dfrac{Y}{P} - b_2 R$

3. $\dfrac{S+T}{P} = \dfrac{I+G+F}{P}$

4. $\dfrac{MT}{P} = g_1 \dfrac{Y}{P}$

5. $\dfrac{MA}{P} = e_0 - e_1 R$

6. $\dfrac{MS}{P} = \dfrac{MT}{P} + \dfrac{MA}{P}$

7. $Y/P = L_d^\alpha K^\beta \,\mathrm{TEC}^\gamma$

8. $W/P = \partial(Y/P)/\partial L_d$

9. $W/P = \theta L_s^\lambda$

10. $VU = L_f - L_s$

11. $IU = L_s - L_d$

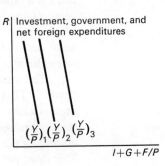

P | Wages and prices

$\overline{W}$

W/P

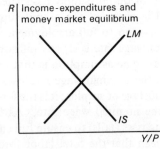

P | Product market

S

D

Y/P

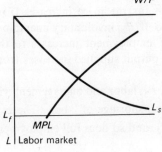

L | Labor market

L_f

MPL

L_s

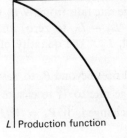

L | Production function

Y/P

the quantity of output supplied. Moreover, as the real wage rate falls, employment increases along the labor demand curve to full employment (labor demand equal to labor supply). If the price level continues to increase, the real wage rate will continue to fall and create a labor shortage (labor demand exceeds labor supply). Since less labor is supplied than demanded, the quantity of output supplied decreases. Thus, the output supply curve is positively sloped when there is a labor surplus and negatively sloped when there is a labor shortage. Consequently, there is a kink in the output supply curve at the level of output supply associated with full employment in the labor market. The shape of the output supply curve is influenced by the labor demand curve up to full employment and by labor supply thereafter when the nominal wage rate is strictly inflexible.

The other extreme assumption is that the nominal wage rate is strictly flexible. That is, the nominal wage rate rises or falls depending on whether there is a labor shortage or surplus; it is the forces of labor supply and demand that determine the nominal wage rate. As the price level rises (falls), the nominal wage rate rises (falls) to ensure full employment in the labor market. This does not mean that the total labor force is employed. It means that although voluntary unemployment can exist as workers are in the process of moving between jobs or unable to work for reasons of immobility, health, or lack of skills, there is no involuntary unemployment. Thus, with a flexible nominal wage rate the shape of the output supply curve is vertical at the level of output supply associated with full employment (labor supply equal to labor demand).

Both of the foregoing extreme assumptions are questionable. Although nominal wage rate flexibility or adjustability may be a reasonable long-run assumption, in the short run it is inconsistent with the observed downward inflexibility of the nominal wage rate when there is a labor surplus. Furthermore, although nominal wage rate inflexibility downward helps to explain short-run labor surpluses, it is inconsistent with the observed upward flexibility of the nominal wage rate in the short run.

A more realistic assumption involves a combination of the two extreme assumptions. Thus, we shall make the short-run assumption that the nominal wage rate is inflexible downward and flexible upward. The shape of the output supply curve which is implied by this assumption is illustrated in Fig. 7.4.8. Given the nominal wage rate $\overline{W}$, as the price increases from P_1 to P_2, the real wage rate falls from $\overline{W}/P_1$ to $\overline{W}/P_2$, involuntary unemployment decreases from $L_3 - L_1$ to zero, and employment increases to the full employment level, L_2. The quantity of output supplied increases from $(Y/P)_1$ to $(Y/P)_2$.

If the price level rises beyond P_2 to, say, P_3, labor and management will raise the nominal wage rate to $\overline{\overline{W}}$ to ensure no shortage of labor. The real wage rate remains unchanged, $\overline{\overline{W}}/P_3 = \overline{W}/P_2$, and so does full employment

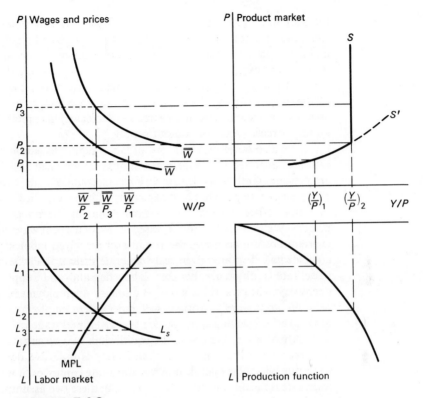

FIGURE 7.4.8

Output Supply with Nominal Wage Rates Which Are Inflexible Downward and Flexible Upward

of labor and the quantity of output supplied. Thus, above price level P_2 the output supply curve is vertical at $(Y/P)_2$.

As we shall see in Chapter 9 labor can be fooled by unexpected price increases into accepting a lower real wage rate and thereby provide additional quantities of labor along the labor demand curve beyond full employment. Thus, the shape of the output supply curve can be positively sloped, S', above the level of output associated with full employment (no involuntary unemployment). But for now we shall work with the output supply curve, S, derived in Fig. 7.4.8.

7.5 SUMMARY

In this chapter we have explained the aggregate production process and the derived demand for labor input for given values of capital and technical inputs. Firms maximize profit when the marginal product of labor equals the real wage rate. When the nominal wage rate is inflexible downward changes in the price level reduce the real wage rate and increase employment and the quantity of output supplied. Thus, changes in the quantity of output supplied are explained by changes in the price level along the output supply curve. Changes (shifts) in the output supply curve occur when at least one of the exogenous variables other than the price level (which is temporarily assumed exogenous) change. Increases (decreases) in capital and/or technical inputs increase (decrease) output supply.

We also developed a theory of labor supply based on worker maximization of expected real wage per unit of labor supplied. Given that workers are predominantly work-leisure diversifiers, changes in the expected real wage rate are positively related to the quantity of labor supplied. Labor's decision to supply labor depends on its expectation of the price level. Thus, the perceived labor supply curve is based on expected real wage rate. Given that expectations are accurate, the actual and perceived labor supply curves are coincidental. For any given real wage rate greater than the equilibrium real wage rate a difference between labor demand and supply is involuntary unemployment or surplus labor. Voluntary unemployment is the difference between labor supply (workers willing to accept employment) and the labor force (workers willing to work) for any given real wage rate.

A real wage rate above the equilibrium real wage rate can exist under the assumption that the nominal wage rate is inflexible downward. A real wage rate below the equilibrium real wage rate cannot exist when the nominal wage rate is flexible upward. By combining these two assumptions the output supply curve is vertical at full employment (labor supply equals labor demand). Only if labor can be fooled into additional supply can employment take place beyond full employment and then only up to the labor force constraint.

APPENDIX
Algebraic Derivation
of the Output Supply Curve

The aggregate supply equation is derived by simultaneously solving the necessary structural equations on the supply side of the model for real income (output supply). By substituting the production function [Eq. (7.1.2)] into the labor demand equation [Eq. (7.2.1)], we derive

$$\frac{\partial(Y/P)}{\partial L_d} = \alpha L_d^{-1} \frac{Y}{P}$$ (7.A.1)

an expression of the marginal product of labor in terms of real income and labor. By substituting (7.A.1) into the equilibrium condition on the supply side of the model [Eq. (7.2.5)], we derive

$$\frac{W}{P} = \alpha L_d^{-1} \frac{Y}{P}$$ (7.A.2)

an expression of the real wage rate in terms of real income and labor. Solving (7.A.2) for real income gives

$$\frac{Y}{P} = \alpha^{-1} W L_d P^{-1}$$ (7.A.3)

Next, the production function (7.1.2) can be solved for labor input,

$$L_d = \left(\frac{Y}{P}\right)^{1/\alpha} K^{-\beta/\alpha} \text{TEC}^{-\gamma/\alpha}$$ (7.A.4)

and substituted into (7.A.3), this gives

$$\frac{Y}{P} = \alpha^{\alpha/(1-\alpha)} W^{\alpha/(\alpha-1)} K^{\beta/(1-\alpha)} \text{TEC}^{\gamma/(1-\alpha)} P^{\alpha/(1-\alpha)}$$ (7.A.5)

the solution for real income (output) on the supply side of the model, i.e., the reduced form for real income (output) on the supply side of the model under the temporary assumption that the price level is exogenous. This is the equation for the aggregate output supply curve. Notice that the quantity of real income (output) supplied is positively related to the price level, i.e., where $0 < \alpha < 1$, $\partial(Y/P)/\partial P > 0$, until labor supply equals labor demand (full employment).

Given a fixed price level, the signs of the reduced-form multipliers which can be derived from (7.A.5) verify the results of graphical analysis: $\partial(Y/P)/\partial W < 0$, $\partial(Y/P)/\partial K > 0$, $\partial(Y/P)/\partial \text{TEC} > 0$.

By substituting the solution for real income into the structural equations of the supply side of the model, we can derive the reduced forms for the other endogenous supply variables. Since the graphical analysis is sufficient for our understanding of the qualitative impacts of changes in the exogenous supply variables on the endogenous variables of the model and since the additional reduced-form equations are complex, we shall not undertake their derivation here.

REVIEW QUESTIONS

1. Draw an individual's total real wage-hours worked indifference map which, when combined with an increasing real wage rate, yields a backward-bending labor supply curve. Rationalize this type of behavior.

2. (a) On a separate piece of paper, copy the table given below. For increases in each of the exogenous variables, indicate the direction of change in the endogenous variables (+ for increases; − for decreases; 0 for no change) when all other exogenous variables remain unchanged. Assume there is less than full employment before and after each change. Examples are given.

END

EXO ↘	W	K	TEC	L_f	P
Y/P	−				
W/P		+			
MPL					
L_d					
L_s					
VU					
IU					

(b) Changes in which exogenous variable(s) from 2(a) explain movement along the aggregate output supply curve and which explain shifts in the supply curve?

3. If the nominal wage rate and the price level were both flexible upward and downward, could involuntary unemployment exist?

SELECTED READINGS

BRANSON, W. H., *Macroeconomic Theory and Policy*, New York: Harper & Row, 1972, Chaps. 6, 7, and 8.

FERGUSON, C. E., *Microeconomic Theory*, Homewood, Ill.: Irwin, 1969.

FLEICHER, B., *Labor Economics: Theory and Evidence*, Englewood Cliffs, N.J.: Prentice-Hall, 1970.

PHELPS, E. S., et al., *Microeconomic Foundations of Employment and Inflation Theory*, New York: Norton, 1970.

CHAPTER **8**

The Complete Model

8.1 GENERAL EQUILIBRIUM

In the *IS-LM* part of our model, we assumed that suppliers of goods and services accommodate demanders of goods and services (demand creates its own supply). By varying the exogenous price level (which implied a horizontal output supply curve), quantities of output demanded were determined. This schedule of quantities demanded at various price levels identified the aggregate demand curve for goods and services. Changes in demand (shifts in the demand curve) occur when any of the values of the other exogenous variables and/or parameters in the *IS-LM* model change.

Similarly, on the supply side of our model, we assumed that demanders of goods and services accommodate suppliers of goods and services (supply creates its own demand). By varying the exogenous price level (which implied a horizontal output demand curve), quantities of output supplied were determined. This schedule of quantities supplied at various price levels identified the aggregate supply curve for goods and services. Changes in supply (shifts in the supply curve) occur when any of the values of the other exogenous variables and/or parameters on the supply side of the model change.

By combining both the theories of output supply and demand, we specify a more general model of aggregate economic behavior. The combination permits us to abandon the exogenous price level assumption. The forces of supply and demand interact in the system to determine the price level as well as the other endogenous variables on both the supply and demand side of the now complete skeleton model.

Producers supply real income generated by output supply in exchange for productive services provided by factor inputs. Real income is demanded so that owners of factor inputs may realize intended expenditures generated by output demand. Thus, suppliers and demanders are mutually accommodative. The decisions in the output market necessarily involve decisions in the bond, money, income-expenditures, and labor sectors. As individuals interact the system moves toward general equilibrium in all sectors.

Figure 8.1.1 shows a general equilibrium position of the model for a given set of exogenous variables and parameters. The values are labeled with the subscript a. It is a short-run general equilibrium because some variables (the exogenous variables) are held fixed. Equilibrium real income, $(Y/P)_a$, determines real saving plus net taxes, $((S + T)/P)_a$, and real transactions money balances, $(MT/P)_a$. The equilibrium interest rate, R_a, determines real asset money balances, $(MA/P)_a$. And both income and the interest rate determine real expenditures $((I + G + F)/P)_a$. Given the nominal wage rate, the equilibrium price level, P_a, determines the real wage rate, $(\overline{W}/P)_a$, and employment, L_a. Less-than-full employment with involuntary unemployment of labor, $L_s - L_a$, exists in the short run. Given the labor force, voluntary unemployment is $L_f - L_s$.

8.2 DISPLACEMENT OF GENERAL EQUILIBRIUM

Monetary policy precipitates changes in output demand through changes in the *LM* schedule. Fiscal policy precipitates changes in output demand through changes in the *IS* schedule. The mechanisms whereby changes in output demand take place were illustrated in Chapter 6. Business and labor precipitate changes in output supply by changing the capital stock, technical progress, and the nominal wage rate. The mechanisms whereby changes in output supply take place were illustrated in Chapter 7. Both changes in output supply and demand cause displacement of general equilibrium in the model. Displacement calls forth market forces whereby disequilibrium adjustment takes place until general equilibrium is restored.

Monetary Authority Displacement

Assume that the Fed initiates an increase in the nominal money stock such that the real money stock increases. The increase creates an excess supply of real money balances in the economy. As the interest rate falls to eliminate the excess supply, real asset money balances increase. Furthermore, the decrease in the interest rate increases intended real investment and thereby creates an excess of intended real expenditures generated from output demand

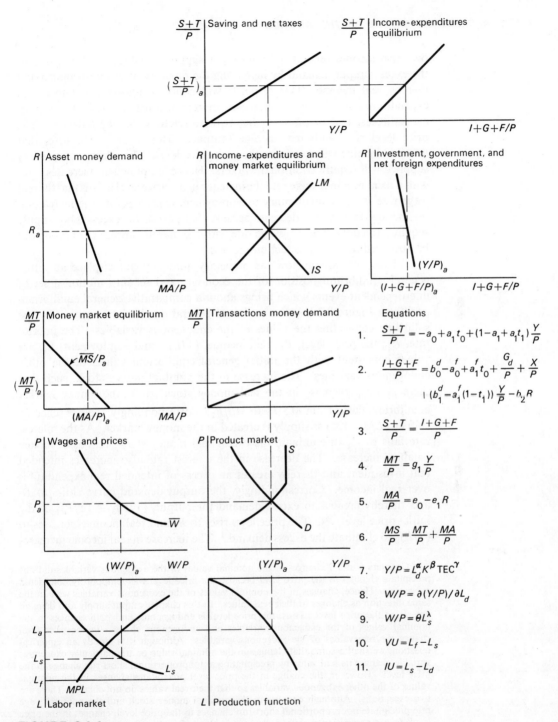

The equations shown in the figure:

1. $\dfrac{S+T}{P} = -a_0 + a_1 t_0 + (1 - a_1 + a_1 t_1)\dfrac{Y}{P}$

2. $\dfrac{I+G+F}{P} = b_0^d - a_0^f + a_1^f t_0 + \dfrac{G_d}{P} + \dfrac{X}{P}$
   $+ (b_1^d - a_1^f(1 - t_1))\dfrac{Y}{P} - h_2 R$

3. $\dfrac{S+T}{P} = \dfrac{I+G+F}{P}$

4. $\dfrac{MT}{P} = g_1 \dfrac{Y}{P}$

5. $\dfrac{MA}{P} = e_0 - e_1 R$

6. $\dfrac{MS}{P} = \dfrac{MT}{P} + \dfrac{MA}{P}$

7. $Y/P = L_d^\alpha K^\beta \text{TEC}^\gamma$

8. $W/P = \partial(Y/P)/\partial L_d$

9. $W/P = \theta L_s^\lambda$

10. $VU = L_f - L_s$

11. $IU = L_s - L_d$

FIGURE 8.1.1

General Equilibrium in the Complete Model

171

over real income generated from output supply. Producers will respond to the excess output demand by increasing the quantity of output supplied and thereby real income. This response will continue until the intended real expenditures are realized. Increases in real income increase real import expenditures, real investment, and real transactions money balances. The price level rises with real income (output). This means, of course, that nominal income will rise more than the price level. The additional quantity supplied will require additional workers. Hence, employment increases. But with a fixed nominal wage rate the increase in the price level means that the real wage rate falls. If involuntary unemployment existed before the increase in the money stock, it will decrease because that part of the excess labor supply required to equate the real wage rate with the marginal product of labor will be absorbed into the production process.

Thus, we explain how the monetary authority can displace an initial general equilibrium position of the economy and set into motion a set of interdependent events which brings about a comparative general equilibrium position. Figure 8.2.1 shows an initial general equilibrium position by the solid line connecting the values of the endogenous variables. The interest rate, R_2; the price level, P_1; real income, $(Y/P)_1$; and employment, L_1, are values consistent with the initial general equilibrium values of the other endogenous variables. The increase in the nominal money stock, such that there is a net increase in the real money stock, shifts the money market equilibrium curve from $\overline{MS}/P_1$ to $\overline{\overline{MS}}/P_2$. Correspondingly, the LM schedule shifts to LM'. Excess supply is created in the money market. As the interest rate falls to R_1 to eliminate the excess real money stock, real asset money balances increase. The decrease in the interest rate also increases intended real investment and thereby creates an excess of intended real expenditures over real income. Correspondingly, the output demand curve shifts to D' and thereby creates an excess demand for output, $(Y/P)_3 - (Y/P)_1$ at the initial price level, P_2. The price level rises to P_2 and real income increases to $(Y/P)_2$ to eliminate the excess demand.[1] The increase in real income increases

---

[1] In Chapters 6 and 7 changes in the nominal values of the exogenous variables did not precipitate changes in the price level because the price level was temporarily considered exogenous. Hence, changes in the nominal values of the exogenous variables were in the same direction as changes in their real values. In this chapter output supply and demand determine the price level. Thus, the price level is endogenous, and both changes in the nominal values of the exogenous variables and endogenous changes in the price level change the real values of the exogenous variables. Although it is strictly an empirical question, we shall assume that changes in the nominal value of any particular exogenous variable changes its real value by precipitating a nonproportional short-run change in the price level. However, the change in the price level precipitates changes in the nominal values of the other exogenous variables so that their real values do not change. There are two exceptions. Although changes in the nominal money stock and the nominal wage rate precipitate nonproportional short-run changes in the price level, changes in the price level *do not* precipitate short-run changes in the nominal money stock or the nominal wage rate. Although these assumptions are questionable in the long run, they simplify our graphical analysis without impairing the short-run qualitative analysis of policy alternatives.

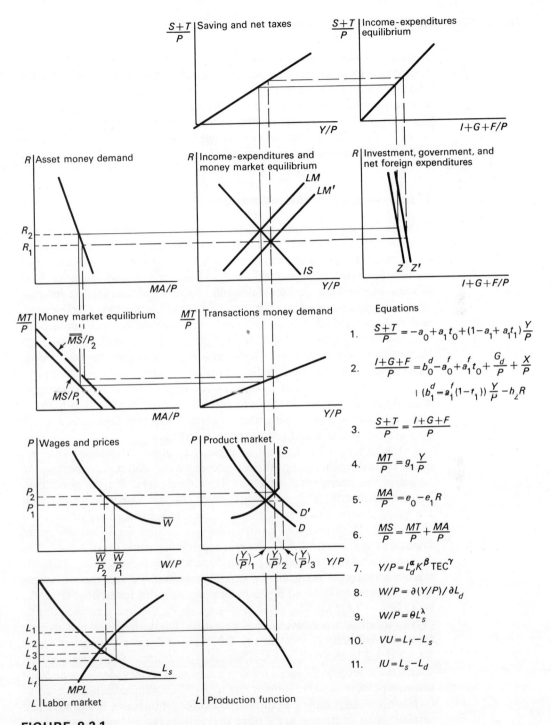

FIGURE 8.2.1

General Equilibrium Displacement by Changes in the Money Stock

transactions money balances, real saving plus net taxes, real investment, and real import expenditures (the real expenditure curve shifts from Z to Z'). The increase in the price level lowers the real wage rate from $\overline{W}/P_1$ to $\overline{W}/P_2$ and employment increases to L_2. Involuntary unemployment falls from $L_4 - L_1$ to $L_3 - L_2$ as voluntary unemployment increases from $L_f - L_4$ to $L_f - L_3$. Full adjustment is complete when all equilibrium conditions of the model are simultaneously satisfied.

Fiscal Authority Displacement

To explain how fiscal policy displaces general equilibrium, assume, for example, that government expenditures are increased. This creates an excess of intended real expenditures generated from output demand over real income generated from output supply. Real income and the price level increase to eliminate the excess demand. Increases in real income increase real saving plus net taxes, real import expenditures, intended real investment, and real transactions money balances. The increase in real transactions money balances creates excess demand in the money market. Thus, the interest rate rises to eliminate excess demand in the money market. Individuals hold more in real bonds and less in real asset money balances. As the price level rises, the real money stock decreases; this raises the interest rate higher and chokes off increases in intended real investment. With a fixed nominal wage rate and a higher price level, the real wage rate falls. As a result employment increases and unemployment decreases.

Figure 8.2.2 illustrates our example of fiscal policy displacement. An initial general equilibrium position is shown by the solid line connecting the values of the endogenous variables. The interest rate, R_1; the price level, P_1; real income, $(Y/P)_1$; and employment, L_1, are values consistent with the initial general equilibrium values of the other endogenous variables of the model. The increase in government expenditures (and the subsequent increase in real income) shifts the real expenditure curve from Z to Z', the *IS* curve from *IS* to *IS'*, and the output demand curve from D to D'. Initially, there is an excess of intended real expenditures over real income and, correspondingly, excess demand in the output market at the initial price level, P_1, by $(Y/P)_3 - (Y/P)_1$. The price level rises to P_2 and real income rises to $(Y/P)_2$ to eliminate excess output demand. The increase in real income increases real transactions money balances, real saving plus net taxes, intended real investment, and real import expenditures. The increase in real transactions money balances creates excess real money demand and the subsequent increase in the interest rate to R_2 which eliminates the excess also increases real asset money balances and chokes off increases in intended real investment. The increase in the price level reduces the real money stock from $\overline{MS}/P_1$ to $\overline{MS}/P_2$ and lowers the real wage rate from $\overline{W}/P_1$ to $\overline{W}/P_2$. Employment increase from L_1 to L_2, and involuntary unemployment falls from

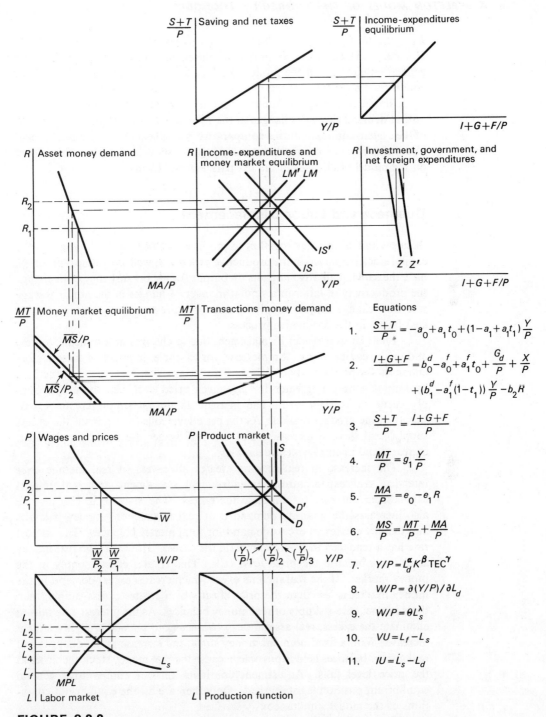

FIGURE 8.2.2

General Equilibrium Displacement by Changes in Government Expenditures

$L_4 - L_1$ to $L_3 - L_2$ as voluntary unemployment rises from $L_f - L_4$ to $L_f - L_3$. Thus, fiscal authority displacement generates a comparative general equilibrium in the model. Full adjustment is complete once all the equilibrium conditions of the model are simultaneously satisfied.

Similarly, changes in the tax parameters are translated into changes in output demand through changes in the *IS* schedule. Subsequent adjustment of the system continues until a comparative general equilibrium is established. Use a duplicate of the final summary page to show and explain the impact on the model of changes in the tax parameters. Do it.

Business and Labor Displacement

Business and labor come together to produce output supply. Changes in the capital stock employed in the productive process, as well as technical progress, have the same qualitative impacts on output supply because they both change the productivity of labor in a similar manner. Changes in the nominal wage rate also change output supply because it represents the primary variable cost factor in the productive process.

First, let us consider displacement due to changes in technical progress and/or the capital stock. An increase, for example, in either of these factors enhances the productivity of labor. This means that real income generated by output supply is greater for any given price level, i.e., the output supply curve shifts rightward. The increase in output supply creates excess supply in the product market. As the price level falls to eliminate the excess supply, real income increases, and the real wage rate falls. Employment increases and unemployment decreases.

The increase in real income creates an excess of real income over intended real expenditures. Intended real investment and real import expenditures increase to eliminate the excess. The increase in real income also increases the quantity demanded of real transactions money balances and thereby creates an excess demand for total money balances. The interest rate has a tendency to rise to eliminate the excess. However, the real money stock rises because the price level falls. This creates excess supply in the money market. If the real income effect which creates excess demand in the money market is less than the price effect which creates excess supply, then there is a net excess supply of real money balances. As the interest rate falls to eliminate the excess, real asset money balances and intended real investment increase. With a fixed nominal money stock, the increase in the quantities of real money balances held is possible because the real money stock increases as the price level falls. Adjustment continues until a comparative general equilibrium position is established. Only then are all the equilibrium conditions of the model simultaneously satisfied.

Figure 8.2.3 shows an initial general equilibrium position of the model by the solid line connecting the values of the endogenous variables. The

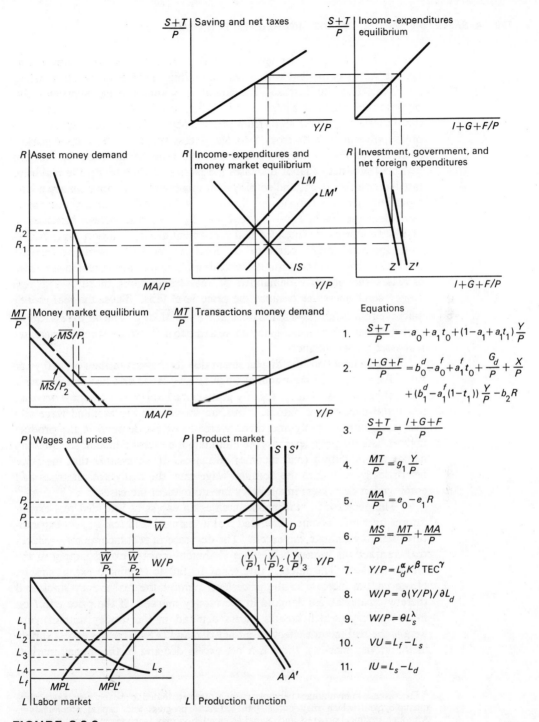

FIGURE 8.2.3

General Equilibrium Displacement by Changes in the Capital Stock and/or Technical Progress

interest rate, R_2; the price level, P_2; real income, $(Y/P)_1$; and employment, L_1, are values consistent with general equilibrium values of the other endogenous variables. An increase in the capital stock and/or technical progress employed in the productive process shifts the production function from A to A'; the labor demand curve shifts from MPL to MPL'. Correspondingly, the output supply curve shifts from S to S'. Excess supply in the output market, $(Y/P)_3 - (Y/P)_1$, is thereby created at the initial price level, P_2. As the marginal product of labor increases the price level falls to P_1, the real wage rate increases to $\overline{W}/P_1$, and employment increases to L_2. Involuntary unemployment increases from $L_3 - L_1$ to $L_4 - L_2$, while voluntary unemployment decreases from $L_f - L_3$ to $L_f - L_4$.[2] As real income increases to $(Y/P)_2$ an increase in intended real investment and real import expenditures shifts the expenditures curve to Z'. Real income will continue to increase until intended real expenditures are realized. The increase in real income also increases the quantity demanded of real transactions money. The real money stock increases because the price level falls. Thus, the real money market equilibrium curve shifts from $\overline{MS}/P_2$ to $\overline{MS}/P_1$. The net excess supply of real money balances causes the interest rate to fall to R_1 and thereby increases real asset money balances.

Let us now consider displacement due to changes in the nominal wage rate. An increase in the nominal wage rate by labor and business increases the cost per unit of output; for any given price level producers must produce less profit-maximizing output. Thus, an increase in the nominal wage rate decreases output supply and thereby creates excess demand in the product market. As the price level rises to eliminate the excess demand, the quantity demanded of output (real income) decreases. If we assume that the price level rises by less than the nominal wage rate, the real wage rate rises and employment decreases; involuntary unemployment increases.

The decrease in real income creates an excess of intended real expenditures over real income. Intended real investment and real import expenditures fall to eliminate the excess. The decrease in real income also reduces real transactions money balances and thereby creates excess supply in the money market. The interest rate tends to fall to eliminate excess supply. However, the increase in the price level reduces the real money stock and thereby creates excess demand in the money market. If the price effect on money supply (which creates excess demand in the money market) outweighs the real income effect on money demand (which creates excess supply in the money market), there is a net excess demand in the money market.

---

[2] The increase in involuntary unemployment is often attributed to the increase in structural unemployment which may occur with technical progress and capital accumulation. Although technical progress and capital accumulation may increase employment in some industries, it may reduce employment in other industries. The net effect may be to increase involuntary unemployment.

As the interest rate rises to eliminate the excess, real asset money balances and intended real investment decrease. The system will continue to adjust until it has moved to a comparative general equilibrium position where all the equilibrium conditions of the model are simultaneously satisfied.

Figure 8.2.4 shows an initial general equilibrium position of the model by the solid line connecting the general equilibrium values of the endogenous variables. The interest rate, R_1; the price level, P_1; real income, $(Y/P)_2$; and employment, L_2, are values consistent with the initial general equilibrium values of the other endogenous variables of the model. An increase in the nominal wage rate shifts the price-real wage rate curve rightward from $\overline{W}$ to $\overline{\overline{W}}$ and thereby the output supply curve from S to S'. Excess demand $(Y/P)_1 - (Y/P)_0$ is created in the product market at the initial price level, P_1. As the price level rises to P_2 the real wage rate rises to $\overline{\overline{W}}/P_2$ (nominal wage rate increases are greater than price increases) and employment decreases to L_1. Involuntary unemployment rises from $L_3 - L_2$ to $L_4 - L_1$, while voluntary unemployment falls from $L_f - L_3$ to $L_f - L_4$. As the quantity of output demanded (real income) falls toward $(Y/P)_1$, downward revisions of intended real investment and real import expenditures shift the expenditure curve to Z'. When intended real expenditures fall enough for them to be realized, real income and intended real expenditures are equal. The decrease in real income also decreases real transactions money balances. The real money stock falls from $\overline{MS}/P_1$ to $\overline{MS}/P_2$ as the price level rises. The net excess demand for real money balances will be reduced as the interest rate rises and people hold less in real asset money balances (more in real bonds). The system will adjust until all the equilibrium conditions of the model are simultaneously satisfied, i.e., a comparative general equilibrium position is established.

8.3 EFFECTIVENESS OF AGGREGATE DEMAND MANAGEMENT

Monetary and fiscal policies are the means of aggregate output demand management. When evaluating the effectiveness of demand management an analyst should bear in mind that there are two parts to the evaluation. First, an analyst must evaluate the effectiveness of monetary and/or fiscal policies in bringing about changes in output demand for any given price level. And, second, he or she should then evaluate the extent to which the change in output demand changes three of the primary target variables of demand management, namely the price level, employment, and output. Clearly, the second part of the evaluation requires knowledge about the state of (the shape of) output supply as well as the reactions (in the form of changes in output supply) of business, labor, and other owners of factor inputs to changes in the price level which results from changes in output demand.

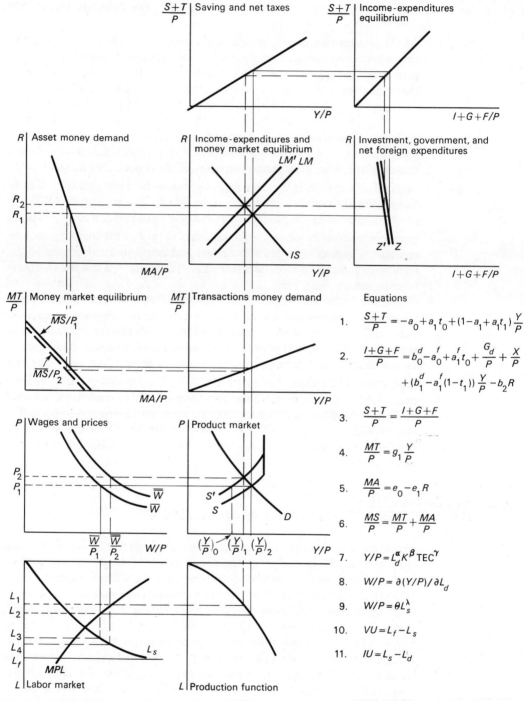

FIGURE 8.2.4

General Equilibrium Displacement by Changes in the Nominal Wage Rate

The following parts of this section will point out some of the factors which have received special consideration in evaluating the effectiveness of output demand management.

The Effectiveness of Monetary Policy

The effectiveness of monetary policy in changing output demand for any given price level depends on the values of the parameters on the demand side of the model. The values of two of these parameters have been given much attention because they play a major role in determining the shape of the *IS* schedule. They are the parameters which relate real income, b_1, and the interest rate, b_2, to intended real investment. To some extent their importance was demonstrated in Chapter 4. The larger the absolute values of these parameters, the more responsive real income is to changes in the interest rate, i.e., the *IS* schedule is more horizontal (or relatively interest elastic).

Figure 8.3.1 illustrates how monetary policy is more effective in changing real income (output demand) for any given price level when the *IS* schedule is more horizontal. The *IS* schedule, *IS'*, indicates smaller absolute values of b_1 and/or b_2 than does *IS"*. The initial equilibrium values of real income and the interest rate are $((Y/P)_1, R_3)$. Suppose that an increase in the nominal money stock for a given price level shifts the *LM* schedule from *LM'* to *LM"*. Along *IS"* the interest rate falls by less and real income increases by more than they do along *IS'*. Monetary policy is more effective in changing real income (output demand) when the *IS* schedule is more horizontal, $(Y/P)_3 > (Y/P)_2$.

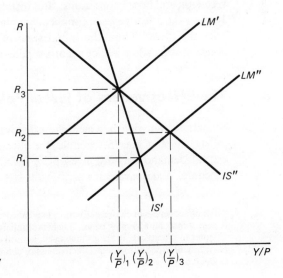

FIGURE 8.3.1

Effectiveness of Monetary Policy

The values of all other parameters which give shape to the *IS* schedule, for example, the marginal propensity to save and the net tax rate, are also very important in evaluating the effectiveness of monetary policy in changing output demand. Moreover, the values of the parameters which determine the extent to which a change in the nominal money stock for any given price level shifts the LM schedule are important; these are the money market parameters. In short, all parameter values on the demand side of the model help to determine the impact of monetary policy on output demand.

One important problem in the application of monetary policy is often overlooked. The magnitudes of the parameters values themselves depend on the initial cyclical position of the economy. That is, their values may vary over the business cycle. Thus, monetary policy may be more or less effective in changing output demand depending on the initial state of the economy over the cycle. At lower levels of real income and the interest rates, intended real investment is likely to be less sensitive to both changes in real income and the interest rate because investors are more pessimistic about the future. Thus, the *IS* schedule will be more vertical, as shown by *IS'* in Fig. 8.3.1, and changes in the nominal money stock for any given price level will be less effective in changing real income (output demand). At higher levels of real income and the interest rates, intended real investment is likely to be more responsive to changes in the interest rate and real income. Optimism reigns. Thus, the *IS* schedule will be more horizontal, as shown by *IS''* in Fig. 8.3.1, and monetary policy will be more effective in changing real income (output demand) for any given price level.

In looking at the data of an economy, we may infer that the parameters are unstable because the parameters vary over the cycle. Of course, they are unstable when the estimates are based on data which include both recession and boom conditions. But instability does not imply ineffectiveness. Rather, the effectiveness of monetary policy, or any policy alternative, varies over the cycle. Thus, the initial state of the economy must be taken into consideration when policy recommendations are considered.

The Effectiveness of Fiscal Policy[3]

Similar to the way in which the effectiveness of monetary policy depends on the shape of the *IS* schedule, the effectiveness of fiscal policy in changing output demand for any given price level depends on the shape of the *LM* schedule. One parameter, e_1, which has been given considerable attention

---

[3] The effectiveness of changes in export expenditures and domestic government expenditures is determined on a similar basis. Their multipliers are equal, as shown in the appendix to Chapter 6. Therefore, in the following evaluation of the effectiveness of change in domestic government expenditures, the effectiveness of change in export expenditures will be likewise evaluated.

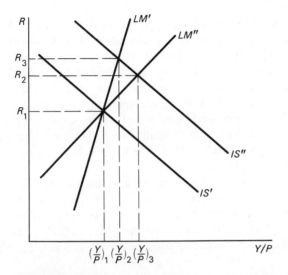

FIGURE 8.3.2

Effectiveness of Fiscal Policies

measures the extent to which changes in the interest rate change real asset money balances. The larger the absolute value of e_1, the greater is the responsiveness of real asset money balances to changes in the interest rate and thereby the more responsive real income (output demand) is to changes in the interest rate for any given price level, i.e., the *LM* schedule is more horizontal (or relatively interest elastic).

Figure 8.3.2 illustrates how shifts in the *IS* schedule due to either changes in domestic government expenditures and/or the tax parameters have a greater impact on real income (output demand) for any given price level when the LM schedule is more horizontal than vertical. The *LM'* schedule indicates a smaller absolute value of e_1 than does *LM"*. The initial equilibrium values of real income and the interest rate, $((Y/P)_1, R_1)$, are shown by the intersection of *LM'* and *IS'*. An increase in government expenditures or a decrease in exogenous net taxes or the net tax rate will cause an increase in the interest rate for any given level of real income, that is, a rightward shift in the *IS* schedule from *IS'* to *IS"*. Along the *LM"* schedule the interest rate rises less and real income increases more than they do along *LM'*. Fiscal policy is more effective in changing real income (output demand) for any given price level when the *LM* schedule is more horizontal, $(Y/P)_3 > (Y/P)_2$.

Again it is important to note that the impact of the government spending as well as the value of the tax parameters on output demand depends on the initial cyclical position of the economy. The *LM* schedule is likely to be more horizontal at lower levels of real income and interest rates because a larger level of real asset money balances is being held. The opportunity cost of holding real asset money (the interest rate) is low relative to that of holding real bonds; real asset money balances are more responsive to changes in the interest rate. Thus, the *LM* schedule indicates that real income (output demand) is more responsive to changes in the interest rate, as shown by *LM″* in Fig. 8.3.2. For a given value of the real money stock, a small increase in the interest rate means that a large quantity of real asset money balances can be drawn out to facilitate a higher level of real income. Thus, the shifts in the *IS* schedule due to fiscal policy will be more effective in changing output demand.

At higher levels of real income and interest rates, the amount held in real asset money balances is small. The opportunity cost of holding real asset money (the interest rate) is high relative to that of holding real bonds. Rightward shifts in the *IS* schedule along the relatively vertical *LM* schedule, *LM′*, in Fig. 8.3.2 means that fiscal policy is less effective in changing output demand.

Monetary policy will be effective in changing output demand for a given price level if the private sector responds to changes in the rate of interest and real income. Similarly, the effectiveness of changes in the tax parameter depends on the private sectors' response. For example, consumers may offset net tax parameter changes, particularly temporary ones like the 1968 surcharge, by changing saving behavior and at least partially maintaining the level of real consumption. Furthermore, at a lower interest rate and level of real income, increases in the nominal money stock for any given price level may be absorbed into real asset money balances with little impact on output demand. Changes in the nominal money stock for any given price level are effective if, in fact, intended real investment spending changes. Changes in the investment parameters over the cycle make monetary policy more uncertain.

Although the effectiveness of changes in government spending in changing output demand is more certain in the sense that the government exogenously changes spending, the impact of government spending depends on how the expenditures are financed. For example, if increases in government expenditures are financed through increased taxes, where the impact on real consumption of the tax increase decreases real consumption by an amount just equal to the increase in government expenditures, government expenditures merely "crowd out" private real consumer expenditures. If increased government expenditures are bond-financed and the interest rate rises sharply, real asset money balances move into real bonds and intended real investment is reduced. Hence, government expenditures partially crowd out private intended real expenditures. If increased government expenditures are financed by new money, than a change in government expenditures is not independent of changes in the money stock.

Interaction between Monetary and Fiscal Policy

Clearly, public policy instruments can be combined to achieve a desired change in the interest rate and real income (output demand) for any given price level. Moreover, since the public, the Fed, and the government initiate changes in the exogenous variables, it is possible that such changes will work in opposite directions in changing real income (output demand) for any given price level.

Pure monetary policy limits the achievement of target rates of interest and real income (output demand) levels to movement along the *IS* schedule. Pure fiscal policy limits the achievement of target rates of interest and real income (output demand) levels to those combinations along the *LM* schedule. Use of both monetary and fiscal policies increase flexibility in the achievement of any desired combination of interest rate and real income (output demand) in the *IS-LM* quadrant. Suppose, for example, the level of output demand necessary to secure the full employment at the current price level requires that real income be $(Y/P)_f$. Initial equilibrium is shown in Fig. 8.3.3 by $((Y/P)_f, R_3)$. But R_3 is too high to give a level of intended real investment sufficient to achieve full employment in the housing market. If we permanently increase the net tax rate, we pivot the *IS* schedule to *IS"* and reduce real consumption demand. The interest rate falls to R_2 to stimulate intended real investment demand, but real income falls to $(Y/P)_1$. To offset the fall in real income while at the same time decreasing the interest rate, we may increase the nominal money stock such that the *LM* schedule shifts from *LM'*

FIGURE 8.3.3

Fiscal-Monetary Policy Mix

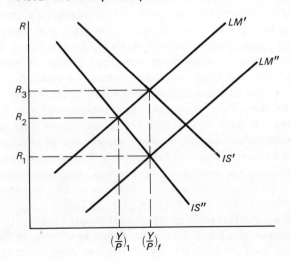

to LM''. Full employment real income is restored. With a net decrease in the interest rate from R_3 to R_1, there is a net increase in intended real investment. Thus, by combining fiscal and monetary policy, we shift the composition of output demand; real consumption is reduced and intended real investment is increased.

Uncoordinated monetary and fiscal policy efforts could be hazardous. In the above example, if the Fed had decreased instead of increased the nominal money stock for any given price level, then along with increases in the net tax rate, real income (output demand) would have decreased for any given price level and the interest rate would have risen. Thus, both real consumption and intended real investment would fall. The possibility of such conflicting policy initiatives suggests a need to consider at least an improvement in the communication between the Fed and the fiscal authorities.

The State of Output Supply

The above evaluation of the effectiveness of output demand management has been limited to the impact of monetary and fiscal policies on output demand *for any given price level.* But as our skeleton model shows, demand alone does not determine the values of the important target variables of the demand managers. Output supply factors are important as well. A change in output demand at the initial price level creates excess output demand (for increases in demand) or excess output supply (for decreases in demand), but it is the shape of the output supply curve which determines the extent to which the price level, output and employment will change.

Figure 8.3.4 shows two output supply curves, one S', is more vertical than the other, S. When compared to the more horizontal output supply curve the more vertical output supply curve shows that the quantity of output supplied is less responsive to changes in the price level (output supply, S', is relatively price inelastic) because under the assumption of profit maximization, for a given nominal wage rate labor demand is less responsive to changes in the real wage rate (labor demand is relatively real wage rate inelastic). Given an increase in output demand from D to D', the price level increases by more, $P_3 - P_2$, and real income by less, $(Y/P)_3 - (Y/P)_2$, when output supply is more vertical than horizontal. Stated differently, the more price inelastic output supply, the more the increase in price and the less the increase in output. Hence, the extent to which changes in demand are effective in changing the price level, output and employment (unemployment) depend on the shape of the output supply curve. One can see that efforts to increase output and employment with a minimal price increase are best served by a more horizontal (price elastic) output supply curve.

Moreover, as we will show more clearly in Chapter 9, the final impact on the price level of changes in output demand depends on the reactions of

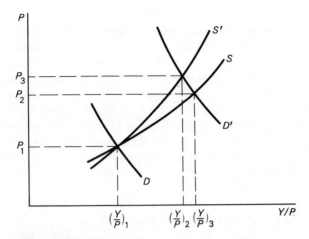

FIGURE 8.3.4

Effectiveness of Demand Management
and the Shape of the Output Supply Curve

business, labor and other owners of factor inputs. Figure 8.3.5 illustrates the
point. Suppose that the purpose of expansionary demand management as
shown by an increase in output demand from D to D' is to increase output
(and employment) along S from $(Y/P)_1$ to $(Y/P)_3$. Further, suppose that
they perceive correctly a relatively horizontal output supply curve, and
therefore, expect a tolerable increase in the price level, $P_2 - P_1$.

FIGURE 8.3.5

Effectiveness of Demand Management
and Subsequent Changes in the Output Supply Curve

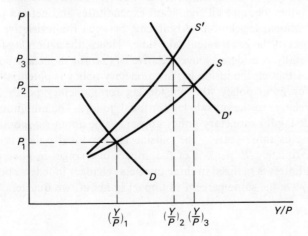

However, suppose the labor and/or other owners of factor inputs respond to demand induced price increases by raising factor prices so that the output supply curve shifts to S'. The price level increases to $P_3 > P_2$ with output rising to $(Y/P)_2 < (Y/P)_3$. Thus, the end result of the change in output demand is not realized. Although output (and thereby employment) increases, they increase by less than the desired amount and the price level increases by more than that which is considered tolerable.

Our discussion has certainly not exhausted the factors which help in evaluating the effectiveness of demand management. But, our discussion does lay the groundwork for further discussion which you should think about and initiate in the classroom.

Lags in Monetary and Fiscal Policy

Although our model includes no lagged relationships between the variables, the effects of monetary and fiscal policies do not work themselves out instantaneously. As our casual dynamic analysis implies, such policies are subject to time lags. There is the lag between a need for discretionary action arising and the recognition of that need; this is *the recognition lag*. Once the need for action is recognized, demand managers must decide on the appropriate action to be taken; this requires time, and the time lapse is called *the action lag*. Both the recognition and action lags make up *the inside lag of policy*. Once action is taken the full effects of policy are not felt immediately. Thus, there is an *outside (or impact) lag of policy*.

Both monetary and fiscal authorities must contend with the recognition lag since they both use the same data. But authority for monetary policy is not as diffused as authority for fiscal policy. The decision-making power of the monetary authority rests with the Board of Governors of the Fed; they can take immediate action to initiate changes in the money stock. Hence, the action lag in monetary policy is relatively short. The same is not true for fiscal policy because all significant expenditures and net tax policies require congressional legislation. Arguments between the legislative and executive branches of the government take time. Hence, the action lag for fiscal policy is generally considered longer relative to that for monetary policy.

Although the inside lag for monetary policy is potentially shorter than that for fiscal policy, the outside lag for monetary policy appears to be long relative to the outside lag for fiscal policy. The minimum length of the outside lag for monetary policy appears to be about six months and may be as long as three years. The outside lag for fiscal policy is much shorter. Approximately 75 percent of the impact of changes in government defense expenditures is realized in three quarters; changes in federal personal income taxes have the same percent of impact in about two quarters.

Another point is worth mentioning. The outside lag for monetary policy appears to be variable in length. And both the inside and outside lags vary depending on whether contractionary or expansionary monetary policy is adopted. Thus, discretionary monetary policy can be poorly timed and thereby destabilizing on the economy. Many economists believe that the discretion of the monetary authority should be removed and a rule of monetary policy imposed. The most widely advocated rule is that the monetary authority should increase the money stock at a rate consistent with that which is necessary to promote economic growth with price stability and full utilization of resources. Recommendations have varied from 3 to 6 percent.

The rules approach has been justified primarily on the grounds of lag variability. However, the strict application of the rules approach for monetary policy reduces our ability to respond to crises (depression and/or recession and/or inflation), should they occur. Perhaps some combination of rules and discretion is appropriate in the use of a combination of monetary and fiscal policy, respectively.

8.4 SUMMARY

In this chapter we pulled the model together in a discussion of short-run general equilibrium. By Walras' law, when the income-expenditures, money, and labor sectors are in general or mutual equilibrium the bond market is in equilibrium as well. The monetary and fiscal authorities, as well as the private sector of the economy (business, labor, and the consumer), can displace general equilibrium. Subsequently, intermarket forces come into play until a comparative general equilibrium is attained. The effectiveness of demand management policy depends on the magnitudes of the parameters of the model, the initial state of the economy when policy is implemented, the length of the inside and outside lags, the degree to which both supply and demand exogenous variables are in fact independent and the state (or shape of) output supply. Hence, the air of determinativeness implied in the construction of our skeleton model must be viewed with reservation.

REVIEW QUESTIONS

1. On a separate piece of paper, copy the table given on page 190. For increases in each of the exogenous variables, indicate the direction of change in the endogenous variables (+ for increases; − for decreases; 0 for no change) when all other exogenous variables remain unchanged. Assume there is less than full employment before and after each change occurs. State any necessary qualification to your answers. Examples are given.

END

EXO

⇄	G	t_0	t_1	X	MS	W	K	TEC	L_f
Y/P	+								
R		−							
C/P									
S/P									
T/P									
I/P									
IM/P									
B/P									
MT/P									
MA/P									
MS/P									
P									
W/P									
MPL			+						
L_d									
L_s									
IU									
VU									

2. Explain the ways in which business and labor can alternatively thwart and enhance the efforts of the fiscal and monetary authorities to curb price increases, stimulate output, and increase employment.

3. Explain the condition(s) under which:
   (a) Only changes in the money stock can change output.
   (b) Only fiscal policy can change output.
   (c) Both monetary and fiscal policy increase the number of attainable combinations of interest rates and output levels.

SELECTED READINGS

ANDO, A., E. C. BROWN, J. KAREKEN, and R. M. SOLOW, "Lags in Fiscal and Monetary Policy," in "Commission on Money and Credit," *Stabilization Policies*, Englewood Cliffs, N.J.: Prentice-Hall, 1963, pp. 1–163.

BARRO, R. J., and H. J. GROSSMAN, "A General Disequilibrium Model of Income and Employment," *American Economic Review*, 61 (March 1971), 82–93.

CLOWER, R. W., "The Keynesian Counterrevolution: A Theoretical Appraisal," in F. H. Hahn and F. P. R. Brechling (eds.), *The Theory of Interest Rates*, New York: St. Martin's, 1965, pp. 103–25.

CULBERTSON, J., "Friedman on the Lag in Effect of Monetary Policy," *Journal of Political Economy*, 68 (Dec. 1960), 617–21.

FRIEDMAN, M., *A Program for Monetary Stability*, New York: Fordham, 1959.

——, "The Role of Monetary Policy," *American Economic Review*, 58 (March 1968), 1–17.

——, *The Optimum Quantity of Money*, Chicago: Aldine, 1969.

FRIEDMAN, M., and A. J. SCHWARTZ, "Money and Business Cycles," *Review of Economics and Statistics*, 45 (Feb. 1963), 32–64.

GRAMLEY, L. E., "Guidelines for Monetary Policy—The Case Against Simple Rules," in W. L. Smith and R. L. Teigen (eds.), *Money, National Income, and Stabilization Policy*, rev. ed., Homewood, Ill.: Irwin, 1970, pp. 488–95.

KEYNES, J. M., *The General Theory of Employment, Interest, and Money*, London: Macmillan, 1936.

LEIJONHUFVED, A., *On Keynesian Economics and the Economics of Keynes*, New York: Oxford University Press, Inc., 1968.

MODIGLIANI, F., "The Monetary Mechanism and Its Interaction with Real Phenomena," *Review of Economics and Statistics*, 45 (Feb. 1963), 79–107.

——, "Some Empirical Tests of Monetary Management and of Rules Versus Discretion," *Journal of Political Economy*, 72 (June 1964), 211–45.

PART **III**

Extensions
of the Skeleton Model

CHAPTER **9**

The Inflation Process

9.1 AN OVERVIEW

This chapter is not a summary of the literature on inflation theory. Neither
is it a catalog of all possible means of explaining the relationship between
inflation and unemployment. Rather, an attempt is made to synthesize the
theories of inflation which help to explain inflation, particularly during periods
of U.S. economic history since 1960.

A rising price level will be used as a working definition of inflation.
Inflation occurs when there is an excess demand for output at last period's
price level. To eliminate the excess, the price level will increase, and either
the quantity of the output supplied will increase (demand induced price
increase) or the quantity demanded will decrease (supply induced price
increase.) That is, the forces of output supply and demand will determine
equilibrium levels of price and output which are acceptable to both buyers
and sellers.

The literature on inflation theory emphasizes two types of inflation.
One type is attributed to monetary and/or fiscal policies which increase
output demand at close to full employment of resources. Because increases
in output demand pull the price level upward, this type of inflation is called
demand pull inflation. The other type is attributed to increasing costs,
particularly labor costs, which decrease output supply. Because increasing
costs per unit of output supplied push the price level upward, this type of
inflation is called *cost push inflation*.

A modern view of inflation does not distinguish between demand pull and cost push inflation. Rather, inflation is a process which exhibits certain characteristic properties or phases. These phases are but connected parts of a single process.

The critical phases of the inflation process generally follow sequential periods of postinflationary recession and recovery. A period of postinflationary recession is characterized by excess productive capacity, including high unemployment (and underemployment) and negligible inflation. The U.S. economy in the late 1950s and early 1960s is an example of the long period of postinflationary recession and price stabilization after the Korean War. The period between late 1961 and mid-1965 is an example of a period where monetary and fiscal policies were used to promote recovery with negligible inflation.

The inflation process begins with increases in aggregate output demand at close to full employment of labor and capital resources. Such increases outstrip increases in output supply which occur because of advances in productivity. The result is that the price level increases along with output and employment. This is the expansion phase of the inflation process, and it is characterized by the dominance of demand pull inflation. Generally, increases in the price level are greater than increases in the nominal wage rate because when the inflation process begins, labor does not expect price increases and initially responds with a delayed increase in nominal wage demands. In about 1965 the U.S. economy was close to full employment of resources. The federal government began to accelerate expenditures for the Vietnam War without any accompanying fiscal and/or monetary measures to prevent inflation. Consequently, the inflation process of the 1960s got underway.

The next phase of the inflation process can be described by increases in the price level and the nominal wage rate as well. But unlike the expansion phase, changes in the nominal wage rate are greater than changes in the price level as labor attempts to restore their real wage rate. The inflation process enters a stabilization phase where increases in output and employment taper off.

As labor continues to increase nominal wage demands to catch up with past price increases, output and employment decrease. As the price level continues to rise, labor may become conditioned to expect future price increases and increase nominal wage demands to compensate not only for past inflation but future expected inflation. The inflation process then enters the inflationary recession phase which is dominated by cost push inflation. If labor begins to overestimate future price increases and raises the nominal wage rate accordingly, problems of an inflationary recession become acute. Decreases in output supply outstrip increases in output demand, and real income and employment decrease below that which is capable of support from an economy's level of productivity.

The severity of the decrease in employment (increase in unemployment) and inflation will depend on the length of time the inflation has been permitted to continue in the past and what steps are finally taken to promote price stability and recovery. It is during the inflationary recession phase of the inflation process that policy alternatives, including fiscal and monetary policies, wage-price guideposts and controls, antitrust policies, and measures to stimulate advances in productivity, become belated considerations of national policy. In the late 1960s and the 1970s the U.S. economy was in such a state. The inflation generated by the boom in the earlier 1960s was out of control.

In this chapter we shall use the skeleton model to explain the inflation process. The formal method of Keynesian short-run analysis (the skeleton model) is in many respects static and comparative static in form but dynamic in substance. Our method of analysis will be to break the inflation process down into short- and long-run comparative static equilibria. The succession of short-run comparative static equilibria should be viewed as an equilibrating process from one long-run equilibrium to another. The short-run equilibria are linked by labor's reaction (adjustments in nominal wage rate demands) to forecast errors in predicting increases in the price level.

Typically, recent expectations models predict a short-run relationship between inflation and unemployment whenever the expected and actual price levels are not equal. Because of forecast errors and subsequent corrective measures (adjustments in nominal wage rate demands) to maintain the real wage rate, the difference between the expected and actual price levels falls to zero. In the long run without advances in productivity, the difference between the expected and actual real wage rates also falls to zero. Only the price level and the nominal wage rate remain higher after full adjustment takes place.

9.2   INFLATION EXPECTATIONS AND THE LABOR MARKET

Zero Inflation Expectations

In the labor market described in Chapter 7 we assumed that there is no difference between labor's expected price level and the actual price level in any time period. In Eq. (7.4.6) the price level forecast error $PE = 0$. Accordingly, we assumed that for a given nominal wage rate in the short run there is no difference between labor's expected and actual real wage rates. In Eq. (7.4.7) the real wage rate forecast error $FE = 0$. However, it is quite possible that decisions based on labor's inflation expectations are wrong. In a world of imperfect foresight there may exist a difference between the expected and actual real wage rates in any period due to labor's error in forecasting the price level.

In Chapter 7 we derived an expression [Eq. (7.4.8)] for labor supply,

$$\frac{W}{P} = -FE + \theta L_s^\lambda \qquad (9.2.1)$$

which can be used to consider the impact of errors in forecasting the actual real wage rate. If there is zero forecast error, $FE = 0$ and the intercept $-(FE) = 0$; the actual and the perceived labor supply curves are coincident [Eqs. (7.4.5) and (7.4.8) are the same]. If the actual is greater than the expected real wage rate, $FE < 0$ and the intercept $-(-FE) > 0$; the actual lies to the left of the perceived labor supply curve. If the actual is less than the expected real wage rate, $FE > 0$ and the intercept $-(+FE) < 0$; the actual lies to the right of the perceived labor supply curve.

Figure 9.2.1 is used to illustrate what happens in the labor market when labor does not expect inflation. We begin our analysis where the actual and perceived labor supply curves are coincident. Labor supply, L_{se}, and labor demand, MPL, determine the initial level of employment, L_2, and the real wage rate, $\overline{W}/P_1$. Although there is voluntary unemployment, $L_f - L_2$, no involuntary unemployment exists.

In period 1 assume that there is an increase in aggregate output demand so that the price level increases to P_2. Also assume that labor does not expect the increase in the price level so that the actual price level is greater than the expected price level, $P_2 > P_1$. Since management is in a position to recognize the actual price increase, it can raise the nominal wage rate by less

FIGURE 9.2.1

Zero Expected Inflation in the Labor Market

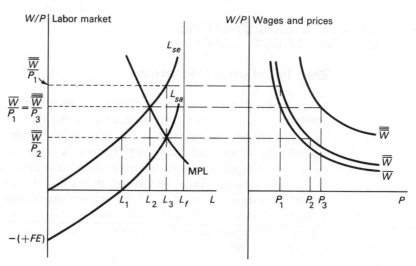

than the price increase and induce labor to increase the quantity of labor supplied at a lower real wage rate.[1] If management raises the nominal wage rate to $\overline{\overline{W}}$ where $\overline{\overline{W}} - \overline{W} < P_2 - P_1$, labor perceives that the real wage rate is increasing along L_{se} to $\overline{\overline{W}}/P_1$. Consequently, labor is willing to accept additional employment, $L_3 - L_2$. However, since labor's expected real wage rate exceeds the actual real wage rate for any given quantity of labor supply, $FE > 0$ and the actual labor supply curve, L_{sa}, lies to the right of the perceived supply curve, L_{se}. Thus, the actual real wage falls from $\overline{\overline{W}}/P_1$ to $\overline{\overline{W}}/P_2$, and management hires the additional labor to maximize profit where $\overline{\overline{W}}/P_2 = \text{MPL}$. Labor is fooled into supplying more units of labor, $L_3 - L_2$, than they would have supplied with zero forecast error. Labor is involuntarily overemployed by $L_3 - L_1$ units of labor, and voluntary unemployment falls to $L_f - L_3$.

Now suppose in period 2 that labor realizes that the price level has increased and they respond by raising the nominal wage rate as a means of restoring the initial period's real wage rate. Since increases in the nominal wage rate will further increase the actual price, labor must increase the nominal wage rate by more than the additional price increase if the real wage rate is to be restored. If labor raises the nominal wage rate to $\overline{\overline{\overline{W}}}$ where $\overline{\overline{\overline{W}}} - \overline{W} > P_2 - P_1$ and $\overline{\overline{\overline{W}}} - \overline{W} = P_3 - P_1$, then the price forecast error falls to zero. The actual labor supply curve shifts back toward the perceived labor supply curve as the difference between the expected and actual real wage rates falls to zero. Employment falls back to L_2, involuntary over-employment falls to zero, and voluntary unemployment returns to $L_f - L_2$. After complete adjustment takes place only the price level and nominal wage rate are permanently higher.

As we can see, unexpected inflation temporarily increases employment (decreases unemployment) by temporarily increasing labor supply; this is a short-run phenomenon. Once the nominal wage rate adjustments are complete, the actual labor supply curve shifts back to the perceived labor supply curve; this is a long-run phenomenon. Thus, the perceived labor supply curve is the long-run labor supply curve. And equilibrium between labor demand and the perceived labor supply curves determines the *critical level of employment*, the highest level that can be achieved permanently in the absence of advances in productivity. With no change in the labor force the *critical level of unemployment* is also determined.[2] Although full adjustment of the system may not take place immediately due to adjustment lags, the labor market will return to long-run equilibrium because the displacement is not acceptable to labor.

[1] Since management is in a better position to know the changes in price level, its perception of labor supply closely approximates the actual labor supply curve.
[2] The critical levels are sometimes called "normal" or "natural" levels of employment and unemployment.

Positive Inflation Expectations

When the expansion phase of the inflation process begins zero inflation expectations is a plausible assumption. But if inflation continues, labor will become conditioned to expect positive inflation. Labor will not only adjust the nominal wage rate to compensate for past inflation but will begin to compensate for future expected inflation. If labor underestimates future price increases, the labor market will behave in a manner similar to the case of zero expected inflation, except that partial nominal wage rate adjustments will take place until labor improves its forecasting methods. If labor adjusts the nominal wage rate to accurately predicted increases in the price level (zero forecast error), the real wage rate will not change; there will be no short-run difference between the perceived and actual labor supply curves, and long-run equilibrium will not be displaced.

If labor overestimates inflation, the situation is quite different. As the inflation process continues labor may begin (although perhaps not intentionally) to expect increases in the price level in excess of actual increases in the price level. In Fig. 9.2.2 suppose that labor supply, L_{se}, and labor demand, MPL, determine employment where the price level is P_1, the nominal wage rate is $\overline{W}$, and the real wage rate is $\overline{W}/P_1$. Now assume that the price level actually increases to P_2, although labor believes that the price level is going to increase to $P_3 > P_2$. In an effort to maintain the real wage rate, labor increases its nominal wage demands in period 1 so that the nominal wage rate increases to $\overline{\overline{W}}$ where $\overline{\overline{W}} - \overline{W} > P_2 - P_1$ and $\overline{\overline{W}} -$

FIGURE 9.2.2

Overestimated Positive Expected Inflation in the Labor Market

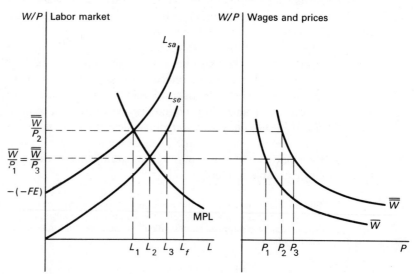

$\overline{W} = P_3 - P_1$. Since labor overestimates the price level, the actual is greater than the expected real wage rate for any given quantity of labor supplied. Hence, $FE < 0$ and the actual labor supply curve, L_{sa}, lies to the left of the perceived labor supply curve, L_{se}. Employment decreases from L_2 to L_1. Involuntary unemployment, $L_3 - L_1$, is created, and although voluntary unemployment decreases to $L_f - L_3$, total unemployment increases to $L_f - L_1$.

In period 2 if labor realizes its error and reduces the nominal wage rate downward so that the net rates of change in the nominal wage rate and the price level are equal, employment will return to its long-run critical level, L_2; voluntary unemployment will return to $L_f = L_2$; and short-run involuntary unemployment, $L_3 - L_1$, will be eliminated.

Downward adjustments in the nominal wage rate are unlikely. Moreover, once labor is conditioned to respond to positive expected inflation, labor is not likely to lower the nominal wage rate. However, after a period during which actual inflation is less than expected, labor is likely to lower nominal wage demands (lower their increases in the nominal wage rate).[3] It is for this reason that those policy measures which potentially lower actual inflation, and thus reduce inflation expectations, become critical issues of national concern. In Fig 9.2.2 suppose that labor makes no additional wage demands, so that the nominal wage rate remains at $\overline{W}$ as the price level moderately increases to P_3. The actual labor supply curve will shift back to the perceived labor supply curve and the labor market will be in long-run equilibrium where $\overline{\overline{W}}/P_3 = \overline{W}/P_1$. Employment returns to L_2, voluntary unemployment returns to $L_f - L_2$, and involuntary unemployment, $L_3 - L_1$, is eliminated.

9.3 INFLATION EXPECTATIONS AND THE PRODUCT MARKET

Zero Expected Inflation

In the product market there are actually two output supply curves. One is for fully perceived inflation (the long-run output supply curve), and the other is for unexpected inflation (the short-run supply curve). If an increase in output demand actually increases the price level above what is expected

---

[3] Labor leaders argue during the phase of the inflation process dominated by cost push inflation that apparent excesses in wage demands are merely a means of "catching up" with past price increases. A cursory inspection of the data for the 1960s can be interpreted to substantiate this claim, because during the expansion phase of the inflation process, prices rose faster than wages. Even if wage demands were adjusted downward, the increases in prices would probably not taper off immediately because management often claims it is catching up with past wage increases. Moreover, management may become conditioned to expect wage increases and raise the price per unit of output (decrease output supply).

by labor, the short-run quantity of output supplied and employment will increase as the actual falls below the expected real wage rate. With a fixed labor force unemployment will decrease as well. The short-run output supply curve is positively sloped throughout because management can hire more labor to produce more output even beyond the critical levels of employment and output. This is possible when labor does not expect inflation and thereby can be fooled into overemployment.

Once labor realizes the forecast error, labor will demand a percentage increase in the nominal wage rate equal to the percentage increase in the price level. Without advances in productivity, output supply and employment will decrease back to their critical levels. Also, given a fixed labor force, unemployment will increase back to its critical level. Once the inflation is fully perceived and full adjustment of nominal wage demands takes place, inflation has no permanent effect on the quantity of output supplied. Thus, the long-run output supply curve is vertical at the critical level of output.

Figure 9.3.1 is a reproduction of the supply side of the skeleton model which will be used to illustrate the interaction between the labor and product markets in the case of zero expected inflation. We begin our analysis where short-run output supply, SR; output demand, D; labor supply, L_{se}; and labor demand, MPL, determine the initial long-run values of the price level, P_1; the real wage rate, $\overline{W}/P_1$; output, Y/P_1; employment, L_2; and voluntary unemployment, $L_f - L_2$. Assume that in period 1 an increase in output demand to D' creates excess demand in the product market at the initial price level, P_1. The price level and output will rise to eliminate the excess. If labor does not expect a price increase, management can increase the nominal wage rate to $\overline{\overline{W}}$ and induce labor to increase the quantity of labor supplied. The increase in the nominal wage rate decreases output supply from SR to SR' and output increases to Y/P_2 as the price level rises to P_2. Since labor does not expect the increase in the price level, the actual exceeds the expected price level, $P_2 > P_1$, and the expected exceeds the actual real wage rate for any given quantity of labor supplied. The actual labor supply curve, L_{sa}, lies to the left of the perceived labor supply curve, L_{se}. The real wage rate falls to $\overline{W}/P_2 < \overline{W}/P_1$. In the short run management hires $L_3 - L_2$ units of additional labor to produce $Y/P_2 - Y/P_1$ units of additional output. Voluntary unemployment decreases from $L_f - L_2$ to $L_f - L_3$ and labor is fooled into overemployment, $L_3 - L_1$.

In period 2 suppose that labor realizes that the price level has increased and increases the nominal wage rate to $\overline{\overline{W}}$ in order to restore the initial real wage rate. The short-run output supply curve decreases to SR'' where the equilibrium price level increases to P_3 and output decreases back to its critical level, $Y/P_3 = Y/P_1$. Because the difference between the actual and expected price levels falls to zero, the actual labor supply curve shifts back to the perceived labor supply curve. The equilibrium real wage rate rises to $\overline{\overline{W}}/P_3 = \overline{W}/P_1$. Employment falls back to L_2 and voluntary unemployment

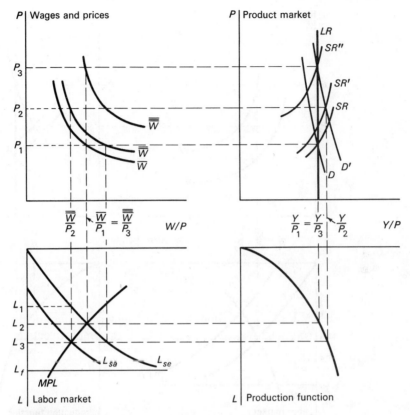

FIGURE 9.3.1

Interaction between the Labor and Product Markets
with Zero Expected Inflation

returns to $L_f - L_2$. After full adjustment occurs only the price level and
nominal wage rate remain higher. In the short run increases in employment
and real income are temporary. Given a fixed labor force there is a short-run
trade-off between changes in the price level and unemployment. However, in
the long run without advances in productivity, employment and real income
return to their critical levels. And there is no permanent trade-off between
changes in the price level and unemployment.

Positive Expected Inflation

If the inflation continues for any length of time, labor will become conditioned
to expect positive inflation. If expected increases in the price level are
underestimated, the interaction between the labor and product markets will
be similar to the case of zero expected inflation described above, except that

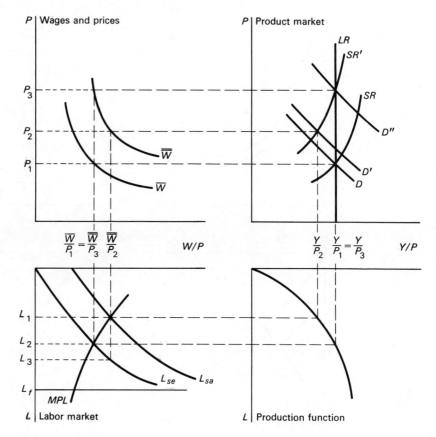

FIGURE 9.3.2

Interaction between the Labor and Product Markets with Overestimated Positive Expected Inflation

the adjustment process will be slower. If labor accurately forecasts increases in the price level and increases the nominal wage rate in period 1 to just offset the actual increase in the price level, real income, the real wage rate, and employment will not change. If initially in long-run equilibrium, the system will move directly from one long-run equilibrium position to another where only the price level and the nominal wage rate are higher.

If labor overestimates increases in the price level, the interaction between the labor and product markets can be explained as follows: In Fig. 9.3.2 suppose that in period 1 output demand, D, and output supply, SR, determines the equilibrium price level, P_1, and output, Y/P_1. The real wage rate is $\overline{W}/P_1$, employment is L_2, voluntary unemployment is $L_f - L_2$, and no involuntary unemployment exists. Now suppose that labor erroneously expects output demand to increase from D to D''. If labor increases the nominal wage rate to $\overline{\overline{W}}$ (output supply decreases to SR') to offset the expected price increase from P_1 to P_3 and if expectations were not erroneous, the real wage rate would not change, $\overline{\overline{W}}/P_3 = \overline{W}/P_1$. However, suppose that output demand increases only from D to D'. The price level increases to $P_2 < P_3$ and output decreases from Y/P_1 to Y/P_2. Due to forecast error the expected is greater than the actual price level ($P_3 > P_2$) and the actual is greater than the expected real wage rate for any given quantity of labor supplied (L_{sa} lies to the right of L_{se}). In the short run the equilibrium real wage rate increases to $\overline{\overline{W}}/P_2 > \overline{W}/P_3$, and firms lay off $L_2 - L_1$ units of labor to produce less output, $Y/P_1 - Y/P_2$. Although voluntary unemployment decreases to $L_f - L_3$, involuntary unemployment, $L_3 - L_1$, is created and total unemployment increases to $L_f - L_1$. As mentioned earlier, the nominal wage rate is generally inflexible downward, even in the long run. Labor will be willing to reduce nominal wage demands (to reduce increases in the nominal wage rate) only after a period where actual is less than expected inflation. In Fig. 9.3.2 suppose that labor demands no additional increase in the nominal wage rate as the price level moderately rises from P_2 to P_3 along SR' as demand increases to D''. The actual labor supply curve will shift back toward the perceived labor supply curve as the real wage falls to its former level, $\overline{\overline{W}}/P_3 = \overline{W}/P_1$. With no advances in productivity, real income and employment will return to their critical levels. With no change in the labor force, unemployment will return to its critical level as well. After long-run adjustment, only the price level and the nominal wage rate remain higher. Once actual inflation is below expected inflation (during a post-inflationary recession) care should be taken to ensure that the inflation process does not get underway again.

Advances in Productivity

It would seem that efforts to permanently increase employment and real income above their critical levels are futile. However, changes in labor's productivity due to changes in technical progress and the capital stock cause changes in both the short- and long-run output supply curves. Figure 9.3.3 illustrates the interaction between the labor and product markets given an increase in the capital stock and/or technical progress. Such increases shift the production function rightward from A to A'. As a result the labor demand curve increases from MPL to MPL'. Since each unit of product can now be produced at a lower unit cost, management can sell each unit at a lower price. Hence, output supply increases to SR'. The price level falls from P_2 to P_1, and with a fixed nominal wage rate, $\overline{W}$, the real wage rate rises from $\overline{W}/P_2$ to $\overline{W}/P_1$. Employment increases from L_1 to L_2, and real income increases from Y/P_2 to Y/P_1. The increase in both employment and real income is permanent, since neither labor nor management has cause to react. Both are satisfied. The long-run output supply curve shifts from LR to LR' and thereby identifies a new critical level of real income (output). Movement

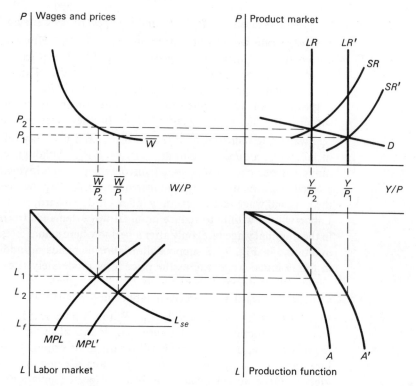

FIGURE 9.3.3

Effect of Changes in the Level of Productivity on the Long-Run Output
Supply Curve

along the long-run labor supply curve, L_{se}, establishes a new critical level of
employment, and with a fixed labor force unemployment permanently falls
to a new critical level, $L_f - L_2$.

9.4 THE IMPACT OF INFLATION EXPECTATIONS ON THE COMPLETE MODEL

Zero Expected Inflation

We are now prepared to explain the impact of labor's reactions to expected
inflation on the complete skeleton model. Figure 9.4.1 illustrates the impact
of inflation on the model when labor expects zero inflation. We begin in
long-run equilibrium where the initial nominal values of the endogenous
variables are deflated by the initial price level, P_1. These correspond to the
initial values of the interest rate, R_1, employment, L_2, and voluntary unemployment, $L_f - L_2$. Involuntary unemployment does not exist.

Assume that in period 1 the net short run effect of an increase in

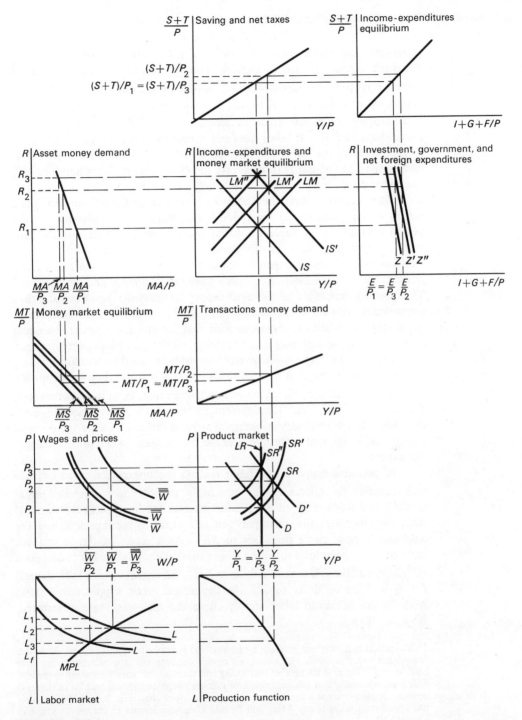

FIGURE 9.4.1

Impact of Zero Expected Inflation on the Complete Model

government expenditures is to shift the real $I + G + F$ curve from Z to Z'', the IS schedule from IS to IS', and aggregate output demand from D to D'. With a small change by management in the nominal wage rate to $\overline{W}$ the short-run supply curve shifts from SR to SR' and the price level rises to P_2. As the real value of the money stock decreases from $\overline{MS}/P_1$ to $\overline{MS}/P_2$, the LM curve shifts to LM'. If labor does not expect the price increase, the actual is greater than the expected price level $(P_2 > P_1)$ and the expected is greater than the actual real wage rate for every unit of labor supplied (L_{sa} lies below L_{se}).

The second column in Table 9.4.1 summarizes the initial long-run values of the variables in the model. The third column summarizes the period 1 values of the variables in our model; the first symbol in the fifth column shows the short-run directions of change. The net impact of the increase in government expenditures and of the decline in the real money stock as the price level rises is to increase the rate of interest and real income.[4] The quantity demanded of real asset money balances decreases because they are inversely related to the interest rate. Real investment + government + net foreign expenditures increases with real income (government spending crowds out investment only if the negative interest rate effect is greater than the positive real income effect on real investment). Real transactions money balances, real saving, and real net taxes increase because they are positively related to real income. Given the nominal wage rate, $\overline{W}$, in the labor market, the real wage rate falls. Employment increases, voluntary unemployment decreases, and involuntary overemployment is created. Labor temporarily accepts the lower real wage rate because the increase in the price level was not expected.

In period 2 suppose that labor realizes the unexpected price increase and increases the nominal wage rate to $\overline{\overline{W}}$ in order to restore the initial period's real wage rate. In the product market the increase in the nominal wage rate increases the costs per unit of output to management and the aggregate supply curve decreases to SR''. As a result of the subsequent increase in the price level to P_3 the money market equilibrium curve decreases to $\overline{MS}/P_3$ and the LM schedule shifts to LM''. Since real income falls, the real $I + G + F$ curve shifts to Z'. As the actual labor supply curve shifts back to the perceived labor supply curve the real wage rate is restored, $\overline{\overline{W}}/P_3 = \overline{W}/P_1$.

---

[4] The interest rate may not increase by as much as is implied in our diagram. If wealth holders act to restore their real wealth which will decrease with the increase in the price level, they will increase the level of real saving and thereby shift the IS schedule to the left. This does not mean that the net impact of nominal wage adjustment will be to decrease output. It simply means the interest rate will be lower than Fig. 9.4.1 indicates after full adjustment takes place. More will be said about the impact of the wealth effect in Chapter 10.

TABLE 9.4.1

Effects of a Change in Government Expenditures with Zero Expected Inflation

Variables	Initial Long-Run Values	Short-Run Values	Final Long-Run Values	Changes
Real saving + net taxes	$(S + T)/P_1$	$(S + T)/P_2$	$(S + T)/P_3$	$(+ - n)$
Real investment + government + net foreign expenditures	E/P_1	E/P_2	E/P_3	$(+ - n)$
Interest rate	R_1	R_2	R_3	$(+ + +)$
Real income	Y/P_1	Y/P_2	Y/P_3	$(+ - n)$
Real money stock	$\overline{MS}/P_1$	$\overline{MS}/P_2$	$\overline{MS}/P_3$	$(- - -)$
Real transactions balances	MT/P_1	MT/P_2	MT/P_3	$(+ - n)$
Real asset money balances	MA/P_1	MA/P_2	MA/P_3	$(- - -)$
Price level	P_1	P_2	P_3	$(+ + +)$
Real wage rate	$\overline{W}/P_1$	$\overline{\overline{W}}/P_2$	$\overline{\overline{\overline{W}}}/P_3$	$(- + n)$
Nominal wage rate	$\overline{W}$	$\overline{\overline{W}}$	$\overline{\overline{\overline{W}}}$	$(+ + +)$
Employment	L_2	L_3	L_2	$(+ - n)$
Involuntary overemployment	0	$L_3 - L_1$	0	$(+ - n)$
Voluntary unemployment	$L_f - L_2$	$L_f - L_3$	$L_f - L_2$	$(- + n)$

Note: In the fifth column there are sets of three symbols, +, −, and *n*, which are used to denote increases, decreases, and no changes in the variables, respectively. The first symbol gives the direction of the short-run change in the variable, the second indicates the direction of change in the variable with long-run adjustments, and the third indicates the direction of net change in the variables after full adjustment.

The fourth column in Table 9.4.1 summarizes the values of the variables after full long-run adjustment in period 2. The second symbol in the fifth column indicates the direction of change in the variables as labor reacts to errors in forecasting inflation; the third symbol indicates the net long-run changes in the variables.

After full adjustment only the nominal wage rate, the price level, and the interest rate are higher. Without advances in productivity the real values of the endogenous variables return to their critical levels. Only the nominal values are higher. There are two exceptions. Although total real expenditures return to their former level, the composition has changed. Real investment is less than before because although real income returns to its former level, the interest rate is higher. Government expenditures crowd out private investment expenditures in the long run. Real asset money balances are less than their former level. Given that the nominal money stock remains fixed an increase in the turnover of money (velocity of money) due to the decrease in asset money balances facilitates the higher level of *nominal* exchange.

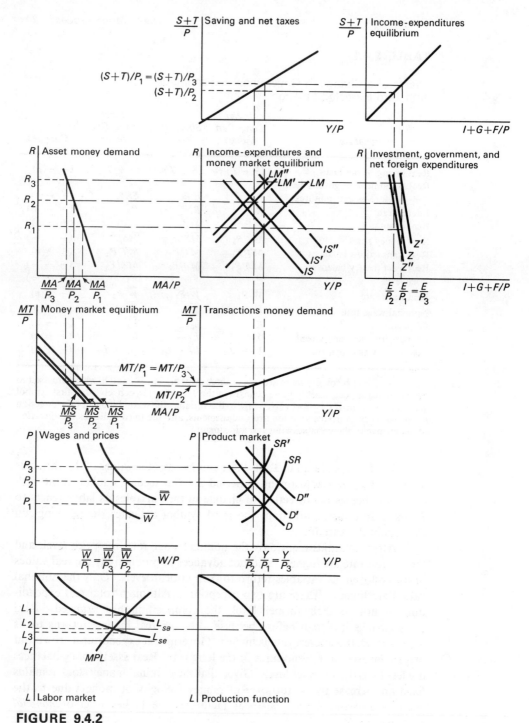

FIGURE 9.4.2

Impact of Overestimated Positive Expected Inflation on the Complete Model

Positive Expected Inflation

Sufficient consideration has been given to the impact of underestimates and perfect estimates of positive expected inflation. In Fig. 9.4.2 we shall consider the impact of overestimations of inflation. The initial nominal values of the endogenous variables are deflated by the initial price level, P_1. These correspond to the interest rate, R_1, employment, L_2, and voluntary unemployment, $L_f - L_2$. There is no involuntary unemployment.

Assume that in period 1 labor expects an increase in government expenditures to shift the output demand from D to D'' and the price level to increase to P_3 (this is consistent with a net short run increase in the real $I + G + F$ curve from Z to Z' and the IS schedule from IS to IS''). In an attempt to maintain the real wage rate labor will increase the nominal wage rate to $\overline{W}$ and thereby the output supply curve shifts to SR'. However, suppose that while the supply curve shifts to SR', the increase in government expenditures actually shifts the IS schedule to IS' and increases the output demand curve to D' so that real income falls to Y/P_2. (Notice that the real $I + G + F$ curve actually shifts to Z'' because real investment decreases more than the increase in real government spending as real income falls and the interest rate rises.) The actual price level increases to $P_2 < P_3$ (the LM schedule shifts to LM'). This means that the real wage rate actually rises to $\overline{W}/P_2$, employment decreases to L_1, involuntary unemployment increases to $L_3 - L_1$, and although voluntary unemployment decreases to $L_f - L_3$, total unemployment increases to $L_f - L_1$.

The second column in Table 9.4.2 summarizes the initial long-run equilibrium values of the variables of the model. The third column shows the short-run values of the variables in period 1, while the first symbol in the fifth column indicates the direction of change in the variables in period 1. Real saving plus net taxes and real transactions money balances fall with decreases in real income. Total real investment + government + net foreign expenditures decrease for reasons already mentioned above. With the money stock fixed, the velocity of money rises because real asset money balances are reduced when the interest rate rises. The increase in the nominal wage rate raises the price level such that the real wage rate increases. Employment decreases, voluntary unemployment decreases, and involuntary unemployment is created.

In period 2 suppose that actual inflation continues to be less than expected and that labor reduces nominal wage demands to zero so that the nominal wage rate remains at $\overline{W}$. Future increases in output demand from D' to D'' (additional government expenditures shift real expenditure curves to Z' and the IS schedule to IS'') will moderately raise the actual price level to P_3 (the LM schedule shifts to LM'') and the real wage rate will be restored, $\overline{W}/P_3 = \overline{W}/P_1$. Without advances in productivity the real values of the endogenous variables of the model return to their former levels. Only their nominal values are higher. There are two exceptions. Although total real expenditures return to their former level, the composition has changed. Real investment is less than before because although real income returns to its former level the interest rate is higher. Government expenditures crowd out private real investment in the long run by raising the interest rate. Real asset money balances are less in the long run than their former level. Given the nominal money stock an increase in the turnover of money due to the decrease in asset money balances facilitates the higher level of nominal exchange.

TABLE 9.4.2

Effects of a Change in Government Expenditures with Overestimated Positive Expected Inflation

Variables	Initial Long-Run Values	Short-Run Values	Final Long-Run Values	Changes
Real saving + net taxes	$(S + T)/P_1$	$(S + T)/P_2$	$(S + T)/P_3$	$(- + n)$
Real investment + government + net foreign expenditures	E/P_1	E/P_2	E/P_3	$(- + n)$
Interest rate	R_1	R_2	R_3	$(+ + +)$
Real income	Y/P_1	Y/P_2	Y/P_3	$(- + n)$
Real money stock	$\overline{MS}/P_1$	$\overline{MS}/P_2$	$\overline{MS}/P_3$	$(- - -)$
Real transactions balances	MT/P_1	MT/P_2	MT/P_3	$(- + n)$
Real asset money balances	MA/P_1	MA/P_2	MA/P_3	$(- - -)$
Price level	P_1	P_2	P_3	$(+ + +)$
Real wage rate	$\overline{W}/P_1$	$\overline{\overline{W}}/P_2$	$\overline{W}/P_3$	$(+ - n)$
Nominal wage rate	$\overline{W}$	$\overline{W}$	$\overline{W}$	$(+ n +)$
Employment	L_2	L_1	L_2	$(- + n)$
Involuntary unemployment	0	$L_3 - L_1$	0	$(+ - n)$
Voluntary unemployment	$L_f - L_2$	$L_f - L_3$	$L_f - L_2$	$(- + n)$

Note: In the fifth column there are sets of three symbols, $+$, $-$, and n, which are used to denote increases, decreases, and no changes in the variables, respectively. The first symbol gives the direction of the short-run change in the variable, the second indicates the direction of change in the variable with long-run adjustments, and the third indicates the direction of net change in the variables after full adjustment.

The fourth column in Table 9.4.2 summarizes the values of the variables after complete long-run adjustment takes place. The second symbol in the fifth column indicates the direction of change which returns the system to long-run equilibrium. The net changes after full long-run adjustment are indicated in the fifth column by the third symbol. After full adjustment only the price level, the interest rate, the nominal wage rates, and the nominal values of the endogenous variable remain permanently higher.

9.5 THE INFLATION PROCESS
IN THE UNITED STATES

Our revised model attempts to explain how labor's adjustments of nominal wage demands to inflation expectations affect an economy. Now we are in a position to consider the applicability of our model to the U.S. economy.

We came out of the 1950s with high unemployment (and underemployment) of resources and negligible inflation. The late 1950s and early 1960s characterized periods of postinflationary recession and price stabilization after the Korean War. President John F. Kennedy took steps to turn the recession into recovery. His prescription for recovery included increases in government spending, increases in the money stock, and decreases in net taxes (decreases in taxes and increases in transfer payments). Monetary policy was primarily accommodative to fiscal policy during these years. In 1964 income and excise taxes were reduced. These measures raised the level of aggregate output demand. Sustained productivity advances occurred during this period and thereby costs per unit of output supplied decreased. In 1962, to speed up productivity advances, tax incentives for investment were provided in the form of more liberal depreciation allowances and investment tax credits. Further, corporate taxes were reduced in 1964. Efforts to improve human capital were made by providing new aids to segments of the war on poverty and education. They were designed to increase the productive quality and mobility of the labor force.

In Fig. 9.5.1 the output demand curve, D_0, and short-run supply curve, SR_0, indicate the initial conditions of the economy. They determine the initial price level, P_0, and real income, Y/P_0. Notice that real income is less than the critical level of real income, Y/P_e.

Beginning in about 1961 the initial effects of the Kennedy efforts increased output demand as indicated by D_1. Productivity advances, falling inflation expectations, and increases in the utilization of employed resources caused a net increase in output supply as indicated by SR_1. There were negligible increases in the price level. Equilibrium real income in period 1 is Y/P_1 and the price level is P_1. At this point we shall assume that there are no further downward expectations adjustments or increases in the utilization of employed resources. From now on only productivity advances increase output supply.

Up until about mid-1965 the multiplier effects of the Kennedy efforts continued to increase output demand as indicated by D_2. Sustained productivity advances continued and increased output supply as indicated by SR_2. Note that productivity advances also increased the long-run output supply curve as indicated by LR'. The new long-run output supply curve identifies a new critical level of real income, $(Y/P)'_e$. Up until about mid-1965 the increases in output supply offset increases in output demand such that

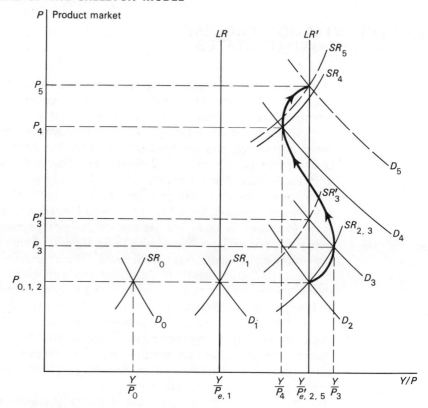

FIGURE 9.5.1

Inflation Process in the United States

increases in the price level were negligible. In period 2 equilibrium real income is Y/P_2 and the price level is P_2.

In mid-1965 government expenditures began to accelerate as the U.S. increased our involvement in the Vietnam War. Output demand increased sharply as indicated by D_3 and outstripped increases in output supply due to productivity advances. For simplification purposes assume that productivity remained unchanged and thereby short-run output supply remained at $SR_2 = SR_3$. In period 3 equilibrium real income is Y/P_3 and the price level is P_3. Since labor had been conditioned to negligible inflation, it is reasonable to assume that labor did not expect the resulting increase in the price level. As real income increased, workers accepted the additional employment (involuntary overemployment) and the real wage rate decreased in the short run.

A significant rise in "defense" outlays necessarily creates problems of demand pull inflation unless accompanied by fiscal and/or monetary restraints. There are several reasons why such anti-inflationary measures were not taken. First, President Lyndon B. Johnson and Congress underestimated the magnitude of the escalation of the war by a wide margin. Second, no one was willing to risk political suicide by suggesting restraint while the economy enjoyed the prosperity of the 1960s. The public was tired of the restraints of the 1950s. Third, and relatedly, Congress and the administration chose to be skeptical of the economic forecasts of impending problems of chronic inflation. Fiscal efforts in the battle against inflation took the form of "moral suasion" or "jawboning," wage price guideposts, and curtailment of the nondefense budget. The monetary authorities took steps to slow down the increase in the money stock, and increases in output demand slacked off in late 1966. The January 1967 budget called for a 6 percent tax surcharge on personal and corporate income. The Fed did not reapply the monetary brakes to the extent that it had previously done under the assumption that prompt tax action was forthcoming. But Congress refused to raise taxes; more facts were needed and not just forecasts of impending disaster.

Fiscal restraint was not forthcoming until the 1968 surtax. And although monetary restraint continued up to early 1970, inflation had become a disease and it could not be halted by preventive measures which would have been effective two or three years earlier. It was during this period that labor became conditioned to expect positive increases in the price level. If the nominal wage rate had been increased just enough to offset previous inflation, the process would have ended. In period 3 if labor had increased the nominal wage rate such that output supply decreased to SR'_3, the equilibrium price level would have been P'_3 and real income could have fallen back to long run equilibrium, Y/P'_e.

Soon labor began to form positive inflation expectations. At first labor either accurately predicted or perhaps underestimated future price increases. However, prolonged conditioning to accelerating inflation caused overestimation of inflation. As output demand continued to increase, the nominal wage rate began to rise faster than the price level, and output supply decreased. In period 4 decreases in output supply to SR_4 outstripped increases in output demand to D_4. The price rose to P_4 and real income fell below its critical level, $Y/P_4 < Y/P'_e$.

At this point government attempts to stabilize the price level and increase employment (reduce unemployment), and real income must be directed toward reducing actual inflation below expected inflation so that inflation expectations can be reduced. Only then will labor reduce nominal wage demands. If inflation has gone on long enough, the public can expect a period of involuntary unemployment and excess capacity until labor adjusts its inflation expectations downward. Thus, there is a connection between today's inflationary recession and yesterday's boom. If the lower unemployment of yesterday's boom is chosen, the higher unemployment of today's inflationary recession must be expected. Economists know something about curbing deflationary depressions and recessions, but they have not yet figured out how to permanently increase real income and employment beyond their critical levels (except by advances in productivity and/or increases in the mobility of workers, i.e., a well-developed labor market) without incurring an inflationary recession. The short-run relationship between inflation and employment (unemployment) obscures this reality.

In the late 1960s and the 1970s President Richard M. Nixon attempted to apply moderate monetary and fiscal restraint as a means of reducing actual inflation below expected inflation. It was hoped that if price expectations fell, increases in nominal wage demands would be reduced and thereby reduce decreases in output supply. Afterward both monetary and fiscal tools would again be used to promote full employment with price stability.

In Fig. 9.5.1 decreases in nominal wage demands would have reduced the increases in output supply as indicated by the decrease in output supply to SR_5. If monetary and fiscal policies were to moderately increase output demand to D_5, the price level would increase to P_5 and real income would increase to $Y/P_5 = Y/P_e'$. Nixon's goal was to stop the inflation and eliminate involuntary unemployment. He also attempted to provide stimulus to productivity which would permit permanent increases in real income above Y/P_e' and permanent increases in total employment with negligible inflation.[5]

Invariably, once the inflation process gets "out of hand" so that monetary and/or fiscal policies do not bring quick response, politicians ignore the causes of the problems, i.e., their previous well-meaning policies. They orate loudly on the inhumanity of the symptoms and recommend "quicky" measures to alleviate them.

Prior to the adoption of the wage-price freeze in August 1971, the Nixon Administration relied on traditional monetary and fiscal policies to manage aggregate demand. However, the administration was apparently unwilling to incur the cost of additional unemployment to curb inflation. As rates of inflation and unemployment became increasingly unacceptable, the administration gave in to the proponents of wage-price controls (much to the proponents' surprise).

The short-run outlook of the new Nixon program appeared favorable. Wage-price controls tend to operate more efficiently under conditions of excess supply, and the suddenness of this adoption prevented labor and business from making anticipatory increases in wages and prices.

The justification for an incomes policy like the wage-price freeze (Phase I) is based on the necessity of reducing inflation expectations. As we have shown, a persistent decrease in the inflation during periods of high unemployment (above the critical level) will reduce inflation expectations and thereby increase employment and curb further inflation. The politicians

---

[5] Actually during this period in the United States there were additional shifts to the right in the long-run output supply curve due to productivity advances. Moreover, the rising cost of other input factors, materials, energy, etc., caused additional leftward shifts in the output supply curve. Also, rising wages and other factor input prices alone did not cause increases in unemployment. Unemployment increased in the later 1960s because the "baby boom" of the 1940s entered the labor market. Further, upward pressures on unemployment occurred as the U.S. involvement in the Vietnam War came to an end and veterans entered the labor force.

reasoned from this proposition that an exogenous shock to the "inflationary psychology" would lower inflation expectations and thereby permit unemployment to be reduced by moderate monetary and fiscal expansionary policy.

In the short run through Phase I and part of Phase II, the wage-price controls decreased the annual inflation rate by 1.2 percent (CPI) to 2.5 percent (WPI) during the period from August 1971 through December 1972. However, beginning in Phase II the controls, along with the energy crisis (which is another cost inducing inflationary factor), appear to have made the situation worse.

Many proponents of the wage-price controls suggest that Phases I and II should have been extended. They argue that the controls would have been effective in permanently lowering inflation except that the administration "botched" the job. Others believe that a prolonged wage-price control program would not only have induced distortion into the allocation of resources but also could not have avoided the problems of "exiting" from a short-run wage-price control system, that is, a reoccurrence of a more severe inflation and higher level of unemployment.

Professor W. Poole cites three primary forces which account for the reoccurrence of severe inflation during Phase III. First, there is the catch-up phenomenon. During the exit from the wage-price freeze, business and labor began to raise prices and nominal wages in order to compensate for perceived losses which they incurred due to the suddenness of the freeze. In early 1973 price increases began to accelerate so that the annual inflation rate was 4.0 percent during the period from August 1971 to March 1973. This is only a little lower than the 4.4 percent rate from July 1970 to July 1973. Since March 1973 the rate has been substantially higher.

The second factor was the "fiscal irresponsibility" which was encouraged by the wage-price freeze. Expansionary monetary and particularly fiscal policies were used in conjunction with the wage-price program in an effort to decrease unemployment. Some argue that employment gains were the obvious success of the program and that the wage-price freeze made the expansion possible. However, once we began to exit from the program, demand pressure which had built up during Phases I and II exploded into more inflation. Moreover, as our analysis of the inflation process implies, little is gained from less unemployment now if it means more unemployment and more severe inflation later on.

The third factor underlying price increases after the freeze was due to anticipation of another wage-price freeze. There remains the real possibility that political expediency will again give way to the realities of the inflation process and again the economy would be subjected to stopgap measures. Business and labor prepare for the possibility by anticipatory wage and price increases.

Unfortunately, there is no empirically verified means of reducing inflation and decreasing unemployment except by noninflationary monetary and fiscal policies. Even these means are questionable when there are shortages in raw material markets. As long as wage-price controls are regarded as a political panacea, the economic realities of the inflation process will remain obscure.

One can readily see where the wage-price spiral got its name. The succession of short-run equilibria between output supply and demand form a spiral which can be characterized as a long-run equilibrating process (see the heavy line in Fig. 9.5.1). The various phases of the process are linked by labor's reaction to errors in forecasting the price level. In the short run given a fixed labor force there is an inverse relationship between the price level and unemployment as output rises above its critical level. Furthermore, there is a positive relationship between the price level and unemployment when labor's nominal wage demands are so excessive as to push the price level to a level where real income falls below its critical level. Both positive and inverse relationships have been the experience of the U.S. economy since 1960. In the long run after full adjustment, a rising price level has no effect on employment and output, and given a fixed labor force, neither will a rising price level affect unemployment.

9.6 THE PHILLIPS' CURVE

Professor A. W. Phillips was one of the first economists to recognize the apparent trade-off between the rates of inflation and unemployment; i.e., when the inflation rate is high unemployment is low and vice versa. For this reason relationships which summarize associated rates of inflation and unemployment are called *Phillips' curves*.

If our description of the inflation process is correct, there is a short-run Phillips' curve which shows a trade-off between rates of inflation and unemployment that result from labor's short-run forecast errors. Moreover, there is a short-run Phillips' curve for each level of inflation expectations. However, in the long run forecast errors fall to zero, and with no change in productivity, changes in the inflation rate have no effect on the unemployment rate. Thus, the long-run Phillips' curve shows no trade-off between rates of inflation and unemployment.[6]

[6] Professors O. Eckstein and R. Brinner agree with our definition of the critical rate of unemployment and that below the critical rate of unemployment there is no long-run trade-off between rates of inflation and unemployment. However, they contend that there is a long-run trade-off above the critical unemployment rate. They base their contention on the imperfectly competitive structure of U.S. labor and business. Even if the un-employment rate is above the critical rate, unions can increase wages in excess of advances in productivity. Because of rigidities in price setting, wage increases are not fully translated into price increases (business does not fully adjust prices to close the gap between actual and perceived labor costs). Thus, increases in the unemployment rate above the critical rate are associated with decreases in the inflation rate.

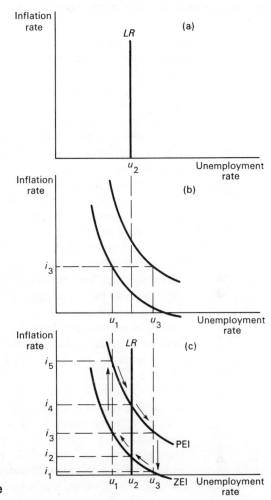

FIGURE 9.6.1

The Short- and Long-Run Phillips' Curve

Figure 9.6.1(a) shows the long-run Phillips' curve, LR, implied by our analysis of the inflation process. It is vertical at the critical rate of unemployment, u_2. In the long run inflation is fully forecast and cannot change unemployment because price increases are offset by equal increases in the nominal wage rate. The only possible equilibrium in the labor market is the intersection of the long-run labor supply curve and the labor demand curve,

---

As the unemployment rate falls, imperfection in price setting and wage setting falls toward zero, and an increasing proportion of rising labor cost increases the price level. The rate of unemployment falls as the inflation rate rises. Once the system returns to the critical rate of unemployment prices rise proportionally with wages. No further decrease in unemployment can occur because the inflation rate and the rate at which wage increases exceed advances in productivity are equal. Thus, the long-run Phillips' curve is vertical at the critical unemployment rate and negatively slopped above the critical rate of unemployment.

which simultaneously determine employment and the real wage rate. No involuntary unemployment or overemployment exists. Voluntary unemployment exists depending on the difference between the labor force and full employment, and advances in productivity which close the gap between the two. Price increases will lower the real wage rate and thereby increase the number of workers business is willing to employ. However, once labor fully adjusts nominal wages to offset price increases so that the real wage rate is maintained, no additional workers will be willing to accept employment.

Figure 9.6.1(b) shows two of a whole family of short-run Phillips' curves, one for each level of inflation expectations. If labor expects zero inflation, we can explain a trade-off when there is an increase in the inflation rate along ZEI. Similarly, for every positive level of inflation expectations there is a short-run Phillips' curve which lies to the right of ZEI. The higher the level of inflation expectations, the farther to the right the relevant Phillips' curve will lie. The curve labeled PEI is one such curve. For any given inflation rate, the unemployment rate will be greater the greater the level of inflation expectations. For example, if the inflation rate is i_3 and inflation expectations are zero along ZEI, the unemployment rate is $u_1 < u_3$ where inflation expectations are positive along PEI.

Figure 9.6.1(c) combines Figs. 9.6.1(a) and (b) and can be used to reiterate the inflation process described in more detail in the earlier sections of this chapter. We can begin our description of long-run equilibrium at the critical rate of unemployment, u_2, where inflation expectations are zero and the inflation rate is i_2. If there are no adjustments of expectations in an expansionary economy and the inflation rate increases to i_3, the unemployment rate falls to u_1 along ZEI. As wage demands increase to catch up with price increases, the unemployment rate falls back to the critical rate, u_2, along ZEI. However, if labor adjusts expectations to the new inflation, i.e., they develop positive inflation expectations when unexpected inflation persists, the short-run Phillips' curve shifts to PEI. As the inflation rate increases from i_3 to i_5 further nominal wage adjustments will increase the unemployment rate back to u_2 along PEI. Notice that once positive inflation expectations set in, the economy cannot move back to its former inflation rate, i_2, unless expectations decrease. Also notice that the decrease in the unemployment rate is temporary when increases in the price level rise above their expected rate; it is the change in the rate that produces this result.

If positive inflation expectations persist and labor overestimates actual price increases, the inflation rate will decrease as the unemployment rate increases above the critical rate along PEI to u_3. If labor adjusts inflation expectations downward during a period in which actual inflation is persistently less than expected, the short-run Phillips' curve will decrease to ZEI. As fiscal and/or monetary authorities stimulate output demand, labor will lower wage demands as the inflation rate increases and the economy returns to its critical level of unemployment, u_2 (with no changes in productivity).

Once positive inflation expectations set in, the economy does not simply increase inflation for a reduction in unemployment. Rather, the full cost of less unemployment now is not only more inflation later but more unemployment as well.

9.7 SUMMARY

In this chapter we have used the skeleton model to explain the inflation process. The method of analysis was to break the inflation process down into both short- and long-run comparative static equilibria. The succession of short-run equilibria can be characterized as a long-run equilibrating process where the short-run equilibria are linked by labor's reaction (nominal wage adjustments) to forecast errors in predicting the price level. Our analysis is helpful in explaining the inflation since the 1960s and the problems we face in the 1970s to promote price stability, full employment, and growth in real income. Our analysis indicates that the inflation process gets underway when there are rapid increases in output demand at close to full employment of resources with little or no accompanying measures to curb inflation. As the price level rises, labor's initial reaction is one of delayed increases in nominal wage demands. Employment and output increase in the short run. But as the inflation continues, labor increases its nominal wage demands on the basis of positive expected inflation. Employment and output stabilize for a time and then fall back toward their critical levels. If labor should begin to overestimate inflation, employment and output may fall below their critical levels. Involuntary unemployment is then created. When the expected inflation falls below actual inflation during a period of postinflationary recession and price stabilization, labor will lower its nominal wage demands. Afterward, monetary and fiscal policies can be used to promote recovery. Once full adjustment occurs employment and output return to their critical levels. Given a fixed labor force, unemployment returns to its critical level as well. Permanent increases in output and employment (decreases in unemployment) occur when there are sustained advances in productivity.

REVIEW QUESTIONS

1. In the short run, increases in government expenditures increase real income and the price level while the real value of fixed money balances fall. How can less real money balances support a higher level of real income?

2. To what extent is there a short-run "crowding out effect" in the beginning of the inflation process?

3. Labor's increases in wage demands during an inflationary recession have been sharply criticized. Discuss.

4. Explain how technical progress and capital accumulation are the most effective means of bringing an economy out of an inflationary recession, and explain why they are difficult to encourage in an inflationary recession.

5. In light of the Phillips' curve analysis in this chapter, is the politician who promises both less inflation *and* less unemployment credible?

SELECTED READINGS

BALL, R. J., and R. DOYLE (eds.), *Inflation*, Baltimore: Penguin, 1969.

BARRO, R. J., and H. I. GROSSMAN, "A General Disequilibrium Model of Income and Employment," *American Economic Review*, 61 (March 1971), 82–93.

BRONFENBRENNER, M., and F. D. HOLZMAN, "Survey of Inflation Theory," *American Economic Review*, 53 (Sept. 1963), 593–661.

CAGAN, P., "The Monetary Dynamics of Hyperinflation," in M. Friedman (ed.), *Studies in the Quantity Theory of Money*, Chicago: University of Chicago Press, 1956, pp. 25–117.

CLOWER, R. W., "Keynes and the Classics: A Dynamical Perspective," *Quarterly Journal of Economics*, 74 (May 1960), 318–23.

DUESENBERRY, J., "Mechanics of Inflation," *Review of Economics and Statistics*, 32 (May 1950), 144–49.

DUNLOP, J. T. (ed.), *The Theory of Wage Determination*, New York: St. Martin's, 1957.

ECKSTEIN, O., and R. BRINNER, "The Inflation Process in the United States," Joint Economics Committee, Congress of the United States, Washington, D.C.: U.S. Government Printing Office, 1972.

FEIGE, E. L., "The 1972 Report of the President's Council of Economic Advisers: Inflation and Unemployment," *American Economic Review*, 62 (Sept. 1972), 509–39.

FELLNER, W., "Demand Inflation, Cost Inflation, and Collective Bargaining," in P. Bradley (ed.), *The Public Stake in Union Power*, Charlottesville: University Press of Virginia, 1959, pp. 225–54.

FRIEDMAN, M., "The Role of Monetary Policy," *American Economic Review*, 58 (March 1968), 17.

GORDON, R. A., *The Goal of Full Employment*, New York: Wiley, 1967.

GORDON, R. J., "Inflation in Recession and Recovery," *Brookings Papers on Economic Activity*, Vol. 1, 1971, 105–66.

HALL, R. E., "Why Is the Unemployment Rate So High at Full Employment?" *Brookings Papers on Economic Activity*, Vol. 3, 1970.

HANSEN, B., "Excess Demand, Unemployment, Vacancies and Wages," *Quarterly Journal of Economics*, 84 (Feb. 1970), 1–23.

JOHNSON, H. G. (ed.), "A Survey of Theories of Inflation," in *Essays in Monetary Economics*, Cambridge, Mass.: Harvard University Press, 1967, pp. 104–42.

KESSEL, R. A., and A. A. ALCHIAN, "The Inflation-Induced Lag of Wages," *American Economic Review*, 50 (March 1960), 43–66.

LEIJONHUFVED, A., *On Keynesian Economics and the Economics of Keynes*, New York: Oxford University Press, 1968.

LIPSEY, R. G., "The Relation Between Unemployment and the Rate of Change of Money Wage Rates in the United Kingdom, 1862–1957: A Further Analysis," *Economica*, 27 (Feb. 1960), 1–31.

MACHLUP, F., "Another View of Cost-Push and Demand-Pull Inflation," *Review of Economics and Statistics*, 42 (May 1960), 125–39.

OKUN, A. M., *The Political Economy of Prosperity*, New York: Norton, 1970.

PERRY, G. L., *Unemployment, Money Wage Rates and Inflation*, Cambridge, Mass.: M.I.T. Press, 1966.

———, "Wages and the Guideposts," *American Economic Review*, 57 (Sept. 1967), 897–904.

PHELPS, E. S., et al., *Microeconomic Foundations of Employment and Inflation Theory*, New York: Norton, 1970.

———, *Inflation Policy and Unemployment Theory*, New York: Norton, 1972.

PHILLIPS, A. W., "The Relation between Unemployment and the Rate of Change in Money Wage Rates in the United Kingdom, 1862–1957," *Economica*, 25 (Nov. 1958), 283–99.

PITCHFORD, J. D., "Cost and Demand Elements in the Inflationary Process," *Review of Economics Studies*, 24 (Feb. 1957), 139–48.

POOLE, W., "Thoughts on the Wage-Price Freeze," from A. M. Okun and G. L. Perry, *Brookings Papers on Economic Activity*, Vol. 2 (1971), pp. 429–43.

———, "Wage-Price Controls: Where Do We Go From Here?," from A. M. Okun and G. L. Perry, *Brookings Papers on Economic Activity*, Vol. 1 (1973), pp. 285–99.

REES, A., "Wage Determination and Involuntary Unemployment," *Journal of Political Economy*, 59 (April 1951), 143–53.

———, "The Phillips' Curve as a Menu for Policy Choice," *Economica*, 37 (Aug. 1970), 277–88.

SAMUELSON, P. A., and R. M. SOLOW, "Analytical Aspects of Anti-Inflation Policy," *American Economic Review*, 50 (May 1960), 177–94.

SARGENT, T. J., "Anticipated Inflation and Nominal Interest," *Quarterly Journal of Economics*, 86 (May 1972), 212–25.

SCHULTZ, G. P., and R. Z. ALIBER (eds.), *Guidelines: Formal Control and the Marketplace*, Chicago: University of Chicago Press, 1966.

SCHULTZE, C. L., "Recent Inflation in the United States," Study Paper No. 1, Joint Economic Committee, Congress of the United States, Washington, D.C.: U.S. Government Printing Office, Sept. 1959.

———, "Has the Phillips' Curve Shifted? Some Additional Evidence," *Brookings Papers on Economic Activity*, Vol. 2 (1971), 452–67.

STIGLER, G. J., "Information in the Labor Market," *Journal of Political Economy*, 70 (Oct. 1962), 94–105.

THORP, W., and R. QUANDT, *The New Inflation*, New York: McGraw-Hill, 1959.

CHAPTER 10

Consumption and Wealth

10.1 A PROBLEM OF INTERPRETATION

Professor J. M. Keynes made the consumption function discussed in Chapter 4 one of the most important relationships of macroeconomic theory. He characterized the consumption function by hypothesizing that (1) consumption is a stable function of income, (2) the marginal propensity to consume is less in the short-run than in the long-run, (3) as income increases the average propensity to consume will fall in the long-run and thus the marginal is less than the average propensity to consume, and (4) household wealth will also influence consumption.

Hypothesis 1 means that consumption can be predicted. Hypothesis 2 implies that changes in income will affect consumption less in the short-run than in the long-run because people adjust consumption to new income levels with a lag. Hypothesis 3 implies that as income increases, the proportion of consumption from income will decrease. Thus, investment and/or government spending must continue to increase to provide for economic growth and to maintain full employment. Finally, hypothesis 4 implies that other variables besides income (such as household wealth) can affect consumption.

Since these hypotheses lend themselves to verification, empirical work was undertaken and for many years both cross-sectional household budget studies and short-period time series data so strongly supported hypotheses 1 and 3 that hypotheses 2 and 4 were forgotten temporarily.

During World War II government expenditures increased income. But economists feared that when the war was over, the economy would slip back into depression without continued government expenditures. They reasoned by hypothesis 3 that since the average propensity to consume falls as income increases (and under these circumstances there is no reason to expect the average propensity to invest to increase), the government must continue to supplement the private sector if economic growth were to continue and full employment were to be maintained. In fact, government spending must increase more than income or at best the economy would become stagnate.

The long-run predictions of these economists (who were called stagnationists) were disproved after the war when both consumer and investment demand increased. Moreover, Professor S. Kuznets' study of U.S. data indicated that the average propensity to consume in the long run is fairly constant so that the long-run marginal propensity to consume, MPC, equals the long-run average propensity to consume, APC, MPC = APC. Thus, there appears to be a proportional relationship between consumption and income in the long-run. In Fig. 10.1.1 the straight line from the origin, C_{LR}, shows the apparent long-run relationship in real terms.

Kuznets' study also indicated that the average propensity to consume was below its long-run average during boom periods and above its long-run average during recession periods. This implies that the average propensity to consume varies inversely with income over the business cycle. In the short-run the average propensity to consume falls as income rises and the marginal is less than the average propensity to consume, MPC < APC. Thus, short-run consumer behavior indicates a nonproportional relationship, C_{SR}, between consumption and income as shown in Fig. 10.1.1 in real terms.

While budget studies at any point in time indicate a nonproportional relationship between consumption and income, additional evidence from a

FIGURE 10.1.1

Long- and Short-Run Consumer Behavior

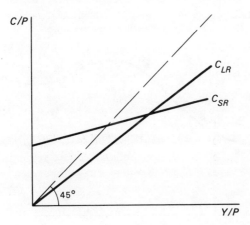

comparison of budget studies at different points in time indicates that the average and marginal propensities to consume are approximately equal. Thus, a closer look at budget studies amplified the apparent contradiction between short- and long-run consumer behavior.

Since Kuznets' study had shaken confidence in the popular view of the Keynesian consumption function, it became apparent that a theory of consumption must account for (1) budget studies which show the average propensity to consume falling as income increases so that in a cross section of households MPC < APC, (2) short-run time series (or business cycle) data which show that the average propensity to consume is less than its average during booms and greater than average during recessions so that in the short-run over the business cycle MPC < APC, and (3) long-run time series data which show that the average propensity to consume is constant so that in the long-run MPC = APC.

Theoretical reconciliation of the observed differences between cross-sectional and short-run time series data and long-run time series data takes a variety of forms. To understand the various hypotheses, one must first understand that they attempt to reconcile interpretations of cross-sectional and short-run time series data with long-run time series data. Short- and long-run behavior relate to the business cycle. Downswings in the business cycle (recessions) are short-run departures from the long-run growth path of income (or trend); upswings (expansions) are just the opposite. Points of turnaround from recession to expansion are called troughs, and points of turnaround from expansion to recession are called peaks. Figure 10.1.2 shows the short-run phases of the business cycle around trend or the long-run growth path.

FIGURE 10.1.2

Phases of the Business Cycle

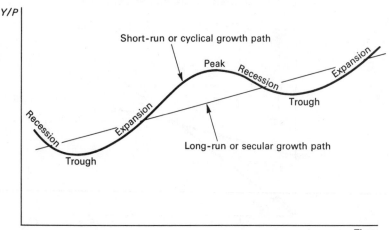

The possible explanation for upward shifts in the short-run consumption function, which potentially reconcile apparent contradictions in the periods covering Kuznets' data, include the following: (1) Medical advances have decreased infant mortality and increased life expectancy and thereby decreased the proportion of the relatively low-consuming working age adults. (2) The rural-urban migration has reduced the number of families in the low-consuming rural sector and increased the number in the high-consuming urban sector. (3) Growth of social benefit programs may have reduced the incentive to set aside funds for retirement. (4) The minimum standard of living rose as additional goods which were luxuries became necessities. (5) A more equal distribution of income reduced the proportion of income going to the relatively low-consuming wealthy classes. (6) Increases in the availability of credit permits increases in consumption in excess of disposable income. (7) Increases in both financial and real wealth have reduced the propensity to save. These are some of the more important factors which help to explain consumption. Various concepts of income as a surrogate for changes in wealth have received special attention.

10.2 THE RELATIVE INCOME HYPOTHESIS

Professor J. S. Duesenberry developed a theory of consumption based on two relative income hypotheses. His first hypothesis recognized that consumers are concerned with their consumption relative to the consumption of others; i.e., they attempt to keep up with the "Joneses." This phenomenon means that the average propensity to consume depends on the consumer's position in the income distribution. If a consumer earns above average income, he will consume a smaller proportion of his income. If the consumer earns below average income, he will consume a larger proportion of his income. Thus, the average propensity to consume falls as income increases. As an individual's relative income position increases, his consumption will increase less than proportionally, and the marginal is less than the average propensity to consume, MPC < APC. However, as income increases, if the distribution of income does not change, there is no reason to expect changes in the average propensity to consume because the relative income position does not change; i.e., the long-run marginal propensity to consume is constant, and MPC = APC. As income increases, people will increase consumption in proportion to income in order to maintain their consumption relative to others.

Thus, the first relative income hypothesis provides an explanation which reconciles cross-sectional data where MPC < APC with long-run times series data where the average propensity to consume is constant so that MPC = APC.

The second hypothesis is that consumers are concerned with their consumption relative to levels of consumption attained in previous periods. Once a consumer attains a level of consumption, decreases in consumption

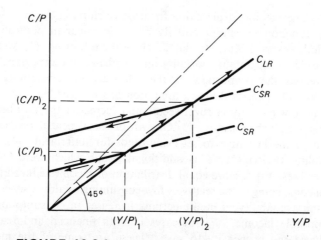

FIGURE 10.2.1

Consumption and Relative Income

are more difficult than decreases in saving. Thus, consumption depends on the current level of income relative to its previous peak.

Suppose that income falls in the short-run during an economic recession. Consumers will reduce consumption by as little as possible and sharply reduce saving; as income falls the average propensity to consume rises. When recovery begins, consumption and saving again increase as income rises to its former peak; as income rises the average propensity to consume falls. In the short-run past peak income exceeds current income and the marginal is less than the average propensity to consume, MPC < APC; there is a nonproportional relationship between consumption and income.

Once current income again reaches the past peak level, further increases in income mean that consumers may increase consumption beyond its past peak level. In the long-run past peak income equals current income and the marginal and average propensities to consume are equal, MPC = APC; there is a proportional relationship between consumption and income.

Thus, the second relative income hypothesis reconciles short- and long-run time series data over the business cycle so that in the short-run MPC < APC and in the long-run MPC = APC. Figure 10.2.1 shows the short- and long-run consumption functions in real terms. As real income increases along the long-run consumption function, C_{LR}, to $(Y/P)_1$, real consumption increases proportionally to $(C/P)_1$. If real income should then decrease in a period of recession, people will reduce real consumption by as little as possible along the short-run consumption function, C_{SR}, and cut real saving sharply. In recovery, as real income increases back to the past peak, $(Y/P)_1$, real consumption increases nonproportionally back to $(C/P)_1$ along C_{SR}. Once the past peak levels of real consumption, real saving, and real income are attained, increases in real income to $(Y/P)_2$ will again increase real consumption proportionally to $(C/P)_2$ along C_{LR} as long as the distribution of real income does not change and people maintain their relative real consumption levels. If real income again decreases in a recession period from $(Y/P)_2$, then real consumption decreases nonproportionally along C'_{SR} in the short-run. In recovery real consumption increases back along C'_{SR} until $(C/P)_2$ is attained. After recovery, further increases in real income above $(Y/P)_2$ means that real consumption again increases proportionally along C_{LR}. Thus, the combination of short- and long-run behavior implies a *ratchet effect* where real consumption falls and rises in the short-run away from past peak levels in the downswing of the business cycle. In the recovery phase of the upswing, real consumption and real income increase back to their past peak levels. The long-run past peak levels indicate a proportional relationship between real consumption and real income.

10.3 THE PERMANENT INCOME HYPOTHESIS

Duesenberry's hypotheses improve our understanding of the consumption-income relationship. But in terms of present acceptance among economists, theories which include concepts of wealth have been more successful. Shortly after publication of Duesenberry's work, Professor J. Tobin suggested a modification of the consumption function to include the amount of wealth possessed by households. Tobin argued that the growth in household wealth has caused upward shifts in the short-run nonproportional consumption function along the long-run proportional relationship between consumption and income. Figure 10.3.1 illustrates Tobin's contention in real terms. Increases in real household wealth from $(\overline{A/P})$ to $(\overline{\overline{A/P}})$ to $(\overline{\overline{\overline{A/P}}})$ shift the

FIGURE 10.3.1

Tobin's Wealth Hypothesis

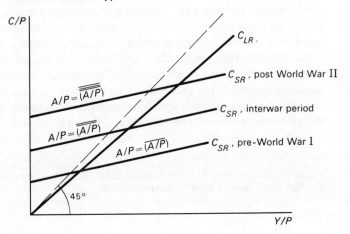

short-run consumption function upward. Thus, there is a secular increase in real consumption as real income increases such that the average propensity to consume is constant along C_{LR}, even though in the short-run the average propensity to consume falls with real income along the short-run consumption functions, C_{SR}. Although Tobin's conclusions were not intuitively clear, they refocused attention on the importance of wealth in determining the levels of consumption and saving.

The first such effort was made by Professor M. Friedman who hypothesized that consumption is based on future expected income rather than the current measure of income. In some months income is lower than expected, while in other months it is higher. Instead of basing consumption on erratic changes in measured income, consumers base it on the present value of expected income or *permanent income* (a surrogate for wealth). Thus, the long-run average propensity to consume is constant so that there is a proportional relationship between consumption and permanent income so that MPC = APC. In the short-run the difference between measured and permanent income due to unexpected changes in measured income is called *transitory income*. When transitory income is either positive or negative, it temporarily creates an apparent nonproportional relationship between consumption and measured income so that MPC < APC. In the long-run both positive and negative instances of transitory income tend to cancel each other out so that average transitory income is zero.

Permanent income is defined as the flow of expected income from the stock of human wealth (labor services), and from nonhuman wealth (bonds, stocks, real estate, money, and durable goods).[1] Since most wealth estimates are considered unreliable, Friedman calculated the present value of expected future income based on income from both human and nonhuman wealth (see Chapter 4 for an explanation of present value).

Measured income includes both permanent and transitory (measured derivations from permanent income) components. Similarly, measured consumption includes permanent and transitory (deviations from permanent consumption) components. Friedman's basic hypothesis is that the average propensity to consume from permanent income is constant. However, because of the transitory component of measured income, MPC < APC, as indicated by budget studies data. A below average income class has measured income below the population's average with negative average transitory income; measured income is less than permanent income. An above average income class has measured income above the population's average; measured income is greater than permanent income. If we assume that transitory consumption,

---

[1] Remember that consumer durables are not consumed monetarily and as such cannot be treated as consumption. It is the imputed value of the flow of services from consumer durables that Friedman included in consumption.

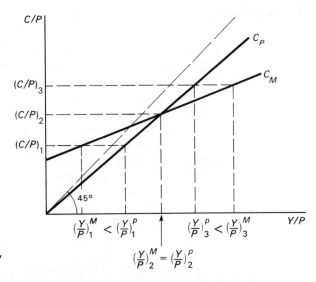

$(C/P)_3$

$(C/P)_2$

$(C/P)_1$

$45°$

$\left(\dfrac{Y}{P}\right)_1^M < \left(\dfrac{Y}{P}\right)_1^P$ $\left(\dfrac{Y}{P}\right)_3^P < \left(\dfrac{Y}{P}\right)_3^M$ Y/P

$\left(\dfrac{Y}{P}\right)_2^M = \left(\dfrac{Y}{P}\right)_2^P$

FIGURE 10.3.2

Consumption, Permanent Income,
and Measured Income

permanent consumption, and transitory income are not related,[2] all groups have zero average transitory consumption such that consumption is proportionally related to permanent income so that MPC = APC. A below average income class has average measured consumption equal to permanent consumption but average measured income less than permanent income such that the measured average propensity to consume is greater than its permanent income counterpart. Similarly, the above average income group has a measured average propensity to consume which is less than its permanent income counterpart. Thus, both negative and positive transitory deviations of measured income from the national average explain the cross-section result that the measured consumption-income relationship exhibits MPC < APC, while the permanent consumption-income relationship exhibits MPC = APC.

Figure 10.3.2 illustrates the permanent income hypothesis in real terms. Points on the consumption function, C_M, show values of real consumption which correspond to measured real income, $(Y/P)^M$, and points on the con-

---

[2] Friedman assumes that there is no correlation between permanent and transitory components of income so that their covariance across individuals is zero. Thus, in cross-section budget studies (1) the income class that centers on the population's average income will have a zero average transitory component of income, (2) the income class above the population's average will have a positive transitory component of income, and (3) the income class below the population's average will have a negative transitory component of income. Moreover, Friedman assumes that there is zero correlation between transitory and permanent consumption such that their covariance is zero. And, finally, there is zero correlation between transitory income and consumption such that their covariance is zero. That is, changes in transitory income have no immediate effect on transitory consumption. The latter assumption is not readily apparent. However, consumption includes nondurable goods and services as well as *use of durable goods*; it excludes *purchases of durable goods*. Transitory income is either saved (dissaved) or used to purchase durable goods. Hence, transitory income has no effect on consumption.

sumption function, C_P, show values of real consumption which correspond to permanent real income, $(Y/P)^P$. The horizontal difference between the two consumption functions for any given level of real consumption is the transitory component of real income. The measured real income of consumers in an average income class equals their permanent real income, $(Y/P)_2^M = (Y/P)_2^P$, and transitory real income is zero when real consumption is $(C/P)_2$. The measured real income of consumers in an above average income class exceeds their average or permanent level, $(Y/P)_3^M > (Y/P)_3^P$, and transitory real income is positive when real consumption is $(C/P)_3$. The measured real income of a consumer in a below average income class is below the average or permanent level, $(Y/P)_1^M < (Y/P)_1^P$, and transitory real income is negative when real consumption is $(C/P)_1$.

As the economy's permanent real income grows along trend C_P, the cross-section consumption function shifts upward, where we observe a constant average propensity to consume in the long-run. In downturns of the business cycles, average transitory real income is negative and the average propensity to consume in the short-run is greater than in the long-run. In a boom year when transitory real income is positive the average propensity to consume in the short-run is less than in the long-run.

Thus, Friedman's hypothesis reconciles cross section budget studies *at any one time* and short-run time series data where MPC < APC with long-run time series data where MPC = APC.

10.4 THE LIFE CYCLE HYPOTHESIS

Professors A. Ando and F. Modigliani hypothesize that an individual's income is relatively low at the beginning of his life, while income is relatively high in his middle years and again relatively low at the end of his life. This generally occurs because of life cycle changes in productivity. Although income varies over the life cycle, consumption remains more-or-less constant.[3] This is called the life cycle hypothesis of consumer behavior. It is an important improvement in the permanent income hypothesis because it explains transitory deviations of measured income from permanent income. Above average income classes have a higher than average proportion of consumers with high incomes because they are in the middle age group; their APC is relatively low. Below average income classes have a higher than average proportion of consumers with low incomes because they are in the lower and higher age groups; their APC is relatively high.

---

[3] If we assume that the present value of his total consumption may not exceed the present value of income, an individual will be a net borrower in his early years, save to repay debts and provide for retirement in his middle years, and dissave in his later years. For this equality to hold we would have to assume that inheritances are passed on in equal amounts when each individual dies.

Thus, the life cycle hypothesis provides an explanation of cross-section budget studies such that MPC < APC. Moreover, given the assumption that there is no reason to favor consumption in any one period over any other, as the present value of consumer income increases in the long run, consumption increases proportionally such that MPC = APC.

Since World War II the age and income distribution in the United States has changed gradually so that Ando and Modigliani's aggregation of individual consumption functions is reasonable. That is, if the age and income distribution of a population and tastes are constant, we can derive a stable aggregate consumption function by summing all individual's consumption for given levels of income.

Another important improvement of the permanent income hypothesis is Ando and Modigliani's separation of permanent income into two parts, the present expected value of income from labor (human wealth) and the present value of expected income from property (nonhuman wealth). They assumed that expected real income from labor was proportional to the present value of labor real income, $(Y/P)_L$,[4] and that if capital markets are efficient, the present value of the real income from property or assets is equal to the real value of the asset, A/P.

Thus, real consumption depends not only on real income of labor, but on the stock of real assets,

$$\frac{C}{P} = q_1 \left(\frac{Y}{P}\right)_L + q_2 \frac{A}{P} \qquad (10.4.1)$$

where the marginal propensity to consume out of the real income of labor is $\partial(C/P)/\partial(Y/P)_L = q_1$ and the marginal propensity to consume out of real assets is $\partial(C/P)/\partial(A/P) = q_2$.

Figure 10.4.1 illustrates the Ando-Modigliani consumption function in real terms under both long- and short-run conditions. Given the real value of assets, $(\overline{A/P})$, the intercept of the short-run consumption function is $q_2(\overline{A/P})$. The slope of the function is the marginal propensity to consume out of real labor income, q_1. In the short run the value of real assets remain fixed and real consumption varies nonproportionally with real labor income along C_{SR} over the cycle such that MPC < APC. In the long run real saving creates additional real assets. When the real value of assets increases to $(\overline{\overline{A/P}})$ the consumption function shifts upward to C'_{SR}. In the long run we observe a set of points which indicates that real income and real consumption

---

[4] Estimates of permanent income have been criticized on the grounds that it is not necessarily true that all households have the same permanent income and that those with high incomes do not cancel out households with low income. To get a homogeneous group of households, Ando and Modigliani used the income data of non-self-employed households. They considered other groupings as well but found that this grouping yields the best results.

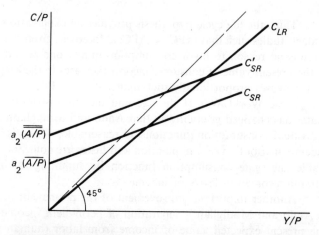

FIGURE 10.4.1

Consumption and Wealth

are proportional along C_{LR}; that is, the average propensity to consume is constant so that MPC = APC.

A numerical example will help to illustrate long-run consumer behavior à la Ando-Modigliani. By dividing (10.4.1) through by real income, we get

$$\frac{C/P}{Y/P} = q_1 \frac{(Y/P)_L}{Y/P} + q_2 \frac{A/P}{Y/P} \tag{10.4.2}$$

$$\frac{C}{Y} = q_1 \frac{Y_L}{Y} + q_2 \frac{A}{Y} \tag{10.4.3}$$

an expression for the average propensity to consume, C/Y. The average propensity to consume is constant if labor's share of income, Y_L/Y, and the average propensity to accumulate wealth out of income, A/Y, are constant. U.S. data confirm that labor's share is roughly constant at about .76 and that the asset-income ratio is roughly constant at about 2.8. Estimates of q_1 and q_2 are approximately .7 and .06, respectively. Substituting these values in (10.4.3) yields

$$\frac{C}{Y} = (.7)(.76) + .06(2.8) = .532 + .168 = .7$$

Thus, in the long-run the average propensity to consume is constant at .7 along C_{LR}, as shown by the straight line through the origin in Fig. 10.4.1. This means that MPC = APC in the long-run.

In the short-run where the value of assets is fairly constant consumption varies over the cycle with changes in labor's share of income. Equation

(10.4.3) indicates that $\partial(C/Y)/\partial(Y_L/Y) = q_1 > 0$. This means that MPC < APC in the short-run.

Thus, the Ando-Modigliani model explains the three observed consumption-income phenomena: (1) the cross-sectional budget studies result that MPC < APC, (2) the short-run time series result that APC falls as income increases, and (3) the long-run constancy of APC such that MPC = APC.

The relative, permanent, and life cycle income hypotheses imply that government expenditures are not essential for continued growth as was feared by the stagnationists in the 1940s. The theories of Ando-Modigliani and Friedman are widely accepted explanations which reconcile cross-section budget studies and time series data. Both theories tie consumption to expected income rather than erratic changes in current income. The Ando-Modigliani theory has the relative strength in its explicit inclusion of both assets and current income in explaining consumption.

10.5 CHANGES IN REAL WEALTH

People save in real terms that part of their real disposable income which is not consumed as a means of accumulating real wealth. Real saving depends on their preferences for real assets relative to real consumption and subject to their real disposable income constraint. Just as changes in real wealth positively affect real consumption for any given level of real disposable income (shifts the consumption function upward), changes in real wealth negatively affect real saving for any given level of real disposable income (shifts the saving function downward). For example, an increase in real wealth increases real consumption and decreases real saving for any given level of real disposable income.

The inclusion of real wealth in our analysis means that the short-run consumption function, Eq. (4.1.4), in real terms,

$$\frac{C}{P} = a_0 + a_1 \frac{DY}{P} \tag{10.5.1}$$

must be respecified to include a real wealth variable. If we assume that $a_0 = a_2(A/P)$, Eq. (10.5.1) then becomes

$$\frac{C}{P} = a_2 \frac{A}{P} + a_1 \frac{DY}{P} \tag{10.5.2}$$

The corresponding short-run saving function is

$$\frac{S}{P} = -a_2 \frac{A}{P} + (1 - a_1) \frac{DY}{P} \tag{10.5.3}$$

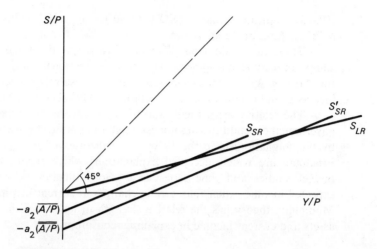

FIGURE 10.5.1

Saving and Wealth

Figure 10.5.1 shows the short-run saving function S_{SR} where the initial level of real wealth is $\overline{A/P}$. An increase in real wealth to $\overline{\overline{A/P}}$ means that people will consume more and save less in real terms for any given level of real income so that the saving function shifts rightward to S'_{SR}. Points along S_{LR} identify long-run real saving-disposable income behavior. Note that in the short-run just as MPC < APC, MPS > APS. And in the long-run just as MPC = APC, MPS = APS.

The foregoing analysis means that the saving plus net taxes function of our model can be rewritten in real terms as

$$\frac{S + T}{P} = -a_2 \frac{A}{P} + a_1 t_0 + (1 - a_1 + a_1 t_1) \frac{Y}{P} \qquad (10.5.4)$$

This function is shown in Fig. 10.5.2 by $(S + T)_{SR}$. When real wealth increases from $\overline{A/P}$ to $\overline{\overline{A/P}}$, just as the short-run saving function shifts rightward along S_{LR} in Fig. 10.5.1, the short-run saving plus net taxes function shifts rightward along the long-run saving plus net taxes relationship, $(S + T)_{LR}$.

The difference between the short- and long-run saving plus net taxes curves means that there is a difference between the short- and long-run IS schedules. In Fig. 10.5.3, the IS_{SR} schedule is derived from the income-expenditures side of our model using the short-run saving plus net taxes function, $(S + T)_{SR}$. The IS_{LR} schedule is the long-run IS schedule as changes in real wealth shift the short-run $S + T$ curve and the short-run IS schedule. For example, an increase in real wealth from $\overline{A/P}$ to $\overline{\overline{A/P}}$ shifts the $S + T$ curve to $(S + T)'_{SR}$ and thereby the IS schedule to IS'_{SR} along IS_{LR}.

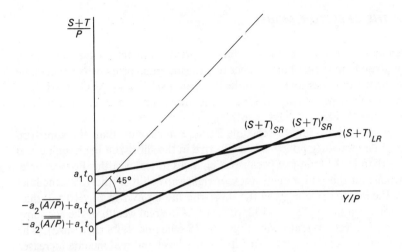

FIGURE 10.5.2

Saving, Net Taxes, and Wealth

FIGURE 10.5.3

IS Schedule and Wealth

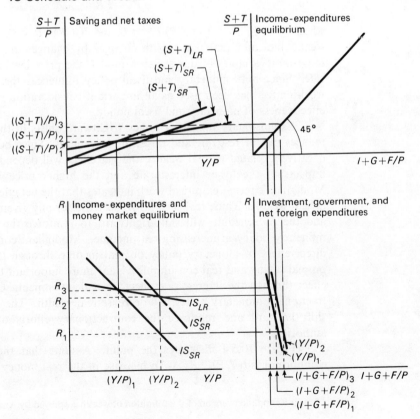

Thus, changes in the interest rate have a greater impact on real income in the long-run than in the short-run because the marginal propensity to consume in the short-run is less than it is in the long-run ($MPC_{LR} = APC > MPC_{SR}$), or the marginal propensity to save in the short-run is greater than it is in the long-run ($MPS_{LR} = APS < MPS_{SR}$).

Since the long-run *IS* schedule is more horizontal than the short-run *IS* schedule monetary policy is less effective in the short-run in changing real income than in the long-run because of changes in real wealth. For example, an increase in the real money stock (a rightward shift in the *LM* schedule) lowers the interest rate more in the short-run (along IS_{SR} in Fig. 10.5.3) than in the long-run (along IS_{LR} in Fig. 10.5.3). As the real wealth of the economy increases, the level of real saving falls (the *IS* schedule shifts rightward). The interest rate increases back toward its former level and real income increases more in the long-run than in the short-run.

If we assume that the rate of interest, R, is a rough estimate of the rate of return on the flow of real asset income, Z/P, to real wealth, A/P (in perpetuity), then real wealth can be approximated by

$$\frac{A}{P} = \frac{Z}{PR} \qquad (10.5.5)[5]$$

where $\partial(A/P)/\partial Z > 0$, $\partial(A/P)/\partial P < 0$, and $\partial(A/P)/\partial R < 0$. This measure of wealth indicates that real wealth changes by changes in two of the most important variables in our skeleton model, the price level and the interest rate. Since both monetary and fiscal policy influences these variables, the wealth effect has been used as an important consideration in evaluating the effectiveness of monetary and fiscal policy.

Expansionary monetary policy (rightward shifts in the *LM* schedule) reduces the interest rate and raises the price level. Since both variables are negatively related to real wealth, the net effect will depend on the relative impacts of the lower interest rate and the higher price level. Professor Modigliani's recent empirical work indicates that the net effect is an increase in real wealth. Thus, real saving will decrease for any given level of income and the *IS* schedule will shift rightward to reinforce the effectiveness of monetary policy in increasing real income. Modigliani concluded that the direct effect of monetary policy on real income through the wealth effect on real saving and real consumption is far more important than the indirect effect through the interest rate effect on real investment. Conversely, contractionary monetary policy will decrease real wealth. The *IS* schedule will shift leftward and reinforce the contractionary efforts of the monetary authority.

Figure 10.5.4 illustrates the point. Assume that the initial *IS-LM* equilibrium is $((Y/P)_1, R_3)$. An increase in the real money stock shifts the

---

[5] This is a simplified version of the definition of wealth employed by Ando and Modigliani.

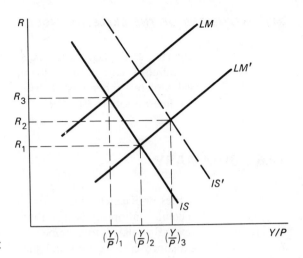

FIGURE 10.5.4

Monetary Policy and the Wealth Effect

LM schedule to *LM'*. As a result the interest rate falls toward R_1 and real income increases toward $(Y/P)_2$ along *IS*. If the net effect of the interest rate decrease and the price level increase is an increase in real wealth, then the level of real saving falls and the *IS* schedule shifts the *IS'* such that final equilibrium values of the interest rate and real income are $((Y/P)_3, R_2)$. Thus, the wealth effect reinforces monetary policy and links monetary policy to output demand through changes in the interest rate and price level.

Expansionary fiscal policy increases the interest rate and level of real income, and under the conditions stated above reduces the value of wealth. For example, an increase in government spending shifts the *IS* schedule rightward. The resulting price level increase will shift the *IS* and *LM* schedules leftward and thereby partially offset the effects of fiscal policy. In Fig. 10.5.5 an increase in government expenditures shifts the *IS* schedule from *IS* to *IS'*, the resulting increase in the price level shifts the *LM* schedule leftward to *LM'*, and the wealth effect (through price and interest rate

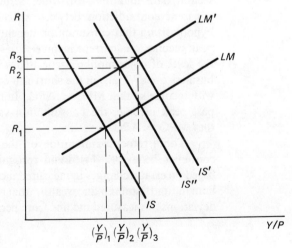

FIGURE 10.5.5

Fiscal Policy and the Wealth Effect

239

changes) shifts the *IS* schedule leftward to *IS"*. Thus, the wealth effect tends to offset at least partially the effect of fiscal policy. The final equilibrium value of real income is $(Y/P)_2 < (Y/P)_3$ and the final equilibrium value of the interest rate is $R_2 < R_3$.

10.6 SUMMARY

Professor Kuznets' study cast doubt on the view that "the" consumption-income relationship is such that the average propensity to consume, APC, is inversely related to income. His analysis of the data indicated that this explained cross-section and short-run time series data but that in the long-run the average propensity to consume is roughly constant. Reconciliation of this apparent contradiction is important because if the APC falls with increases in income so that MPC < APC, government expenditures must continually increase if full employment is to be maintained and the economy is to continue to grow. If MPC = APC, economic growth via consumption (and investment) expenditures could continue to promote full employment and economic growth.

In response to this problem, Professors Duesenberry, Tobin, Friedman, Ando, and Modigliani have made major contributions to our understanding of the consumption-income relationship. In each of their models they hypothesized that the long-run relationship is proportional, i.e., APC is constant so that the MPC = APC, and explained why the short-run consumption-income relationship is nonproportional; i.e., the APC falls with increases in income so that MPC < APC.

Duesenberry emphasized the importance of a consumer's income relative to others in reconciling the apparent contradiction between cross-section data and long-run times series data. Further, he reconciled the apparent contradiction between short- and long-run time series data by hypothesizing that consumption depends on current income relative to past peak income. As current income varies consumers will attempt to maintain the level of consumption associated with their past peak income over the business cycle. Thus, in the short-run consumption varies nonproportionally with income so that MPC < APC. In the long-run as income increases with past peak income, the consumption varies proportionally with income so that MPC = APC.

Tobin refocused attention on the importance of wealth in explaining consumer behavior. Friedman recognized that consumer behavior is not based on erratic changes in measured income but on the expected flow of both human and nonhuman wealth, that is, permanent income. Transitory deviations of measured income from permanent income explain the short-run nonproportional relationship between consumption and measured income, so that MPC < APC. In the long-run transitory income averages out to zero and consumption is proportional to permanent income, so that MPC = APC.

Ando and Modigliani provide the life cycle hypothesis as a theoretical explanation of transitory deviations of measured income from permanent income. Transitory income for the young and the old is negative because measured income is relatively low. Transitory income for the middle-age group is positive because the measured income is relatively low. Although the life cycle hypothesis is an important contribution to our understanding of consumer behavior, Ando and Modigliani's empirical work is their most impressive contribution. They separated permanent income into two components, expected income from human and nonhuman wealth. They hypothesize that given nonhuman wealth in the short-run, APC falls with real human income. In the long-run nonhuman wealth increases so that the short-run nonproportional consumption function shifts upward along the long-run (or trend) consumption-income relationship. The data lend support to the hypothesis.

The difference between short- and long-run consumer behavior implies a difference between short- and long-run saving behavior. The average propensity to save is positively related to changes in real income in the short-run so that MPS > APS and roughly constant in the long-run so that MPS = APS. As real wealth increases, the short-run saving function falls along the long-run saving-income relationship.

Likewise, as real wealth increases the short-run saving plus net taxes function will fall along the long-run saving-net taxes-income relationship, and the short-run *IS* schedule will shift rightward along the long-run *IS* schedule. This means that the long-run *IS* schedule is more horizontal than its short-run counterpart. Thus, monetary policy (shifts in the *LM* schedule) is more effective in changing real income in the long-run than in the short-run.

In the remainder of the chapter we considered in more detail the ways in which changes in real wealth induce a wealth effect on the economy. The wealth effect is simply a reaction to changes in real wealth by increases in real saving as a means of maintaining real wealth. For example, when real wealth falls because nominal wealth increases less than the price level and/or the rate of interest, people will increase real saving in an effort to maintain their real wealth position. The wealth effect links monetary policy to consumer demand through changes in the price level and the interest rate where monetary policy affects interest rates and the price level less in the long-run than in the short-run. The wealth effect links fiscal policy to consumer demand through the price level and the interest rate but tends to reduce the immediate impact of fiscal policy as people attempt to maintain their real wealth position.

REVIEW QUESTIONS

1. Based on the analyses in this chapter explain consumption and saving behavior over the business cycle by reference to changes in the APC and APS when the MPS and MPC are constant.

2. Why does an increase in real wealth due to expansionary monetary policy have a greater impact on output demand in the short-run than in the long-run?

3. Why does the wealth effect dampen the impact of expansionary fiscal policy on output demand?

SELECTED READINGS

ANDO, A., and F. MODIGLIANI, "The Life Cycle Hypothesis of Saving: Aggregate Implications and Tests," *American Economic Review*, 53 (March 1963), 55–84.

————, "Econometric Analysis of Stabilization Policies," *American Economic Review*, 59 (May 1969), 296–314.

DUESENBERRY, J. S., *Income, Saving, and the Theory of Consumer Behavior*, Cambridge, Mass.: Harvard University Press, 1952.

FRIEDMAN, M., *A Theory of the Consumption Function*, Princeton, N.J.: Princeton University Press, 1957.

GURLEY, J. G., and E. S. SHAW, *Money in a Theory of Finance*, Washington, D.C.: The Brookings Institution, 1960.

JOHNSON, H. G., *Macroeconomics and Monetary Theory*, London: Gray Mills Publishing Ltd., 1971, pp. 116–17.

JOHNSON, M. B., *Household Behavior: Consumption, Income, and Wealth*, Baltimore: Penguin, 1970.

KALECKI, M., "Professor Pigou on the 'Classical Stationary State': A Comment," *Economic Journal*, 54 (April 1944), 131–32.

KEYNES, J. M., *The General Theory of Employment, Interest, and Money*, New York: Macmillan, 1936.

KUZNETS, S., *National Product since 1869*, New York: National Bureau of Economic Research, 1946.

MODIGLIANI, F., "Monetary Policy and Consumption: Linkages via Interest Rate and Wealth Effects in the FMP Model," *Consumer Spending and Monetary Policy: The Linkages*, Boston: Federal Reserve Bank of Boston, 1971.

————, and R. BRUMBERG, "Utility Analysis and the Consumption Function: An Interpretation of Cross-section Data," in K. K. Kurihara (ed.), *Post-Keynesian Economics*, New Brunswick, N.J.: Rutgers University Press, 1954, pp. 388–436.

METZLER, L. A., "Wealth, Saving and the Rate of Interest," *Journal of Political Economy,* 59 (April 1951), 93–116.

PATINKIN, D., *Money, Interest, and Prices,* 2nd ed., New York: Harper & Row, 1965.

———, "Money and Wealth," *Journal of Economic Literature,* 7 (Dec. 1969), 1140–60.

PESEK, B. P., and T. R. SAVING, *Money, Wealth, and Economic Theory,* New York: Macmillan, 1967.

PIGOU, A. C., "The Classical Stationary State," *Economic Journal,* 53 (Dec. 1943), 343–51.

SUITS, D., "The Determinants of Consumer Expenditure: A Review of the Present Knowledge," in *Impacts of Monetary Policy,* Commission on Money and Credit, Englewood Cliffs, N.J.: Prentice-Hall, 1963, pp. 1–57.

TOBIN, J., "Relative Income, Absolute Income, and Savings," in *Money, Trade, and Economic Growth,* New York: Macmillan, 1951, pp. 135–56.

CHAPTER 11

Capital Theory and Economic Growth

11.1 THE MARGINAL PRODUCTIVITY APPROACH TO CAPITAL THEORY

The economy's capital stock is not used up in a time period. It yields a flow of services per time period which is used in the production process. In the development of the skeleton model we implicitly assumed that there is a proportional relationship between the capital stock and the flow of capital services. Thus, a theory which determines the capital stock uniquely determines the flow of capital services. Our simplifying assumption means, for example, that if the capital stock doubles, the flow of capital services will double.

Competitive firms maximize profit by hiring inputs used in the production process where their marginal products equal their respective real user cost. Just as labor is hired where the marginal product of labor, MPL, equals labor's real user cost (the real wage rate, W/P),

$$\text{MPL} = \frac{W}{P} \tag{11.1.1}$$

capital is used where the marginal product of capital, MPK, equals capital's real user cost, UC/P,

$$\text{MPK} = \frac{UC}{P} \tag{11.1.2}[1]$$

---

[1] Moreover, traditional microtheory shows that firms will use that combination of input factors which minimizes cost. The cost minimizing rule states that firms equate the marginal product to factor price ratios of all input factors. If, for example, capital's marginal product

The marginal product of capital is derived from the production function. The real user cost of capital is the real opportunity cost of capital, i.e., the implicit real rental price of capital which users (firms) pay if they rent a unit of capital or the price capital owners charge when they rent a unit of capital to someone else. Since user cost data are not readily available, their value must be estimated. Estimates of net nominal user cost include both interest and depreciation costs. The interest rate is the opportunity cost of tying up funds (the market rate of interest, R) times the price of investment goods, P^I. Depreciation costs can also be expressed as a percent of the price of investment goods. However, we shall exclude depreciation costs in our analysis because gross estimates of user cost are generally used in capital theory. Thus, gross real user cost can be measured,

$$\frac{UC}{P} = \frac{P^I}{P} R \qquad\qquad (11.1.3)^2$$

where $\partial(UC/P)/\partial R > 0$, $\partial(UC/P)/\partial P < 0$, and $\partial(UC/P)/\partial P^I > 0$.

When the capital market is not in equilibrium, such that $\partial(Y/P)/\partial K > UC/P$, firms will increase net investment. As long as capital's productivity at the margin is greater than capital's real user cost at the margin, the desired capital stock is greater than the actual capital stock, and net investment will take place until they are equal. Net disinvestment will occur when $\partial(Y/P)/\partial K < UC/P$ because capital's real user cost at the margin is greater than capital's productivity at the margin. That is, the desired capital stock is less than the actual capital stock; net disinvestment will occur until they are equal. When the capital market is in equilibrium net investment is zero and the capital stock is said to be optimal.

Given the production function in our skeleton model,

$$\frac{Y}{P} = L_d^\alpha K^\beta \text{TEC}^\gamma, \qquad 0 < \alpha, \beta, \gamma < 1 \qquad\qquad (11.1.4)$$

the derived demand for capital or the marginal product of capital is

$$\frac{\partial(Y/P)}{\partial K} = \text{MPK} = \beta L_d^\alpha K^{\beta-1}\text{TEC}^\gamma \qquad\qquad (11.1.5)$$

---

per dollar spent on capital exceeds that of labor, it would be profitable to use more capital and less labor. As more capital is used the marginal product of labor rises until the marginal product per dollar spent on both input factors equal.

[2] Any change in the market price of a unit of capital once purchased causes either a capital loss or gain. Consequently, price changes should be included in the measure of user costs, particularly in times of chronic inflation. In this way the nominal interest rate less the rate of change in the price, that is, the real rate of interest, would be included in our measure of user cost. However, for the present we shall assume that firms ignore this factor.

Given labor and technical progress, increases in capital increase output but at a decreasing rate because

$$\frac{\partial \text{MPK}}{\partial K} = (\beta - 1)\beta L_d^{\alpha} K^{\beta - 2} \text{TEC}^{\gamma} < 0 \qquad (11.1.6)$$

Since $0 < \beta < 1$ this means that as the production process becomes more capital intensive there are diminishing returns to capital.

Figure 11.1.1 shows the aggregate capital demand curve (11.1.2) for given values of labor, $\bar{L}_d$, and technical progress, $\overline{\text{TEC}}$. The marginal product of capital is on the vertical axis along with the real user cost; quantities demanded of capital are on the horizontal axis. The curve is downward sloping because of diminishing returns. If the real user cost is $(UC/P)_2$, the desired capital stock is K_1. If the real user cost falls to $(UC/P)_1$, the desired capital stock increases to K_2. Net investment will take place until the actual and desired levels become equal, i.e., the capital stock is optimal.

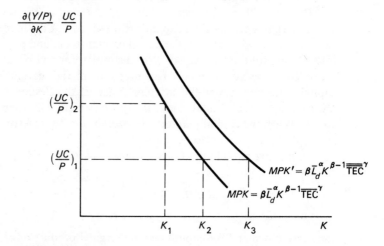

FIGURE 11.1.1

Capital Market

Changes in technical progress and labor positively affect the marginal product of capital for any given unit of capital input as indicated by differentiating (11.1.5) with respect to labor,

$$\frac{\partial \text{MPK}}{\partial L_d} = \alpha\beta L_d^{\alpha - 1} K^{\beta - 1} \text{TEC}^{\gamma} > 0 \qquad (11.1.7)$$

and with respect to technical progress,

$$\frac{\partial \text{MPK}}{\partial \text{TEC}} = \gamma \beta L_d^\alpha K^{\beta-1} \text{TEC}^{\gamma-1} > 0 \qquad (11.1.8)$$

For example, Fig. 11.1.1 shows that an increase in technical progress from $\overline{\text{TEC}}$ to $\overline{\overline{\text{TEC}}}$ raises the marginal product of capital, i.e., the capital demand curve shifts upward. This means that if the real user cost is $(UC/P)_1$, the desired capital stock will increase from K_2 to K_3. Net investment will take place until the capital stock is optimal.

We can think in terms of a comparison which firms make between the productivity of capital (in real dollars) and the user cost of capital (in real dollars) as shown by (11.1.2), or, alternatively, we can translate this comparison into one between the yield on capital and the yield on the next best alternative earning asset, namely the market rate of interest.

Substituting (11.1.3) into (11.1.2) and solving for the interest rate give

$$R = \frac{P \cdot \partial(Y/P)/\partial K}{P^I} \qquad (11.1.9)$$

an expression of the capital market equilibrium condition which states that the capital stock is optimal when the interest rate equals the yield on capital, i.e., the value of capital's marginal product relative to the price of investment goods.

Substituting (11.1.5) into (11.1.9) gives

$$R = \frac{P \cdot \beta L_d^\alpha K^{\beta-1} \text{TEC}^\gamma}{P^I} \qquad (11.1.10)$$

an alternative expression of the capital market equilibrium condition implied by our skeleton model.

But, wait just a minute! There is an ambiguity in the concept of the optimum capital stock, since one of its determinants is the price of investment goods (a marginal unit of capital), P^I. Although the price of investment goods can be taken as given by the firm, in the aggregate the price of investment goods varies with the decisions of all firms. To remove the ambiguity, suppose that the price of investment goods is the price level P_0^I which would prevail if gross investment included only replacement through depreciation, i.e., the price which would prevail if capital stock were optimal and net investment were zero. Equation (11.1.10) can then be rewritten as

$$R = \frac{P(\beta L_d^\alpha K^\beta \text{TEC}^\gamma)}{P_0^I K} \qquad (11.1.11)$$

or, since $Y/P = L_d^\alpha K^\beta \text{TEC}^\gamma$,

$$R = \frac{\beta Y}{P_0^I K} \qquad (11.1.12)$$

or, by solving (11.1.12) for K,

$$K = \frac{\beta Y}{R P_0^I} \qquad (11.1.13)$$

we derive an expression for the optimum capital stock in terms of income, the interest rate, and the two parameters P_0^I and β.

11.2 THE MARGINAL EFFICIENCY APPROACH TO CAPITAL THEORY

Generally, when firms purchase additional capital, they do not realize the total return on the outlay in the period of purchase. As the flow of services from a capital asset is used up over its productive life, a firm receives a corresponding flow of return. Thus, the decision to purchase additional capital requires that a firm estimate the expected future return for each period of the additional capital's productive life. Estimates of the expected return per time period consist of the sum of the expected market values of the additional output that is to be produced by the additional capital and the additional noncapital inputs (primarily labor) less the expected additional noncapital costs (excluding interest and depreciation costs),

$$E_i^e = (P \cdot \text{MPK})_i^e + (P \cdot \text{MPO})_i^e - \text{MCO}_i^e, \qquad i=1,\ldots,n \qquad (11.2.1)$$

where E is the net return, P is the price of output, MPK is the marginal product of capital, MPO is the marginal product of other inputs, MCO is the additional cost of other inputs, e denotes the expected value of the variables, and i refers to the periods of the productive life of the additional capital asset.

Given the estimates of expected return per time period, firms can estimate the yield on the additional capital. The yield is the internal rate of return on a marginal unit of capital which will discount the sum of returns per time period so that it just equals the price of investment goods which would prevail if the capital stock were optimal and net investment were zero. This rate of return on the economy's capital stock is called the *marginal efficiency of capital*, MEC. The equation for calculating MEC is

$$P_0^I = \frac{E_1^e}{1 + \text{MEC}} + \frac{E_2^e}{(1 + \text{MEC})^2} + \cdots + \frac{E_n^e}{(1 + \text{MEC})^n} \qquad (11.2.2)$$

The equation is similar to the marginal efficiency of investment, MEI, equation developed in Chapter 4. The one important difference is that *the price of the capital asset in (11.2.2) is the one which would prevail when the optimum capital stock is realized and net investment is zero.* In calculating the MEI schedule, the price of assets varies with net investment above or below its replacement level.

If MEC is at least as great as the market rate of interest, net investment will increase until the capital stock is optimal. Thus, the equilibrium condition in the capital market is

$$R = \text{MEC} \tag{11.2.3}$$

It can be shown that if we assume that the life of a capital asset is infinite and the expected return per time period is constant,

$$P_0^I = \frac{E^e}{\text{MEC}} \tag{11.2.4}^3$$

or

$$\text{MEC} = \frac{E^e}{P_0^I} \tag{11.2.5}$$

This means that MEC is a constant expected yield per time period. If expectations are realized, then

$$E^e = E \tag{11.2.6}$$

---

[3] If $E_1^e = E_2^e = \cdots = E_n^e = E^e$, (11.2.2) can be rewritten

$$P_0^I = E^e[(1 + \text{MEC})^{-1} + (1 + \text{MEC})^{-2} + \cdots + (1 + \text{MEC})^{-n}] \tag{1}$$

Since this equation is a geometric series, we can find its sum by first multiplying both sides by $(1 + \text{MEC})^{-1}$,

$$P_0^I(1 + \text{MEC})^{-1} = E^e[(1 + \text{MEC})^{-2} + (1 + \text{MEC})^{-3} + \cdots + (1 + \text{MEC})^{-(n+1)}] \tag{2}$$

Second, by subtracting Eq. (2) from (1) and cancelling out terms,

$$P_0^I[1 - (1 + \text{MEC})^{-1}] = E^e[(1 + \text{MEC})^{-1} - (1 + \text{MEC})^{-(n+1)}] \tag{3}$$

And third, by multiplying both sides of (3) by $1 + \text{MEC}$ and rearranging terms,

$$P_0^I = \frac{E^e}{\text{MEC}}[1 - (1 + \text{MEC})^{-n}] \tag{4}$$

as $n \to \infty$, $(1 + \text{MEC}) \to 0$ and $[1 - (1 + \text{MEC})^{-n}] \to 1$. Thus,

$$P_0^I = \frac{E^e}{\text{MEC}}$$

or

$$\text{MEC} = \frac{E^e}{P_0^I}$$

and by (11.2.1)

$$(P \cdot \text{MPK})^e + (P \cdot \text{MPO})^e - \text{MCO}^e = (P \cdot \text{MPK}) + (P \cdot \text{MPO}) - \text{MCO}$$

$$(11.2.7)$$

In equilibrium since the values of the marginal products of other inputs equals their marginal costs,

$$P \cdot \text{MPO} = \text{MCO} \qquad (11.2.8)$$

and since the interest rate equals the marginal efficiency of capital,

$$R = \text{MEC} = \frac{E}{P_0^I} \qquad (11.2.9)$$

the capital market equilibrium conditions per time period implied by (11.1.9) and (11.2.9) are equivalent,

$$\text{MEC} = \frac{E}{P_0^I} = \frac{P \cdot \text{MPK}}{P_0^I} = R \qquad (11.2.10)$$

Thus, the marginal efficiency approach builds on the marginal productivity approach by including consideration of expectations and time in the theory of capital. When expectations are realized and the yield per time period on additional capital is constant, both approaches give the same results.

The specification of (11.2.10) based on our skeleton model is

$$\text{MEC} = \frac{P}{P_0^I} \beta L_d^\alpha K^{\beta-1} \text{TEC}^\gamma \qquad (11.2.11)$$

or since $Y/P = L_d^\alpha K^\beta \text{TEC}^\gamma$,

$$\text{MEC} = \frac{\beta Y}{P_0^I K} \qquad (11.2.12)$$

Figure 11.2.1 graphically illustrates the correspondence between the two alternative approaches of the capital market. The upper quadrant shows the capital demand curve à la the marginal productivity approach. The lower quadrant shows the capital demand curve (11.2.12) à la the marginal efficiency approach. Capital demand in both cases is downward sloping because as production becomes more capital intensive there are diminishing returns to capital.

If the interest rate is R_2 and the price of replacement investment that would prevail if net investment were zero is P_0^I, the real user cost is $(UC/P)_2$

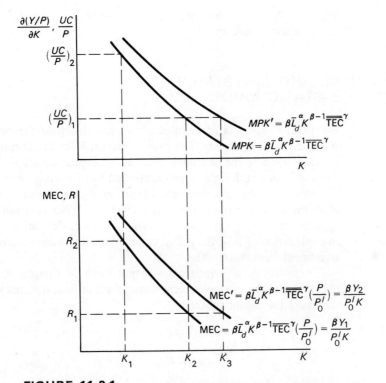

FIGURE 11.2.1
Relationship between MPK and MEC

and the capital stock is optimal at K_1 where $\text{MPK} = (UC/P)_2$ and MEC $= R_2$.

Suppose that the Fed engages in expansionary monetary policy such that the interest rate and thereby the real user cost fall to R_1 and $(UC/P)_1$, respectively. The new optimum capital stock is K_2 where $\text{MPK} = (UC/P)_1$ and $\text{MEC} = R_1$. Since the actual capital stock, K_1 is less than the new optimum capital stock, firms will undertake net investment until the K_2 is realized. In this illustration output demand policy induced the increase in the capital stock.

Changes in output supply can also induce changes in the capital stock. For example, in Fig. 11.2.1 suppose that technical progress increases from $\overline{\text{TEC}}$ to $\overline{\overline{\text{TEC}}}$ such that output supply increases from Y_1 to Y_2. For simplification purposes assume that all other variables remain unchanged. The MPK curve shifts upward because the increase in technical progress raises MPK for any given unit of capital. The MEC curve shifts upward since income increases. With no changes in the interest rate and real user cost, the optimum capital stock increases to K_3 where $\text{MPK}' = (U/P)_1$ and

MEC$' = R_1$. Firms will increase net investment until the new optimum capital stock is realized.

11.3 CAPITAL AND INVESTMENT IN THE STATIC MODEL

The theory of capital developed above explains how the optimum stock of capital is determined. The capital market is in equilibrium when firms use capital where the marginal efficiency of capital equals the interest rate. However, none of the related propositions directly explain investment because investment occurs only when the capital market is not in equilibrium, i.e., when the capital market is in disequilibrium. What is required then is an explanation of how the optimum capital stock is determined together with an explanation of how the actual capital stock increases (decreases) through investment (disinvestment).

Our theory of investment was put forth in Chapter 4. Part (a) of Fig. 11.3.1 shows the investment demand curve in real terms which we can express in the functional form,

$$\frac{I}{P} = I\left(R, \frac{Y}{P}\right) \tag{11.3.1}$$

Part (b) shows the aggregate supply curve for real investment goods, S_I. The aggregate supply curve is the horizontal sum of all the marginal cost curves of all producers in the investment goods industry. Rising marginal costs per unit of additional output produced imply a positively sloped aggregate supply curve. Notice that when real net investment in part (a) is zero, only real replacement investment, REP, takes place in part (b). The price of replacement goods when real net investment is zero is P_0^I.[4]

If equilibrium $Y/P = (Y/P)_1$ and $R = R_2$, the investment demand curve, $I(R, (Y/P)_1)$, in Fig. 11.3.1 indicates that real net investment is zero; only real replacement investment, REP, takes place in part (b) at a supply price P_0^I. If the interest rate falls to R_1, real net investment will increase to I_3 in the short run, while real gross investment will increase to REP $+ I_3$ and the supply price of investment goods will rise along S_I to P_3^I. If real income increases simultaneously with the decrease in the interest rate (à la an increase in the real money stock), the investment demand curve will shift rightward to $I(R, (Y/P)_2)$. For any given interest rate, say R_1, real net

---

[4] The replacement price level is a variable. When the capital stock increases (decreases) the replacement investment required to maintain the capital stock increases (decreases). Hence, the replacement price level when net investment is zero increases (decreases). For simplification purposes, in our analysis we shall assume that the variation in the replacement price level is negligible.

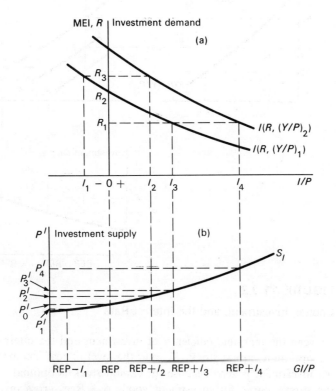

FIGURE 11.3.1

Short-Run Investment

investment will increase to I_4, the price of investment goods will increase to P_4^I, and real gross investment will increase to REP $+ I_4$.

If equilibrium $Y/P = (Y/P)_1$ in Fig. 11.3.1 and the interest rate increases from R_2 and R_3, real net investment will decrease to I_1 in the short-run along $I(R, (Y/P)_1)$. The price of investment goods will fall to P_1^I, which is below the initial replacement level; real gross disinvestment, REP $- I_1$, will take place. However, if real income increases to $(Y/P)_2$ simultaneously with the increase in the interest rate (à la an increase in real government spending), then the investment demand curve shifts to $I(R, (Y/P)_2)$ where short-run real net investment will increase to I_2, real gross investment will increase to REP $+ I_2$, and the price of investment goods will increase to P_2^I.

We are now ready to pull together our theories of capital and investment. Figure 11.3.2 illustrates the interrelationship between the two theories. Part (a) shows the aggregate demand for capital, $K(R, (Y/P)_1)$, based on the equality of the marginal efficiency of capital and the interest rate. For $Y/P = (Y/P)_1$ assume that the actual and desired capital stocks are equal at the interest rate R_3, and therefore the capital stock, K_1, is optimal. Part (b) shows the short-run investment demand curve, $I(R, (Y/P)_1, K_1)$, based on the equality

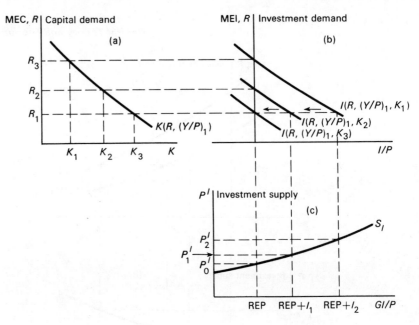

FIGURE 11.3.2

Capital, Investment, and the Interest Rate

between the marginal efficiency of investment and the interest rate, R_3, for the optimum capital stock, K_1, and the level of real income, $(Y/P)_1$. Real net investment is zero because the capital stock is optimal. Part (c) shows the supply curve for investment goods S_I. Real gross investment equals real replacement investment, REP, and the price of investment goods is P_0^I.

Suppose that the interest rate falls to R_1 (assume that real income remains unchanged). The desired capital stock increases to K_3; it is greater than the actual capital stock K_1 (the old optimum capital stock). In the short-run real net investment increases to I_2 along $I(R, (Y/P)_1, K_1)$, while real gross investment increases to REP $+ I_2$ and the supply price rises to P_2^I. As real net investment takes place the actual capital stock increases and closes the gap between the actual and desired capital stocks. Thus, the level of real net investment falls off. When the actual capital stock increases to K_2, the investment demand curve shifts to $I(R, (Y/P)_1, K_2)$ and real net investment decreases to I_1. Real gross investment falls off to REP $+ I_1$ and the price of investment goods decreases to P_1^I.

As real net investment continues to take place, the actual capital stock increases to K_3. The investment demand curve decreases to $I(R, (Y/P)_1, K_3)$ where real net investment falls to zero. Real gross investment decreases to its replacement level and the price of investment goods returns to P_0^I.[5] After

---

[5] Actually the price of investment goods will be higher than P_0^I. Since the new optimum capital stock requires greater replacement investment to maintain the new optimum capital stock, the price will be higher. If we wish to be more precise, in Fig. 11.3.2 we would shift the origin of part (c) leftward so replacement investment and its price would be higher once the capital stock increases from K_1 to K_3.

full adjustment, the interest rate equals the marginal efficiency of capital where the capital stock is optimal at K_3. Although there is a short-run relationship between real net investment and the interest rate, there is no such long-run relationship.

Figure 11.3.3 illustrates the effects of a change in real income on the capital-investment relationship. Part (a) shows the economy's capital demand curve, $K(R, (Y/P)_1)$ when real income is $(Y/P)_1$. If the interest rate is R_1, the optimum capital stock is K_1. Part (b) shows the corresponding investment demand curve, $I(R, (Y/P)_1, K_1)$. Since the capital market is in equilibrium, real net investment is zero. Part (c) shows the supply curve for investment

FIGURE 11.3.3

Capital, Investment, the Interest Rate, and Real Income

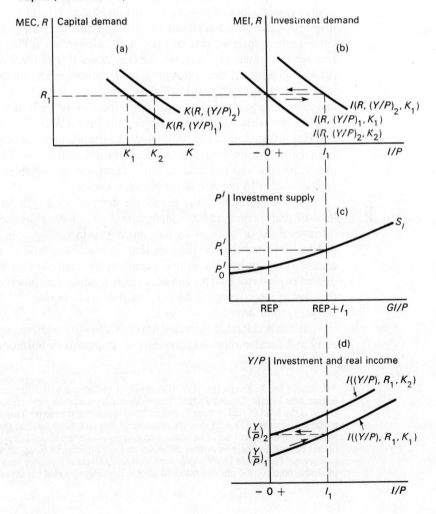

goods where only real replacement investment, REP, takes place at a price P_0^I. Part (d) shows the positive relationship between real net investment and real income, $I(Y/P, R_1, K_1)$, when the capital stock is optimal at (K_1, R_1). Since the capital market is in equilibrium, real net investment is zero with respect to real income as well.

If real income increases to $(Y/P)_2$, for example, because of changes in either labor or technical progress, firms will revise their expectations upward with respect to future returns on capital. Thus, the desired capital stock will be higher for each level of MEC and rate of interest, i.e., the capital demand curve shifts rightward in Fig. 11.3.3 to $K(R, (Y/P)_2)$. Correspondingly, the investment demand curve shifts rightward to $I(R, (Y/P)_2, K_1)$. If the interest rate remains at R_1, the desired capital stock is K_2. Since the actual capital stock, K_1, is less than K_2, real net investment, I_1, will take place. Real gross investment will be REP + I_1. As the actual capital stock approaches the desired capital stock, $K_1 \rightarrow K_2$, real net investment falls to zero and real gross investment falls to the replacement level. In part (d) the investment demand curve (with respect to real income) shifts leftward to $I(Y/P, R_1, K_2)$ where real net investment is zero when the capital stock is optimal at K_2. In part (b), the investment demand curve (with respect to the interest rate) shifts leftward to $I(R, (Y/P)_2, K_2)$, which is identical to $I(R, (Y/P)_1, K_1)$. Real net investment is again equal to zero with respect to the interest rate.[6]

In this section we have explained the interrelationship between capital and real investment in the static model as firms adjust the economy's actual capital stock to its desired level. Equilibrium is displaced by both changes in real income and the interest rate. These are the variables which link the capital market to the rest of the skeleton model.

In the short-run static model the demand for capital depends on the level of real income and the interest rate. We have considered the impact on investment of changes in real income from one level to another. But implicit in the analysis is the idea that an increasing level of net investment cannot occur unless the actual capital stock continues to lag behind the desired capital stock. This can occur only if ouput continues to grow. Thus, the level of net investment depends on changes in output. This idea is called the *accelerator principle*.

If the accelerator principle holds, it adds to the difficulties which monetary and fiscal authorities encounter in short-run stabilization policies. In

---

[6] Professor M. K. Evans (pp. 133–42) examined and summarized the empirical evidence in this area for the United States. The evidence supports the importance of the interest rate and the level of real income in determining real net investment. Two statements are of particular interest: (1) a 25 percent decrease in the long-term interest rate causes a 5–10 percent increase in real net investment over two years after an initial lag period of one year; (2) a 1 percent increase in output increases real net investment from 1.5 to 2 percent over two years. Professors D. W. Jorgenson and C. D. Siebert's studies also lend support to the importance of the interest rate and output in explaining real net investment.

the interim period of adjusting the actual to the desired capital stock, the growth rate of investment is higher than that for the real income. If the economy is at less-than-full employment of the labor supply (involuntary unemployment exists) and the monetary and/or fiscal authorities further stimulate real income to bring about full employment, they run the risk of overstimulating demand. When the rate of growth in investment subsides once the optimum capital stock is realized, the economy may be stuck with surplus capital and thereby a business slump.

In upswings of the business cycle it is reasonable to expect an acceleration in net investment as income changes from one rate of change to another in order to realize a higher equilibrium capital stock. But in the downswings when firms are stuck with more capital than required for sales, the rate of reduction in the capital stock is limited to the rate of depreciation. Thus, in the downswings there is no accelerated disinvestment. Disinvestment is tied to the depreciation rate. Professors J. R. Meyer and E. Kuh suggest that during the upswings of the business cycle the accelerator does well in predicting investment behavior but that during the downswings the accelerator does poorly. The implications of their study suggest that in general the accelerator may not be the best predictor of short-run net investment. Net investment takes place in the downswing of the business cycle, particularly when firms plan to employ new cost-saving technology to improve existing products and/or produce new products. Under these circumstances (even in a downswing) firms are not so much interested in expected changes in real income but rather in the absolute size of real income. Moreover, firms appear to prefer internal to external financing. That is, they prefer financing investment expenditures from depreciation allowances and retained earnings rather than borrowing or issuing stocks. Such funds are highly correlated to the level of income (through profits). Thus, expecting short-run investment to be an increasing function of the level of income may have more general applicability than the accelerator principle.

A more recent study by Professors D. W. Jorgenson and C. D. Siebert compares the various theories which have been used to explain investment behavior. Their empirical work suggests that the neoclassical theory of investment behavior, where the optimum capital stock is determined by the equality of the marginal product of capital and capital's real user cost, does a better job of explaining investment behavior (once the appropriate lag between the desired and actual capital stock is determined) than theories based on the accelerator principle (desired capital is proportional to output), expected profits (measured by the market value of a firm so that desired capital is proportional to market value), and liquidity or current profits (measured by the flow of internal funds available for investment). In fact, the neoclassical theory of investment is superior to both the accelerator and profit expectations theories, and these theories are superior to the liquidity theory of investment.

11.4 CAPITAL ACCUMULATION AND ECONOMIC GROWTH

In this chapter we have developed a theory of capital and related it to the theory of investment in the static model. The analysis magnifies the inconsistency in our skeleton model of assuming that the capital stock is fixed while net investment takes place. You will remember that inconsistency was resolved in our short-run analysis by assuming that changes in the capital stock due to net investment are relatively small so that the capital stock is roughly fixed. In the long-run, however, the growth of the capital stock is one of the primary means of economic growth.

The problems of economic growth are best analyzed within the framework of a dynamic model. Although it is beyond the scope of this book to present a comprehensive discussion of macrodynamics, it is useful to extend our treatment of capital theory by introducing a very simple growth model which emphasizes the importance of capital accumulation in the growth process.

In the 1950s Professors J. Tobin, R. M. Solow, and T. W. Swan introduced the first neoclassical growth models into the economic literature. Many economists accept them as a good first approximation of the growth process. They are called *neoclassical* because their assumptions are the same as those of the neoclassical economists such as A. Marshall and K. Wicksell. Capital and labor are assumed to be substitutes for each other in the production process. Hence, there is a continuous set of alternative capital-labor ratios which will produce a given level of output. This assumption also means that there are alternative values of the capital-output ratio. The neoclassical models also assume that the production process exhibits *diminishing marginal productivity* (diminishing returns) and *constant returns to scale*. Diminishing marginal productivity was explained in Chapter 7. Constant returns to scale means that if all inputs are increased proportionally, output will increase by the same proportional amount. For example, if all inputs are doubled, output will double.

The one-sector neoclassical growth models are structured by (1) a production function which specifies a relationship between capital and labor inputs and output, (2) an assumption that labor supply is exogenous and grows at a constant rate, and (3) a saving and investment relationship which determines the amount of current output that will be saved and invested in order to increase the capital stock. They provide a simple explanation of the growth process, which is considered applicable to most industrial economies. Labor in period t, L_t, is combined with capital in period t, K_t, to produce output in period t, Q_t. A portion of Q_t is saved and invested so that a larger capital stock in period $t + 1$, K_{t+1}, combined with a larger labor supply, L_{t+1}, can produce a larger output, Q_{t+1}. The process repeats itself again and again as the economy grows. The extent to which technical progress increases the productivity of labor and/or capital will also add to the growth of output.

On the output supply side of our growth model we shall assume that capital, labor, and technical progress produce the economy's output. We shall assume that all technical progress is labor-saving and introduce it through the concept of *effective labor input*. Units of effective labor input include not only the traditional notion of labor units (number of workers or man hours), L, but also a term, A, which represents the coefficient of labor-saving technical progress. As each worker becomes more productive he is able to produce greater output with the same amount of capital.

The production function is specified by

$$y = E^{1-\beta}K^{\beta}, \qquad 0 < \beta < 1 \qquad (11.4.1)$$

where $y \equiv Y/P$ is output, $E \equiv AL$ is effective labor input, and K is capital input. This is the Cobb-Douglas form of the production process, which possesses all the neoclassical characteristics.[7]

It can be shown that (11.4.1) can be solved for the growth rate of output,

$$\frac{\Delta y}{y} = (1 - \beta)\frac{\Delta E}{E} + \beta \frac{\Delta K}{K} \qquad (11.4.2)$$

where $\Delta y/y$, $\Delta E/E$, and $\Delta K/K$ are the growth rates of output, effective labor, and capital respectively.[8]

---

[7] This form of the production function exhibits diminishing returns because if $0 < \beta < 1$, the marginal products of both inputs are positive and decreasing. The marginal products of effective labor and capital, $\partial y/\partial E = (1 - \beta)(y/E)$ and $\partial y/\partial K = \beta(y/K)$, respectively, indicate that the marginal products are positive and as effective labor and/or capital increases, their marginal products diminish.

The production function also exhibits constant returns to scale because it is homogeneous of degree 1. If we increase E and K by a constant λ,

$$(\lambda E)^{1-\beta}(\lambda K)^{\beta} = \lambda^{1-\beta}\lambda^{\beta}E^{1-\beta}K^{\beta} = \lambda y$$

When all inputs increase by the same constant, λ, output also increases by λ.

Moreover, $1 - \beta$ and β are effective labor's and capital's shares of output when effective labor is paid (the real wage rate) its marginal product and capital is paid (the real user cost) its marginal product. Capital's absolute share is the marginal product of K times the units of capital, $K(\partial y/\partial K) = \beta y$. If we divide by y, $[K(\partial y/\partial K)]/y = \beta$. Thus, we can see that β is capital's relative share of output. Similarly, when output is fully distributed, effective labor's share is $1 - \beta$.

[8] By taking the total differential of (11.4.1),

$$dy = (1 - \beta)K^{\beta}E^{-\beta}\, dE + \beta E^{1-\beta}K^{\beta-1}\, dK$$

Dividing the total differential by $y = E^{1-\beta}K^{\beta}$ gives

$$\frac{dy}{y} = (1 - \beta)\frac{dE}{E} + \beta \frac{dK}{K}$$

which is closely approximated by (11.4.2) if the changes in the variables are very small.

If we assume that the growth rate of labor supply is constant,

$$\frac{\Delta L}{L} = n \tag{11.4.3}$$

and that the growth rate of labor productivity is constant,

$$\frac{\Delta A}{A} = \rho \tag{11.4.4}$$

such that

$$\frac{\Delta E}{E} = n + \rho$$

then if labor is fully employed, (11.4.2) becomes

$$\frac{\Delta y}{y} = (1 - \beta)(n + \rho) + \beta \frac{\Delta K}{K} \tag{11.4.5}$$

This expression states that the full labor employment growth rate of output depends on the growth rate of the capital stock.

On the demand side of the model, we shall assume that saving is proportional to output and that in each time period saving equals intended or planned investment,

$$S = sy = I \tag{11.4.6}$$

where S is both private and public saving (private saving plus net taxes), I is both private and public investment, and s is the social marginal propensity to save. Since $I \equiv \Delta K$, (11.4.6) can be rewritten as

$$\Delta K = sy \tag{11.4.7}$$

Dividing (11.4.7) by K gives

$$\frac{\Delta K}{K} = s \frac{y}{K} \tag{11.4.8}$$

an expression which states that the growth rate of capital which will permit investors to realize planned investment depends on both the social marginal propensity to save and the output per unit of capital (the output-capital ratio).

The growth rate of output which will not only maintain full employment of labor but also maintain full employment of capital and permit investors to realize planned investment ($S = I$) can be derived by substituting (11.4.8) into (11.4.5),

$$\frac{\Delta y}{y} = (1 - \beta)(n + \rho) + \beta s \frac{y}{K} \qquad (11.4.9)$$

This is the growth rate of output that is warranted by the importance of full employment of resources and saving sufficient for investors to realize investment plans which are based on the level of output through the saving income relationship and changes in the output through changes in the capital stock.

Equation (11.4.9) is one equation in two unknowns, y/K, $\Delta y/y$. To close the system for solution we must recognize that the growth rate of the output-capital ratio is the difference between the growth rates of output and capital.

$$\frac{\Delta(y/K)}{y/K} = \frac{\Delta y}{y} - \frac{\Delta K}{K} \qquad (11.4.10)^9$$

Substituting (11.4.8) and (11.4.9) into (11.4.10) gives

$$\frac{\Delta(y/K)}{y/K} = (1 - \beta)(n + \rho) - (1 - \beta)s \frac{y}{K} \qquad (11.4.11)$$

a single equation in one unknown, y/K. By setting $\Delta(y/K)/(y/K)$ equal to zero, we can solve (11.4.11) for the equilibrium output-capital ratio,

$$0 = (1 - \beta)(n + \rho) - (1 - \beta)s \frac{y}{K}$$

or

$$\left(\frac{y}{K}\right)_e = \frac{n + \rho}{s} \qquad (11.4.12)$$

When the output-capital ratio is constant at $(n + \rho)/s$ the economy is on its equilibrium growth path where labor and capital are fully employed and investors realize planned investment. It follows from (11.4.10) that the growth rates of capital and output are equal. Moreover, by substituting (11.4.12) into either (11.4.8) or (11.4.9) we can verify that the growth rate of

---

[9] By differentiating the output capital ratio (by the quotient rule),

$$d\frac{y}{K} = \frac{K\,dy - y\,dK}{K^2}$$

Dividing the results by y/K gives

$$\frac{d(y/K)}{y/K} = \frac{dy}{y} - \frac{dK}{K}$$

which is closely approximated by (11.4.2) if the changes in the variables are very small.

effective labor also equals the growth rates of capital and output when the economy is on its equilibrium growth path,

$$\frac{\Delta y}{y} = \frac{\Delta K}{K} = \frac{\Delta E}{E} \qquad (11.4.13)$$

Since $\Delta E/E = \Delta L/L + \Delta A/A = n + \rho$, (11.4.13) means that the growth rates of output and capital exceed the growth rate of labor by the growth rate of labor-saving technical progress,

$$\frac{\Delta y}{y} = \frac{\Delta K}{K} > \frac{\Delta L}{L} = n \quad \text{by} \quad \frac{\Delta A}{A} = \rho \qquad (11.4.14)$$

Thus, the output-labor and the capital-labor ratios grow at the rate ρ.

These results can be illustrated graphically: For given values of n, ρ, s, and β, the upper quadrant of Fig. 11.4.1 shows the curves for (11.4.7) and (11.4.8). The growth rates of output and capital are on the vertical axis and the output-capital ratio is on the horizontal axis. The slope of the $\Delta y/y$ curve is βs, and the vertical axis intercept is $(1 - \beta)(n + \rho)$. The slope of the $\Delta K/K$ curve is s and the intercept is zero. The lower quadrant shows the curve for (11.4.11) where the growth rate of the output-capital ratio is on the vertical axis and the output-capital ratio is on the horizontal axis. The slope of the curve is $-(1 - \beta)s$, and the vertical axis intercept is $(1 - \beta)(n + \rho)$. Notice that the $\Delta(y/K)/(y/K)$ curve is the vertical difference between the $\Delta y/y$ and $\Delta K/K$ curves in the upper quadrant.

In Fig. 11.4.1 the economy is on its equilibrium growth path when the capital-output ratio is constant at $(y/K)_e = (n + \rho)/s$ and the growth rates of output and capital equal $(\Delta y/y)_e = (\Delta K/K)_e$ [the growth rate of the output-capital ratio equal zero, $\Delta(y/K)/(y/K) = 0$]. If the output-capital ratio were greater or less than $(n + \rho)/s$, the economy would be off the equilibrium growth path. However, the economic forces built into the model will ensure that the equilibrium is attained. For example, if $y/K = (y/K)_1 < (n + \rho)/s$, the rate of growth in capital is less than that which is necessary to achieve a growth rate of output which will provide full employment. That is, planned investment exceeds saving and labor is unemployed. As output increases to eliminate the excess demand, saving and investment increase. Output grows at a greater rate than capital and the output-capital ratio increases toward $(n + \rho)/s$ where labor and capital are fully employed and saving equals planned investment. If $y/K = (y/K)_2 > (n + \rho)/s$, the rate of growth in capital is greater than that which is necessary to achieve a growth rate of output which will provide full employment. That is, saving exceeds planned investment and capital is unemployed. As output decreases to eliminate the excess supply, saving and investment decrease. Capital decreases at a greater rate than that of output, and the output-capital ratio decreases toward $(n + \rho)/s$.

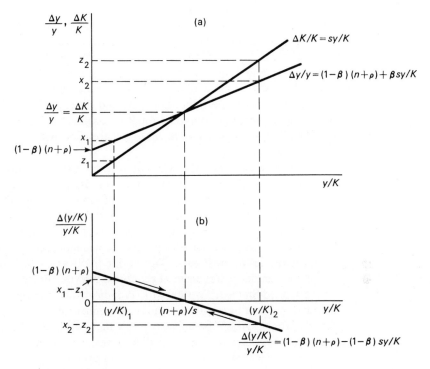

FIGURE 11.4.1

Neoclassical Growth

The implications of our model are clear. We can see that both capital and output grow at the same constant rate. The growth rates in capital and output exceed the growth rate of labor by the growth rate in labor-saving technical progress. This means that the capital-output ratio is constant and that both the capital-labor and output-labor ratios grow at the same rates as labor-saving technical progress. Since capital, effective labor, and output grow at the same rate (11.4.13), the capital-labor ratios grow at the constant rate of growth of labor-saving technical progress.

Moreover, since effective labor's share of output, $1 - \beta$, is constant, since capital's share of output, β, is constant, and since the profit rate is constant (capital does not derive any returns from technical progress), effective labor's share of output is constant, while the real wage rate paid to labor increases by the constant growth rate of labor-saving technical progress.

The model is supported by a long-run analysis of post-World War II data for the United States. Capital and full employment output in the United States grow around a trend at about 4 percent per year, which is roughly equal to the 1.2 percent per-year growth rate in the labor force (averaging in the effects of the post-World War II baby boom) plus the 3 percent per-year growth rate in labor productivity so that the capital-output ratio is roughly constant. This means that growth rates in capital and full employment output roughly exceed the growth rate in labor by the average growth rate of labor productivity so that the output-labor ratio and capital-labor (in man-hours) ratio is roughly 2.6 percent per year along trend. The ratio of profits to the capital stock (the profit rate) is roughly constant in the long-run. Since both the profit rate and the capital-output ratio are constant, capital's share of output is roughly constant at .23. Since labor's share of output is 1 − capital's share, labor's share of output is roughly constant at 1 − .23 = .77.

We have assumed that technical progress is strictly labor-saving. Other theoretical possibilities exist. Technical progress is capital-saving when it increases output with the same amount of labor. It is neutral when its impact falls equally on both labor and capital. Regardless of the kind of technical progress assumed, it is often considered *disembodied*. This means that technical progress increases productivity independently of changes in any of the quantities of the inputs. This notion implies that capital accumulation is not an essential prerequisite of economic growth. Professor Solow's study of the United States from 1909 to 1949 indicated that if technical progress is assumed to be disembodied, capital accumulation only slightly increased labor's productivity. These results imply that output may be more effectively increased by encouraging intangible investment such as education and research rather than tangible investment in capital.

In recent years, however, economists have criticized the disembodiment assumption. Technical progress is more often being considered as embodied in gross investment. Hence, additional capital and its modernization are the vehicle by which technical progress is introduced into the production process. Capital is composed of different "vintages." The older capital embodies older technical progress than the newer capital. Thus, the new capital yields a greater output per worker than the old. Investment reduces the average age of capital by introducing technical progress. As a result the growth of output is not constrained by the number of units of capital available. However, the resulting increase in productivity does not last. Increases in current investment will create a larger older vintage capital stock in the future. Moreover, increases in investment require increases in saving. As the average age of capital eventually reaches its long-run value, the growth rate in the economy will return to its previous level. Modernization cannot permanently increase the equilibrium rate of output growth. However, it can move the economy onto a higher equilibrium growth path and thereby raise the *level* of output.

This recent view of investment restores the previous importance of capital accumulation as a means of increasing the level of output. What we must do is calculate the rate of return of the alternatives. Professor E. S. Phelps' estimate of the rate of return on the U.S. capital stock is about 14 percent. Professor W. L. Hansen's estimate of the rate of return to education (males who complete high school) is about 12 percent. Thus, we may tentatively conclude that tangible investment is an appropriate means of output growth.

11.5 SUMMARY

In this chapter we developed a theory that explained how the optimum capital stock is determined together with an explanation of how the capital stock grows through investment. The demand for capital is based on the marginal product of capital. When the desired capital stock exceeds the actual capital stock, net investment will increase until the desired and actual capital stocks are equal. The decision to increase the capital stock can be explained by either the marginal productivity or the marginal efficiency approach. The former involves a comparison between the real user cost of capital (the real dollar return on an alternative earning asset) and the marginal product of capital, while the latter involves a comparison between the internal yield on capital (the marginal efficiency of capital) and the external yield (the market rate of interest). The marginal efficiency approach builds on the marginal productivity approach by considering expectations of future returns in the capital decision.

Firms maximize profit by using capital where capital's marginal product equals its real user cost. Changes in real user cost displace capital market equilibrium by creating a difference between the desired and actual capital stocks. For example, a decrease in the real user cost increases the desired capital stock because of diminishing returns. This means that the desired capital stock is greater than the actual capital stock so that real net investment increases until the actual and desired levels are equal. When this occurs the marginal product of capital equals capital's real user cost and the capital stock is said to be optimal. Conversely, when the real user cost rises so that the actual exceeds the desired capital stock, real net disinvestment will increase until capital's marginal product equals its real user cost. Not only changes in real user cost displace equilibrium in the capital market. Changes in output through changes in technical progress and/or labor employment also create differences between the actual and desired capital stock by changing the marginal product of capital. Again real net investment (disinvestment) will occur until the capital market is in equilibrium.

Since the return on additional capital (the sum of the values of the marginal products of capital and other associated inputs less the additional noncapital costs excluding interest and depreciation costs) is not realized within the time period of purchase, firms must estimate expected future returns for each period of the additional capital productive life. The marginal efficiency of capital is the internal rate of return on the economy's capital stock, which discounts the stream of expected income so that it equals the price of investment goods that would prevail if the capital market were in equilibrium and net investment is zero. The capital market is in equilibrium when the internal yield on capital, MEC, equals the external yield, the interest rate. Changes in the interest rate create a difference between the desired and actual capital stock. Changes in the capital stock will occur until the capital market is in equilibrium.

Clearly, if the expected return is the same per time period and expectations are realized, the marginal productivity and marginal efficiency approaches yield the same optimum capital stock per time period.

Net investment occurs in the short run when the interest rate and/or income displace capital market equilibrium. In the long-run as the actual capital stock adjusts to the desired capital stock, net investment decreases to zero. Thus, in the long-run net investment is not related to the interest rate or the level of real income.

Capital accumulation is a major factor in the process of economic growth. The one-sector neoclassical growth model helps to explain some of the regularities of the growth process of most industrial economies. Given constant growth rates of labor supply and labor-saving technical progress, capital accumulation makes possible a growth rate of output that will maintain full employment of capital and labor and permit investors to realize planned investment. When an economy is on its equilibrium growth path the growth rates of capital, output, and effective labor (includes labor and an element of labor productivity through labor-saving technical progress) are equal. This means that output and capital grow at a rate that exceeds the growth rate of labor by the growth rate of technical progress. Moreover, both the capital-labor and the output-labor ratios increase by the growth rate of technical progress, while the output-capital ratio is constant. Factor shares are constant, and since the profit rate is constant, the real wage increases by the growth rate of labor productivity through labor-saving technical progress.

Our model assumes that technical progress takes place independently of changes in the quantities of the inputs. This assumption led many economists to recommend the encouragement of education and research (intangible investment) as a primary means of increasing labor productivity and to deemphasize the role of capital accumulation. In recent years, economists have recognized that technical progress is introduced into the production process through new vintages of capital. Hence, the important role of capital accumulation is partially restored.

REVIEW QUESTIONS

1. Carefully distinguish between the concepts of MEI and MEC.

2. Why is the MEC downward sloping?

3. What factors distinguish the MEC and MPK approaches to capital demand theory?

4. Why does the price of investment goods rise when the actual capital stock is less than desired? Why does it fall as the gap closes?

5. Explain how an increase in growth of the labor force and technical progress effect the output-capital ratio and the growth rates of output and capital.

SELECTED READINGS

ACKLEY, G., *Macroeconomic Theory*, New York: Macmillan, 1961, Chap. 17.

ALLEN, R. G. D., *Macroeconomic Theory*, New York: St. Martin's, 1967, Chaps. 6–7.

BISCHOFF, C. W., "Business Investment in the 1970's: A Comparison of Models," in *Brookings Papers on Economic Activity*, Vol. 1, Washington, D.C.: The Brookings Institution, 1971.

BURMEISTER, E., and A. R. DOBELL, *Mathematical Theories of Economic Growth*, New York: Macmillan, 1972.

CLOWER, R. W., "An Investigation into the Dynamics of Investment," *American Economic Review*, 44 (March 1954), 64–81.

DOMAR, E. D., *Essays in the Theory of Economic Growth*, New York: Oxford University Press, 1957.

DORFMAN, R., "An Economic Interpretation of Optimal Control Theory," *American Economic Review*, 59 (Dec. 1969), 817–31.

EISNER, R., "A Distributed Lag Investment Function," *Econometrica*, 28 (Jan. 1960), 1–29.

——, "Investment: Fact and Fancy," *American Economic Review*, 53 (May 1963), 237–46.

——, "Capital Expenditures, Profits and the Acceleration Principle," in *Models of Income Determination*, Studies in Income and Wealth, Vol. 28, National Bureau of Economic Research, 1964, pp. 137–76.

——, "A Permanent Income Theory for Investment," *American Economic Review*, 57 (June 1967), 364–90.

——, and R. H. STROTZ, "Determinants of Business Investment," in *Impacts of Monetary Policy*, Commission on Money and Credit, Englewood Cliffs, N.J.: Prentice-Hall, 1963, pp. 59–337.

EVANS, M. K., *Macroeconomic Activity: Theory, Forecasting and Control*, New York: Harper & Row, 1969, pp. 133–42 and 220.

HANSEN, W. L., "Total and Private Rates of Return to Investment in Schooling," *Journal of Political Economy*, 71 (April 1963), 128–40.

HARROD, R. F., *Towards a Dynamic Economics*, London: Macmillan, 1948.

HIRSHLEIFER, J., "On the Theory of Optimal Investment Decisions," *Journal of Political Economy*, 66 (Aug. 1958), 329–52.

JORGENSON, D. W., "Econometric Studies of Investment Behavior: A Survey," *Journal of Economic Literature*, 9 (Dec. 1971), 1111–47.

————, and Z. GRILICHES, "The Explanation of Productivity Change," *Review of Economics and Statistics*, 34 (July 1967), 249–83.

————, and C. D. SIEBERT, "A Comparison of Alternative Theories of Corporate Investment Behavior," *American Economic Review*, 58 (Sept. 1968), 681–712.

————, and C. D. SIEBERT, "Optimal Capital Accumulation and Corporate Investment Behavior," *Journal of Political Economy*, 76 (Nov./Dec. 1968), 1123–51.

————, and J. A. STEPHENSON, "Investment Behavior in U.S. Manufacturing, 1947–60," *Econometrica*, 35 (April 1967), 169–220.

————, and J. A. STEPHENSON, "Issues in the Development of the Neo-classical Theory of Investment Behavior," *Review of Economics and Statistics*, 51 (Aug. 1969), 346–53.

KALDOR, N., "Capital Accumulation and Economic Growth," in F. Lutz and D. C. Hague (eds.), *The Theory of Capital*, New York: Macmillan, 1961, pp. 177–222.

KEYNES, J. M., *The General Theory of Employment, Interest, and Money*, London: Macmillan, 1936, Chaps. 11 and 12.

KNOX, A. D., "The Acceleration Principle and the Theory of Investment: A Survey," *Economica*, 19 (Aug. 1952), 269–97.

LEIJONHUFVED, A., *On Keynesian Economics and the Economics of Keynes*, New York: Oxford University Press, 1968, Chap. 3.

LERNER, A. P., *The Econmoics of Control*, New York: Macmillan, 1944.

————, "On the Marginal Product of Capital and the Marginal Efficiency of Investment," *Journal of Political Economy*, 61 (Feb. 1953), 1–14.

————, "On Some Recent Developments in Capital Theory," *American Economic Review Papers and Proceedings*, 55 (May 1965), 284–95.

MARGLIN, S. A., "Investment and Interest: A Reformulation and Extension of Keynesian Theory," *Economic Journal*, 80 (Dec. 1970), 910–31.

MEYER, J. R., and E. KUH, *The Investment Decision*, Cambridge, Mass.: Harvard University Press, 1957.

NELSON, R. R., "Aggregate Production Functions and Medium-Range Growth Projections," *American Economic Review*, 54 (Sept. 1964), 575–606.

PHELPS, E. S., "The New View of Investment: A Neoclassical Analysis," *Quarterly Journal of Economics*, 76 (Nov. 1962), 548–67.

———— (ed.), "Tangible Investment as an Instrument of Growth," in *Goals of Economic Growth*, New York: Norton, 1962, pp. 94–105.

SOLOW, R. M., "A Contribution to the Theory of Economic Growth," *Quarterly Journal of Economics*, 70 (Feb. 1956), 65–94.

———, "Technical Change and the Aggregate Production Function," *Review of Economics and Statistics*, 39 (Aug. 1957), 312–20.

———, "Investment and Technical Progress," in K. J. Arrow, S. Karlin, and P. Suppes (eds.), *Mathematical Methods in the Social Sciences*, Stanford, Calif.: Stanford University Press, 1960.

———, *Capital Theory and the Rate of Return*, Skokie, Ill.: Rand McNally, 1964.

TARSHIS, L., "The Elasticity of the Marginal Efficiency Function," *American Economic Review*, 51 (Dec. 1961), 958–85.

TOBIN, J., "A Dynamic Aggregate Model," *Journal of Political Economy*, 63 (April 1955), 103–15.

———, "Economic Growth as an Objective of Government Policy," *American Economic Review*, 63 (May 1964), 103–15.

WHITE, W. H., "Interest Inelasticity of Investment Demand—The Case from Business Attitude Surveys Re-examined," *American Economic Review*, 46 (Sept. 1956), 565–87.

WITTE, J. G., "The Microfoundations of the Social Investment Function," *Journal of Political Economy*, 71 (Oct. 1963), 441–56.

CHAPTER 12

International Flow of Funds

12.1 THE CURRENT ACCOUNT

People purchase goods and services that are produced in foreign economies because they are unable to buy comparatively priced items in the domestic economy. These goods and services include such items as merchandise, insurance, transportation, and the use of domestic capital abroad. The *current account* records the flow of funds from foreigners for purchases of currently produced goods and services and the flow of funds to foreigners for purchases of foreign-produced goods and services. While receipts from foreigners appear in the current account as export expenditures, payment to foreigners appear as import expenditures.

You will recall that the difference between export and import expenditures is net foreign expenditures. This value may be zero, negative, or positive. Clearly, if it is positive the domestic economy enjoys a surplus of receipts over payments in its current account. If it is negative, a deficit exists in its current account. If it is zero, there is neither a surplus nor a deficit in its current account.

In the past, the U.S. economy has not been particularly sensitive to foreign economic developments. However, in recent years the United States has become concerned with the first current account deficits in many years. Moreover, other smaller and more open economies such as England, Japan, and many underdeveloped economies have been (and still are) very sensitive to external economic developments. For these reasons, we shall consider more extensively the factors which influence the current account.

Domestic producers may conduct international transactions in the domestic currency (dollars) or in foreign currencies (pounds, yen, marks, francs) because all currencies are exchangeable. The rate at which different currencies are exchanged is called the exchange rate; it is measured in units of foreign currency per unit of domestic currency. For example, if it takes 4 francs to acquire 1 dollar, the exchange rate is 4. The exchange rate is important because it translates the price in dollar denominations into the price in foreign currency denominations of domestic goods which are traded in international markets. For example, if 1 dollar costs 4 francs, a good that sells for 20 dollars will sell for 80 francs since the exchange rate if 4. It follows that the foreign price of domestic goods is

$$P_f = P_d \cdot r \tag{12.1.1}$$

where P_f is the foreign price of domestic goods, P_d is the domestic price of domestic goods traded in the international markets, and $r = P_f/P_d$ is the exchange rate. In our example,

$$P_f = \$20 \times 4 = 80 \text{ francs}$$

For simplification purposes, we shall assume that the domestic price level of goods and services traded in the international markets, P_d, is proportional to the domestic price level for all currently produced domestic goods and services, P,

$$P_d = \delta P \tag{12.1.2}$$

such that the rates of change in the two price levels are equal.[1] By substituting (12.1.2) into (12.1.1) we derive

$$P_f = \delta P \cdot r \tag{12.1.3}$$

an expression for the foreign price of domestic goods traded in the international market in terms of the exchange rate and the domestic price level.

For any given level of aggregate foreign demand and prices, real export expenditures, X/P, depend on the domestic price level and the exchange rate, or simply the foreign price of domestic goods. We shall assume that the relationship is linear,

$$\frac{X}{P} = x_0 - x_1 P_f \tag{12.1.4}$$

---

[1] Taking the full differential of (12.1.1),

$$dP_d = \delta \, dP$$

and dividing by $P_d = \delta P$ give

$$\frac{dP_d}{P_d} = \frac{dP}{P}$$

or by (12.1.3),

$$\frac{X}{P} = x_0 - x_1 \, \delta Pr \qquad (12.1.5)$$

An increase in the domestic price level or the exchange rate will raise the foreign price level of domestic goods and thereby reduce real export expenditures. Since the domestic price level and the exchange rate are positively related to the foreign price of domestic goods, $\partial(X/P)/\partial P < 0$ and $\partial(X/P)/\partial r < 0$.

Real import expenditures depend on the level of domestic real income and the foreign price of domestic goods. We shall assume that the relationship is linear,

$$\frac{IM}{P} = i_0 + i_1 \frac{Y}{P} + i_2 P_f \qquad (12.1.6)$$

where changes in real income and the foreign price of domestic goods positively affect the real import expenditures, $\partial(IM/P)/\partial(Y/P) > 0$ and $\partial(IM/P)/\partial P_f > 0$. Since the foreign price of domestic goods and both the exchange rate and the domestic price level are positively related, $\partial(IM/P)/\partial P > 0$ and $\partial(IM/P)/\partial r > 0$, at any given level of foreign demand and prices, an increase in either the domestic price level or the exchange rate increases the foreign price of domestic goods and raises real import expenditures. An increase in the domestic price level increases the price of domestic goods which compete with imports. Thus, real import expenditures increase. An increase in the exchange rate decreases the domestic price of foreign goods. Thus, real import expenditures increase.

The difference between real export and real import expenditures is called real net foreign expenditures, F/P, [the difference between (12.1.4) and (12.1.6)],

$$\frac{F}{P} = x_0 - x_1 P_f - i_0 - i_1 \frac{Y}{P} - i_2 P_f \qquad (12.1.7)$$

or, by factoring,

$$\frac{F}{P} = x_0 - i_0 - i_1 \frac{Y}{P} - (x_1 + i_2) P_f \qquad (12.1.8)$$

Increases in domestic real income increase real import expenditures and thereby decrease real net foreign expenditures, $\partial(F/P)/\partial P_f < 0$.[2] Increases in

---

[2] If the foreign price of domestic goods increases because of an increase in the domestic price of domestic goods, real import expenditures increase as the domestic economy substitutes foreign goods for domestic goods. Real export expenditures decrease as foreign economies substitutes foreign goods for domestic goods. Clearly, the domestic money value of imports increases for any given foreign price level and exchange rate. The money

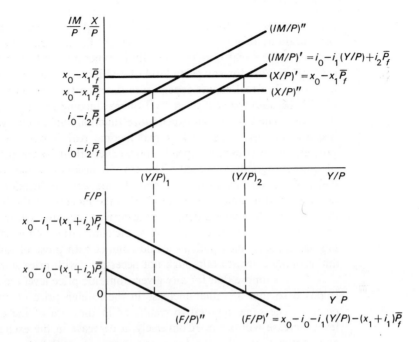

FIGURE 12.1.1

Impact of Changes in Foreign Prices on Net Export Expenditures

the foreign price of domestic goods decrease real export expenditures, increase real import expenditures, and thereby decrease net foreign expenditures, $\partial(F/P)/\partial(Y/P) < 0$.

Figure 12.1.1 illustrates the impact of changes in either the domestic price level and/or the exchange rate on the current account. In the upper quadrant is the important expenditure function, $(IM/P)'$, and the export expenditure function, $(X/P)'$. Notice that real export expenditures are invariant with respect to domestic real income. Given the foreign price of domestic goods, $\bar{P}_f$, the current account shows neither a surplus nor a deficit when domestic real income is $(Y/P)_2$ and real net foreign expenditures are zero as shown in the lower quadrant. At all other levels of real income the current account shows either a surplus or a deficit. If real income is less than $(Y/P)_2$, real export expenditures exceed real import expenditures and real net foreign expenditures are positive (a surplus exists in the current account). If domestic real income is greater than $(Y/P)_2$, real import expenditures exceed real export expenditures and real net foreign expenditures are negative (a deficit exists in the current account).

value of exports will fall if the decrease in real export expenditures outweighs the increase in the price. Professors H. S. Houthakker and S. P. Magee's empirical work indicates that the price elasticity of demand for U.S. exports is less than the price elasticity of U.S. import demand. Hence, increases in the price of U.S. goods decrease net export expenditures.

Suppose that for any given exchange rate and foreign price level, the price of domestic goods increases so that the foreign price of domestic goods increases. The real import expenditure function (12.1.6) shifts upward to $(IM/P)''$ because for any given level of real income, real import expenditures increase. The real export expenditure function (12.1.5) shifts downward to $(X/P)''$, because for any given level of real income real export expenditures decrease. The net foreign expenditure function shifts downward to $(F/P)''$, because for any given level of real income real import expenditures are greater, and real export expenditures are less than before the foreign price of domestic goods increased. The current account would show neither a deficit nor a surplus if domestic real income were to decrease to $(Y/P)_1$. If domestic real income remains at $(Y/P)_2$, the increase in the foreign price of domestic goods creates a deficit in the current account. Clearly, if monetary and fiscal policies were geared toward the elimination of the deficit by reducing real income, such policies would conflict with those of full employment and economic growth (although not necessarily with price stabilization).

Now suppose that for any given domestic price level the exchange rate is raised so that a similar increase in the foreign price of domestic goods occurs. The same qualitative results as in the case of the domestic price level increase will occur. Conversely, a decrease in the exchange rate, i.e., governments agree that the domestic currency is worth less in terms of foreign currencies than before, means that the foreign price of domestic goods will be lower. Consequently, real import expenditures will be lower and real export expenditures higher for any given level of domestic real income. Net foreign expenditures will rise with domestic real income. You may recognize this effect as a consequence of the domestic economy's *devaluation* of its currency.

12.2 THE CAPITAL ACCOUNT

The second major account in the international balance of payments is the *capital account*.[3] This account records the flow of funds between the domestic and foreign economies for purchases of assets such as capital equipment, stocks, bonds, and demand deposits. The difference between outflows and inflows of funds, or the balance of the capital account, is called net capital outflows. This balance is not included in our skeleton model because it reflects asset transfers, not current production.

In the skeleton model we explained why people will allocate their holdings of real liquid assets between real asset money and bonds. Changes

---

[3] Other minor accounts are private and public transfers to foreigners (gifts, pensions to foreigners, government grants-in-aid, etc.). We shall not consider these exogenous factors in our present analysis.

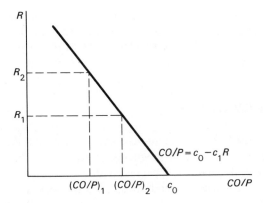

FIGURE 12.2.1

Real Net Capital Outflows

in the quantities demanded depend on changes in the interest rate. Similarly, people will split up their holdings of real domestic and real foreign assets depending on the domestic interest rates relative to foreign interest rates. For a given set of interest rates, there exists an equilibrium distribution of real asset holdings between real domestic and real foreign assets. Given the level of total real asset holdings, changes in domestic interest rates relative to foreign interest rates cause a redistribution of real asset holdings and thereby international capital flows. We shall assume that as domestic real wealth grows a larger percentage of additional real wealth will be held in foreign real assets the higher the foreign interest rates relative to domestic interest rates. As foreign real wealth grows, a smaller fraction of additional real wealth will be held in foreign portfolios the higher the foreign interest rates relative to domestic interest rates.[4] Thus, the real net outflow of capital, (CO/P) (purchases of foreign real assets less foreign purchases of domestic real assets), is inversely related to the domestic interest rate, R. We shall assume that the relationship is linear,

$$\frac{CO}{P} = c_0 - c_1 R \qquad (12.2.1)$$

where increases in the domestic interest rate decrease the net capital outflow (increases the capital inflow by more than the capital outflow), $\partial(CO/P)/\partial R = -c_1 < 0$.

Figure 12.2.1 shows a picture of (12.2.1). If the domestic interest rate decreases, people in both the domestic and foreign economies will adjust

---

[4] If domestic real wealth grows, a larger percentage of foreign real wealth can be held if foreign real wealth grows faster than domestic real wealth. The public can attempt to do as we suggest, resulting in changes in asset prices and interest rates.

their holdings of real assets so as to hold more in foreign and less in domestic real assets. Thus, real net capital outflows occur in the capital account. In Fig. 12.2.1 net capital outflows increase from $(CO/P)_1$ to $(CO/P)_2$ if the interest rate falls from R_2 to R_1.

12.3 BALANCE OF PAYMENTS

We have discussed the two major accounts in the international balance of payments. A real balance of payments surplus (if the balance is negative, it is called a real balance of payments deficit), BOP/P, is the difference between real net foreign expenditures, F/P, and real net capital outflows, CO/P,

$$\frac{BOP}{P} = \frac{F}{P} - \frac{CO}{P} \tag{12.3.1}$$

If a zero balance of payments of surplus (deficit) exists, real net foreign expenditures just equal real net capital outflows,

$$\frac{F}{P} = \frac{CO}{P} \tag{12.3.2}$$

Figure 12.3.1 shows a picture of the real balance of payments equilibrium condition specified in (12.3.2). Points along the 45° line represent equality between F/P and CO/P such that the real balance of payments surplus (deficit) is zero. Points above the 45° line represent combinations of

FIGURE 12.3.1

Real BOP Equilibrium

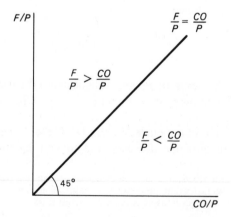

real net capital outflows and real net foreign expenditures which show a real balance of payments surplus because $(F/P) > (CO/P)$. Likewise, points below the 45° line indicate a real balance of payments deficit because $(F/P) < (CO/P)$. So far, we have not specified anything in our model which will automatically ensure that the real balance of payments surplus (deficit) will adjust to zero. We shall attempt this shortly. But for now let us try to bring together the parts of our foreign sector analysis and relate it to our skeleton model.

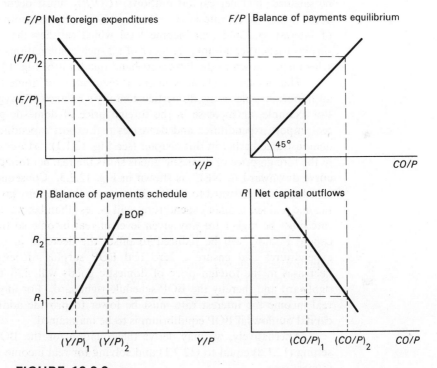

FIGURE 12.3.2

BOP Schedule

In the upper left-hand quadrant of Fig. 12.3.2 is the real net foreign expenditures curve illustrated in Fig. 12.1.1. In the lower right-hand quadrant is the real net capital outflows curve which was illustrated in Fig. 12.2.1. In the upper right-hand quadrant is the 45° line along which the real balance of payments surplus (deficit) is zero.

In the lower left-hand quadrant of Fig. 12.3.2 we derive the real balance of payments (BOP) schedule. It is defined as a locus of points representing combinations of interest rates and real income levels which satisfy the zero balance of payments surplus (deficit) condition that real net foreign expenditures equal real net capital outflows. If the interest rate were R_2, real net capital outflows would be $(CO/P)_1$. If the zero surplus (deficit) condition is to be satisfied, real net foreign expenditures must be $(F/P)_1$. If $(F/P)_1$ real net foreign expenditures are to be forthcoming, then real income must be $(Y/P)_2$. Hence, $((Y/P)_2, R_2)$ is one combination of interest rate and real income level which satisfies the zero real BOP surplus (deficit) condition. If the real income level were $(Y/P)_1$, then $(F/P)_2$ real net foreign expenditures would be forthcoming. If the zero real BOP surplus (deficit) condition is to be satisfied, real net capital outflows, $(CO/P)_2$, must occur, and they will occur if the interest rate is R_1. Hence, $((Y/P)_1, R_1)$ is another combination of interest rate and real income level which satisfies the zero real BOP surplus (deficit) condition. A locus of all such combinations forms the BOP schedule as shown in the lower left-hand quadrant of Fig. 12.3.2.

The impact of changes in the foreign price of domestic goods plays an important role in the domestic economy's balance of payments problem. For example, an increase in the foreign price of domestic goods increases real import expenditures and decreases real export expenditures. This was demonstrated earlier in this chapter (see Fig. 12.1.1). Moreover, an increase in the foreign price of domestic goods shifts the real net foreign expenditures curve downward to NEE' as shown in Fig. 12.3.3. Consequently, the BOP schedule shifts leftward to BOP'. This means that for any given level of real income real net foreign expenditures will be less than before, and the interest rate must be higher for any given level of real income so that the real net capital outflow will be reduced to offset the decrease in real net foreign expenditures and ensure a zero real BOP surplus (deficit). Conversely, decreases in the foreign price of domestic goods will shift the NEE curve rightward and thereby the BOP schedule rightward. For any given level of real income the interest rate must be lower to provide additional real net capital outflows if BOP equilibrium is to be maintained.

Alternatively, we may derive the equation for the BOP schedule by setting (12.1.8) equal to (12.2.1) and solving for real income in terms of the interest rate,

$$\frac{Y}{P} = \frac{x_0 - i_0 - c_0}{i_1} - \frac{x_1 + i_2}{i_1} P_f + \frac{c_1}{i_1} R \qquad (12.3.3)$$

The BOP equation indicates the same qualitative results as our graphical analysis, $\partial(Y/P)/\partial R > 0$, and since $\partial(Y/P)/\partial P_f < 0$, $\partial(Y/P)/\partial P < 0$ and $\partial(Y/P)/\partial r < 0$.

12.4 INTERNAL AND EXTERNAL EQUILIBRIUM

All points along the BOP schedule represent combinations of interest rate and real income levels which satisfy the zero real balance of payments surplus

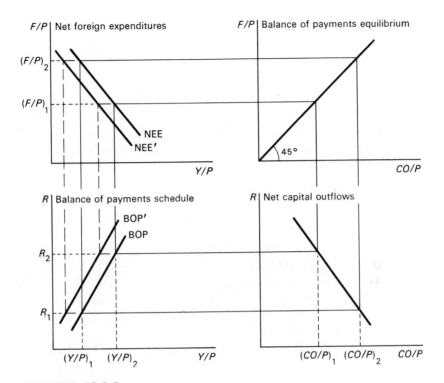

FIGURE 12.3.3

Impact of Changes in the Foreign Price of Domestic Goods
on the BOP Schedule

(deficit) condition, or, as it is sometimes called, the external equilibrium. The
internal equilibrium on the demand side of our basic model is determined by
the intersection of the *IS* and *LM* schedules. To determine whether any
given internal equilibrium combination of interest rate and real income levels
will yield an external equilibrium, we can superimpose the BOP schedule onto
the *IS-LM* diagram as shown in Fig. 12.4.1. The internal equilibrium combination of interest and real income, $((Y/P)_1, R_1)$, is determined by *IS-LM*
equilibrium; this combination yields a balance of payments deficit because
real net capital outflows exceed real net foreign expenditures as shown in the
upper right-hand quadrant at point *d*.

Similarly, if the BOP schedule lies to the right of the *IS-LM* equilibrium,
a balance of payments surplus exists. If the BOP, *IS*, and *LM* schedules
intersect at the same combination of interest rate and real income, an internal-
external equilibrium exists.

A balance of payments deficit means that the internal equilibrium real
income is so high and the interest rate so low that real net capital outflows
exceed real net foreign expenditures. When commercial banks purchase

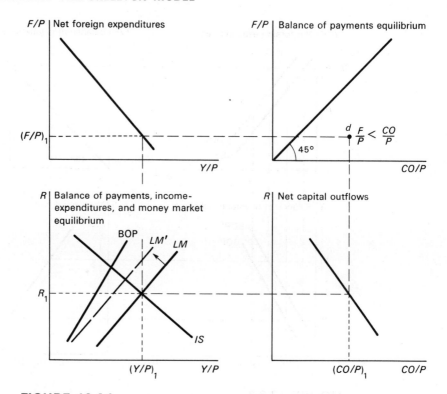

FIGURE 12.4.1

Internal and External Equilibrium

foreign exchange from the Fed, their reserves decrease by the amount of the deficit. With fixed exchange rates, this means that the domestic banking system experiences an external drain on its reserves and the money stock decreases.[5] As our skeleton model shows, the decrease in the nominal money stock will reduce output demand and the domestic price level such that the real money stock decreases (if the nominal money stock decreases more than the domestic price level).

In the absence of open market purchases of government bonds to

[5] With fixed exchange rates a deficit means that unless demand deposits of foreign currencies are owned by foreigners, domestic commercial banks are losing (on balance) demand deposits. Either people in the domestic economy are buying foreign currency with domestic currency checks and paying for their purchases in foreign currencies, or they are paying out domestic currency checks which foreigners are depositing in foreign banks. Regardless of the means of payment, domestic commercial banks are net losers of reserves when a deficit exists.

At this point the Fed is also a net loser of foreign exchange reserves as commercial banks draw down foreign exchange balances equal to the loss of unborrowed reserves held at the Fed. The Fed can restore its foreign exchange balances by either selling gold to foreign central banks or borrowing from foreigners by selling short-term government bonds.

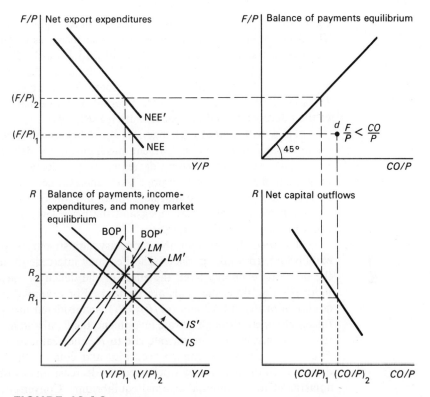

FIGURE 12.4.2

Automatic Monetary Adjustment Mechanism

counter the external reserve drain, the *LM* schedule in Fig. 12.4.1 will shift leftward toward *LM'* as the real money stock decreases. Hence, the internal equilibrium, $((Y/P)_1, R_1)$, is only temporary when a deficit exists. As long as the *IS-LM* intersection is not on the BOP schedule, the deficit shifts the *LM* curve toward the intersection of the *IS* and BOP schedules where both internal and external equilibria are simultaneously attained.

   Not only do decreases in the real money stock shift the *LM* schedule leftward, but the decrease in the domestic price level will shift the *IS* schedule rightward due to the wealth effect. In Fig. 12.4.2 the intersection of the *LM* and *IS* schedules established internal equilibrium at $((Y/P)_2, R_1)$. The BOP schedule again is shown to lie to the left of the *IS-LM* equilibrium values. Decreases in the real money stock that result from decreases in the domestic price level (output demand and the quantity of output supplied decreases) shift the *LM* schedule leftward toward *LM'*. The decrease in the domestic price level also decreases the foreign price of domestic goods (with fixed exchange rates). Consequently, the net foreign expenditures function shifts rightward to NEE′ and the BOP schedule shifts rightward toward BOP′.[6] The decrease in the domestic price level also increases real wealth, and the wealth effect shifts the *IS* schedule rightward toward *IS*′. The temporary equilibrium, $((Y/P)_2, R_1)$, is displaced by domestic decreases which occur as the deficit decreases the real money stock. The price effects shift the *LM*, *IS*, and BOP schedules to where internal and external equilibria values of the interest rate and real income are $((Y/P)_1, R_2)$.

Thus, with a fixed exchange rate the deficit is self-liquidating through an automatic monetary adjustment mechanism. A deficit decreases the real money stock and thereby decreases output demand, the quantity of output supplied, the domestic price level, and real net foreign expenditures; it raises the interest rate so that net capital outflows decrease. Conversely, a surplus increases the money stock and the price level and causes just the opposite changes in the variables.

The Fed can prevent the monetary adjustment to internal-external equilibrium from taking place. The Fed may intercede in order to insulate the domestic economy from the effect of the deficit or surplus until other more pressing domestic goals are realized. For example, if a deficit exists as shown in Fig. 12.4.2 and $((Y/P)_2, R_1)$ is considered necessary to achieve full employment through private investment, the fiscal and monetary authorities would not let the interest rate rise to R_2 and real income fall to $(Y/P)_1$. The Fed can buy government securities and counter the external reserve drain. Then the real money stock need not decrease and cause the automatic adjustment to the internal-external equilibrium. Conversely, in the case of a surplus, the Fed could sell government securities to absorb increases in reserves, or it could simply refuse to accept foreign exchange deposits as reserves.

Monetary and fiscal authorities may wish to attain the internal-external equilibrium but one which is different from that which would be established by the automatic monetary adjustment mechanism. They can use monetary and fiscal policies to shift the *IS* and *LM* schedules to their target values of interest rate and real income. Moreover, direct balance of payments policies may be implemented to shift the BOP schedule so that the desired internal-external equilibrium is established.

The government may adjust exchange rates in order to affect the foreign price of domestic goods. In Fig. 12.4.2 if $((Y/P)_2, R_1)$ is the desired internal-external equilibrium, the government desires to shift the BOP schedule rightward along the *IS* schedule to the intersection of the *IS* and *LM* schedules. A decrease in the exchange rate decreases the foreign price of domestic goods and increases real net foreign expenditures for any given level of domestic real income. Hence, the BOP schedule shifts rightward toward the desired internal-external equilibrium, $((Y/P)_2, R_1)$. Conversely, an increase in the

---

[6] See footnote 2.

exchange rate increases the foreign price on domestic goods. Hence, for any given level of real income, real net foreign expenditures fall. The BOP schedule shifts leftward and tends to liquidate a surplus in the balance of payments.

The government can also change the balance of the current account by changes in import and export tariffs, import quotas, taxes, and subsidies. Such measures change net foreign expenditures for any given level of real income and thereby shift the BOP schedule. However, both tariffs and quota systems reduce the gains in efficiency and welfare between nations, and they are generally imposed only when all else does not correct an extreme situation. Moreover, import restrictions usually cause other countries to retaliate on domestic exports, in which case everyone is worse off.

Still other means of direct balance of payments adjustment are those measures which affect real capital outflows, such as foreign credit restraints on goods, and restrictions on direct investment in foreign production. These measures shift the net capital outflow curve and thereby the BOP schedule.

Freely Fluctuating Exchange Rates

Direct measures which influence the current and capital accounts are usually taken to avoid exchange rate adjustments. Fixed exchange rates minimize the uncertainty in international currency markets and tend to encourage trade. Moreover, if a country is dependant on imports, a devaluation of its currency raises the price of imports. This is politically unpopular. Thus, changes in exchange rates are usually considered a last resort of manipulating the BOP schedule.

Many economists argue that we would eliminate our balance of payments problems and the necessity for stop-gap kinds of policies if we converted to a freely fluctuating exchange rate system. Balance of payments deficits and surpluses can exist because of the fixed exchange rate system. If the exchange rate were free to fluctuate with changes in currency market conditions, it would continue to change. Such changes continue to shift the BOP schedule until the internal-external equilibrium is attained. In this way the domestic economy is insulated from the foreign sector.

Foreigners demand domestic currency to buy domestic exports. Thus, the demand for domestic currency, $D_\$$, depends on the domestic price of domestic goods, $P_d = \delta_P$, times the real export expenditures (12.1.5),

$$D_\$ = P_d(x_0 - x_1\,\delta Pr) \tag{12.4.1}$$

The lower the exchange rate, for example, francs per dollar, the more dollars foreigners demand to purchase exports, $\partial D_\$/\partial r < 0$.

Similarly, people in the domestic economy supply domestic currency to foreigners by buying imports and through net capital outflows. Thus, the supply of domestic currency, $S_\$$, depends on the domestic currency value of imports, P_f/r, times real import expenditures (12.1.6) and net capital outflows (12.2.1),

$$S_\$ = \frac{P_f}{r}\left(i_0 + i_1\frac{Y}{P} + i_2\,\delta Pr + c_0 - c_1 R\right) \tag{12.4.2}$$

or, since $r = P_f/P_d$,

$$S_\$ = P_d\left(i_0 + i_1\frac{Y}{P} + i_2\,\delta Pr + c_0 - c_1 R\right) \tag{12.4.3}$$

The higher the exchange rate, for example, francs per dollar, the more dollars will be supplied by purchasing imports, $\partial S_\$/\partial r > 0$.

By dividing both the supply (12.4.3) and demand (12.4.1) for dollars through by $P_d = P_f/r$ and setting the real value of dollars demanded equal to the real dollars supplied, we can solve for the equilibrium exchange rate in the currency market:

$$r = \frac{x_0 - i_0 - c_0}{(x_1 + \delta i_2)P} - \frac{i_1}{(x_1 + \delta i_2)P}\frac{Y}{P} + \frac{c_1}{(x_1 + \delta i_2)P}R \tag{12.4.4}$$

This operation is equivalent to solving the BOP equation (12.3.3) for the exchange rate. Given the internal equilibrium values of P, Y/P, and R, the equilibrium value of r can be determined. Thus, if the exchange rate is endogenous, it will adjust to a value consistent with internal-external equilibrium. The BOP schedule will intersect the *IS* schedule where the *LM* schedule intersects the *IS* schedule.

Figure 12.4.3 shows the supply, $S_\$$, and demand, $D_\$$, for dollars for given values of P, Y, and R. The equilibrium exchange rate (francs per dollar) is r_2 and the equilibrium quantity of dollars is $\$_1$.

Suppose now that due to expansionary monetary policy domestic real income and the price level increase and the domestic interest rate decreases. Initially a balance of payments deficit would exist. Real import expenditures would increase with the increase in the domestic price level and real income. Real net capital outflows would increase as the interest rate falls. Thus, the supply curve for dollars would increase to $S'_\$$. The increase in the domestic price level will also reduce export expenditures and thereby the demand for domestic dollars to $D'_\$$.

If the supply curve shifts to the left more than the demand curve (as reasonable implied by the equations of the model), the equilibrium quantity of dollars will increase to $\$_2$ and the exchange rate will fall to r_1. Consequently, the BOP schedule would shift rightward to eliminate the deficit and ensure a new internal-external equilibrium.

Conversely, increases in the market determined exchange rate will

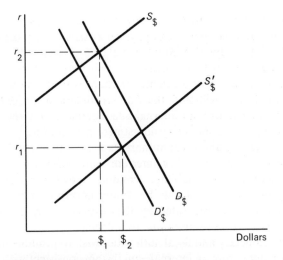

FIGURE 12.4.3

Freely Fluctuating Exchange Rates

eliminate an initial balance of payments surplus automatically as the BOP schedule shifts leftward. With the flexible exchange rate, the changes in the foreign price of domestic goods shift the BOP schedule so that it shifts along the *IS* schedule to the internal equilibrium values of the interest rate and real income.

With fixed exchange rates the Fed buys and sells foreign currency from commercial banks at a fixed rate. It absorbs net balances of foreign currency as international reserves. If the net balance is positive (negative), reserves increase (decrease). Thus, reserves are used to maintain exchange rates. In the case of flexible exchange rates, the central bank need not take any such action. Instead, the commercial banks and traders can buy and sell foreign exchange as they need it and permit *r* to change freely in the currency market. Changes in *r* shift the BOP schedule and insulate the domestic economy from the foreign sector. External equilibrium adjusts to internal equilibrium and monetary and fiscal policies can turn to pursuing domestic problems of full employment, growth, and price stability.

12.5 SUMMARY

In this chapter we expanded the foreign sector of our skeleton model. We discussed the two major accounts in the international balance of payments, the current account and the capital account. The current account balance is called net foreign expenditures, while the capital account balance is called net capital outflows. When the current account balance equals the capital account balance a zero balance of payments exists. When the current exceeds (is less than) the capital account, a balance of payments surplus (deficit) exists. If the Fed does not engage in open market operations to sterilize the impact of a surplus or a deficit, the changes in the money stock and the domestic price level will shift the *LM* schedule and the BOP schedule toward each other until both internal and external equilibria are established. This is the automatic monetary adjustment mechanism.

The monetary and fiscal authorities may not wish to let the automatic adjustments take place if they interfere with other more urgent domestic problems such as price stability, economic growth, and full employment. The Fed can sterilize a surplus by selling government bonds and thereby decrease the reserves generated by the surplus, or by buying government bonds to offset a reserve drain due to a deficit.

If the monetary and fiscal authorities wish to promote internal-external equilibrium but ensure an internal equilibrium consistent with the other goals of the 1946 Employment Act, they can use monetary and fiscal policies to bring about the desired internal equilibrium and then shift the BOP schedule to where internal and external equilibria coincide. They may attempt to do this by direct action on the current account (tariffs, import quotas, taxes, and subsidies) and the capital account (a tax on purchases of foreign assets and restrictions on lending for purchases of foreign assets). Direct actions may relieve the pressure to change exchange rates. However, fixed exchange rates provide the certainty in currency markets which many believe is essential to the encouragement of international trade. Flexible exchange rates create uncertainty but eliminate the necessity for anyone to do anything to correct for balance of payments problems. The flexible exchange rate system means that the international currency market ensures external equilibrium and internal equilibrium simultaneously. There appears to be a movement toward this system, but old ways are hard to put aside.

REVIEW QUESTIONS

1. Given
$$X/P = x_0 - x_1 P_f$$
$$IM/P = i_0 + i_1(Y/P) + i_2 P_f$$

where $x_0 = \$520,$ $x_1 = \$2,$ $P_f = 110$

$i_0 = \$90,$ $i_1 = .1,$ $i_2 = \$1$

(a) Calculate real export and import expenditures if $Y = \$1100$.
(b) Calculate the level of real income at which net foreign expenditures are zero.
(c) If the foreign price level of domestic goods increases to 120 what will be the value of net foreign expenditures?

2. If net foreign expenditures exceed net capital outflows, is the system implied by the model to the left or right of the BOP schedule? Explain the process of adjustment to balance of payments equilibrium when the interest rate is assumed exogenous.

3. Explain the process of automatic adjustment to internal-external equilibrium when a balance of payments surplus exists under a fixed exchange rate system. List the other assumptions on which this automatic adjustment is based.

SELECTED READINGS

HOUTHAKKER, H. S., and S. P. MAGEE, "Income and Price Elasticities in World Trade," *Review of Economics and Statistics*, 5 (May 1969), 111–25.

KINDLEBURGER, C., *International Economics*, Homewood, Ill.: Irwin, 1973.

KRUEGER, A. O., "Balance of Payments Theory," *Journal of Economic Literature*, 7 (March 1969), 1–26.

MUNDELL, R. A., "The Monetary Dynamics of International Adjustment under Fixed and Flexible Exchange Rates," *Quarterly Journal of Economics*, 74 (May 1960), 227–57.

———, "The Appropriate Use of Monetary and Fiscal Policy for External and Internal Balance," *IMF Staff Papers*, 9 (March 1962), 70–7.

———, *International Economics*, New York: Macmillan, 1968.

WRIGHTSMAN, D., "*IS, LM* and External Equilibrium: A Graphical Analysis," *American Economic Review*, 60 (March 1970), 203–8.

CHAPTER 13

Extensions of Monetary Economics

13.1 THE ENDOGENEITY OF MONEY SUPPLY

Throughout this book we have assumed that the money supply is an exogenous variable. In Chapter 5 we explained how the Fed controls the money supply by direct control over base money and reserve requirements. This is the basis for the traditional explanation of the money supply. A new explanation is based on the endogenous character of money supply. It stresses the importance of income, the interest rate, and other market conditions in explaining the money supply.

In this section we shall increase our understanding of the money creation process by exploring the endogenous character of money supply. To do this we shall begin with the generalized expression of the money supply,

$$MS = mB \tag{13.1.1}$$

where MS is the money supply, m is the base money multiplier, and B is base money. In Chapter 5 we used the naive version of the base money multiplier, $m = 1/r_D$, where only changes in base money and/or the required reserve ratio on demand deposits explained changes in the money supply. The money supply is narrowly defined to include currency held by the public, C^P, and demand deposits, DD,

$$MS = C^P + DD \tag{13.1.2}$$

Base money is defined to include currency held by the public and total unborrowed reserves owned by commercial banks, RES,

$$B = C^P + \text{RES} \tag{13.1.3}$$

Solving (13.1.1) for the base money multiplier gives

$$m = \frac{MS}{B} \qquad (13.1.4)$$

Substituting (13.1.2) and (13.1.3) into (13.1.4) gives

$$m = \frac{C^P + DD}{C^P + RES} \qquad (13.1.5)$$

Substituting (5.1.7),

$$RES = r_D DD + r_T TD + (e - br)(DD + TD) \qquad (13.1.6)$$

into (13.1.5) gives

$$m = \frac{C^P + DD}{C^P + r_D DD + r_T TD + (e - br)(DD + TD)} \qquad (13.1.7)$$

and dividing both the numerator and denominator of (13.1.7) by DD gives

$$m = \frac{(C^P/DD) + 1}{(C^P/DD) + r_D + r_T(TD/DD) + (e - br)[1 + (TD/DD)]} \qquad (13.1.8)$$

This is an expanded definition of the base money multiplier which includes not only the required reserve ratios on demand deposits, r_D, and time deposits, r_T, but public preference for currency relative to demand deposits (the currency ratio), C^P/DD, public preferences for time relative to demand deposits (the time deposit ratio), TD/DD, and the commercial banking system's net free reserves ratio, $e - br$.[1] The expanded definition of the base money multi-

---

[1] There are three distinct roles which have been assigned to the net free reserve concept. One is the causal role which free reserves play in the money creation process. The second is its role as a *target*, which the Fed uses to control the money supply. The third is its role as an *indicator*, which the financial community can use to determine whether monetary *ease* or *tightness* is forthcoming.

The target and indicator functions of free reserves are based on the importance of the causal role of free reserves in the money creation process. However, the Fed does not consistently use free reserves as a target for control of the money stock. In fact, in recent years it has used free reserves less frequently in its target package. Thus, free reserves are an inconsistent indicator of Fed intent. Moreover, free reserves are not a good indicator to the financial community of money market conditions. Free reserves are but one factor which play an important role in determining money market conditions. The foolhardiness of placing primary emphasis on one variable on one side of a market is obvious.

Although the importance of the causal role of free reserves in the money creation process is implicit in the arguments for using free reserves as a target and/or an indicator, the evidence which suggests that free reserves are a poor target (if used alone) and indicator of monetary ease or tightness does not imply that free reserves do not play an important causal role on the supply side of the money market.

plier is important because it introduces the variables which indicate that not only the Fed but the behavior of the public and the member banks can influence the money supply.

Substituting (13.1.8) into (13.1.1) gives

$$MS = \frac{(C^P/DD) + 1}{(C^P/DD) + r_D + r_T(TD/DD) + (e - br)[1 + (TD/DD)]} B$$

$$(13.1.9)$$

an expanded version of the money supply equation.

As long as C^P/DD, TD/DD, and $e - br$ are constants, the Fed can control the money supply by controlling, r_D, r_T, and B. However, the constancy of C^P/DD, TD/DD, and $e - br$ is based on given values of income, interest rates, and other market conditions. As income and/or the interest rate change, changes occur in the banking system's desired net free reserve ratio, the public's desired currency ratio, and/or the public's desired time deposit ratio.[2] Unfortunately, the empirical evidence does not consistently support the hypothesized behavior of the public and the banking system, because except for a few variables which include income and the interest rate, many of the market forces have not yet been identified. Hence, the problems of explaining the behavior of the public and the banking system are unresolved.

However, there is some empirical evidence to support the hypothesis that the currency ratio is inversely related to income, $\partial(C^P/DD)/\partial Y < 0$.[3] For example, an increase in income decreases the currency ratio because an increase in income implies that people expect more transactions requiring payment by check than those requiring payment by cash. In (13.1.9) a decrease in the currency ratio increases the money supply, $\partial MS/\partial(C^P/DD) < 0$. Hence, an increase in income increases the money supply, $\partial MS/\partial Y > 0$.

There is also empirical evidence to support the hypothesis that the time deposit ratio is positively related to income, $\partial(TD/DD)/\partial Y > 0$, and inversely related to the interest rate, $\partial(TD/DD)/\partial R < 0$. Time deposits are generally considered a luxury good and demand deposits a necessity. An increase in income increases both time and demand deposits but time deposits more than demand deposits. Moreover, since time deposits are a closer substitute for other interest-bearing assets than non-interest-bearing demand deposits, an increase in market interest rates means that the public will hold less time and demand deposits but that they will decrease time deposits more

---

[2] If changes in C^P/DD, TD/DD, and $e - br$ are predictable, the Fed can use changes in r_D, r_T, and B to offset any undesirable change in the money stock.

[3] The currency ratio appears in both the numerator and the denominator of the base money multiplier. Since the sum of the other parameters of the denominator is less than 1, increases (decreases) in the currency ratio decrease (increase) the base money multiplier.

than demand deposits.[4] In (13.1.9) an increase in the time deposit ratio decreases the money supply, $\partial MS/\partial(TD/DD) < 0$. Hence, an increase in income decreases the money supply, $\partial MS/\partial Y < 0$, and an increase in the interest rate increases the money supply, $\partial MS/\partial R > 0$.

During the depression of the 1930s banks held a very large volume of excess reserves relative to their total deposit liabilities because they were afraid of excessive deposit withdrawals. In "normal times" where this fear motive subsides and the profit motive dominates, the desired excess reserve ratio largely depends on the opportunity cost of holding non-interest-bearing excess reserves, i.e., the interest rates on alternative assets. In Chapter 5 we explained why people will allocate their holdings of assets between non-interest-bearing money and interest-bearing bonds. Changes in the quantities demanded depend on changes in the interest rate. Similarly, banks will split their holdings of assets between non-interest-bearing excess reserves and interest-bearing assets such as bonds. For any given market interest rate, there exists an equilibrium distribution of asset holdings between excess reserves and other assets. Changes in the interest rate causes a redistribution of assets and negatively affect bank holdings of excess reserves, $\partial e/\partial R < 0$. For example, a decrease in the interest rate increases the desired level of excess reserves relative to total deposit liabilities. As the actual level adjusts to the desired level, (13.1.9) shows that an increase in the excess reserve ratio decreases the money supply, $\partial MS/\partial e < 0$. Thus, the decrease in the interest rate decreases the money supply, $\partial MS/\partial R > 0$.

Another important way in which the changes in the interest rate can affect banks' behavior is by changing banks borrowing among themselves and from the Fed. Banks borrow reserves to cover reserve deficiencies or when it is profitable to do so. When market interest rates rise relative to the cost of bank borrowing, banks find it profitable to borrow reserves and purchase assets where the returns exceed the cost. Thus, the borrowed reserve ratio is positively related to the difference between the market rate of interest and the cost of bank borrowing, r_F, i.e., the discount rate at the Fed,

$$br = f(R - r_F) \qquad (13.1.10)$$

where $\partial br/\partial R > 0$, and $\partial br/\partial r_F < 0$.

Since r_F is controlled by the Fed, it is the positive relationship between br and R that concerns us at this point because it reflects in impact of market forces on the borrowed reserve ratio and therefore the money supply. In (13.1.9), the borrowed reserve ratio is positively related to the money supply, $\partial MS/\partial br > 0$. Hence, the money supply is positively related to the interest rate, $\partial MS/\partial R > 0$.

---

[4] Economists do not agree on the expected sign of the relationship between time deposits and the interest rate. If, not generally true, our explanation is realistic when other asset rates rise above the time deposit rate when the time deposit rate is at its ceiling rate.

We can subtract the borrowed from the excess reserve ratio to obtain the net free reserve ratio, $e - br$. Since the excess reserve ratio is inversely related to the interest rate and the borrowed reserve ratio is positively related to the interest rate, the net free reserve ratio is negatively related to the interest rate, $\partial(e - br)/\partial R < 0$. In (13.1.9), since changes in the net free reserve ratio negatively affect the money supply, $\partial MS/\partial(e - br) < 0$, and changes in the interest rate positively affect the money supply, $\partial MS/\partial R > 0$.

We have explained how changes in the interest rate and income can influence the money supply. The money supply is positively related to the interest rate, inversely related to income through the time deposit ratio, and positively related to income through the currency ratio. An increase in the interest rate lowers the net free reserve ratio (lowers the excess reserve ratio and raises the borrowed reserve ratio) and lowers the time deposit ratio, both of which increase the money supply. An increase in income decreases the currency ratio and increases the money supply. An increase in income raises the time deposit ratio and decreases the money supply. Conversely, decreases in the interest rate and income will have the opposite results.

All the variables which determine the money supply are not generally included in the specification of the money supply function. The argument as to which variables to include depends on one's view of each variable's relative as well as absolute importance in explaining money supply. One group of economists holds that base money and reserve requirements are the primary determinants of the money supply and that income and interest rates add very little in terms of predictive ability. This view gives effective control of the money stock to the Fed, as we did in our skeleton model. Another group of economists holds that income, interest rates, and other market conditions are the primary determinants of the money supply and that there is not a predictable relationship between the changes in the money stock and variables under Fed control; i.e., public and commercial bank behavior can inhibit the Fed's ability to control the money stock.

The empirical evidence supports parts of both views. The primary determinants of the money stock appear to be the interest rate and the primary means whereby the Fed influences the money supply, that is, base money.[5] Thus, we can tentatively conclude that the money supply is partially endogenous because of the interest rate and partially exogenous because of base money. Both are important. For this reason the money supply function includes both the interest rate and base money. In real terms it can be written,

$$\frac{MS}{P} = MS\left(R, \frac{B}{P}\right) \qquad (13.1.11)$$

[5] This statement is not strictly accurate. Monetary policy is generally accommodating to fiscal policy, particularly government expenditures. Thus, changes in base money depend on changes in government expenditures. If government expenditures are predetermined, then Fed power to perform its independent function is relinquished.

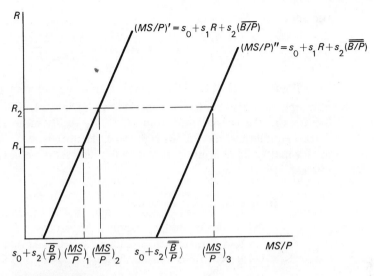

FIGURE 13.1.1

Money Supply Function

where $\partial MS/\partial R > 0$ and $\partial MS/\partial(B/P) > 0$. By assuming that (13.1.11) is linear,

$$\frac{MS}{P} = s_0 + s_1 R + s_2 \frac{B}{P} \tag{13.1.12}$$

Figure 13.1.1 illustrates the theory of money supply specified by (13.1.12). For given values of real base money, $\overline{B/P}$, and the parameters, the horizontal intercept of the money supply curve, $(MS/P)'$, is $s_0 + s_2(\overline{B/P})$ and the slope is $\partial(MS/P)/\partial R = s_1 > 0$. An increase in the interest rate increases the quantity of real money supplied. For example, if the interest rate rises from R_1 to R_2, the quantity of real money supplied increases from $(MS/P)_1$ to $(MS/P)_2$. Conversely, a decrease in the interest rate reduces the quantity of real money supplied. An increase in nominal base money due to Fed purchases of government securities (such that real base money increases) increases the real money supply for any given interest rate. For example, if real base money increases from $\overline{B/P}$ to $\overline{\overline{B/P}}$, the money supply curve shifts rightward to $(MS/P)''$. For any given interest rate, for example, R_2, the real money supply increases to $(MS/P)_3$. Conversely, a decrease in real base money decreases the real money supply for any given interest rate.

The endogeneity of money supply means that the money market equilibrium curve in the skeleton model,

$$\frac{MT}{P} = \frac{MS}{P} - \frac{MA}{P} \tag{13.1.13}$$

becomes

$$\frac{MT}{P} = \left(s_0 + s_1 R + s_2 \frac{B}{P}\right) - \frac{MA}{P} \qquad (13.1.14)$$

Figure 13.1.2 shows the money market equilibrium quadrant. The intercepts now also contain the market rate of interest. Given $B/P = \overline{B/P}$, increases in the interest rate from R_1 to R_2 to R_3 mean that the money market equilibrium curve shifts rightward. Hence, there is a whole family of money market equilibrium curves, one for each set of values for the interest rate and real base money.

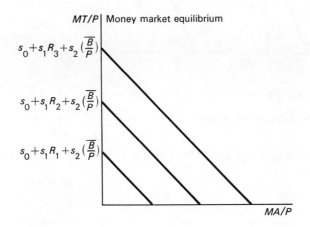

FIGURE 13.1.2

Changes in the Interest Rate and the Money Market Equilibrium Curve

For a given value of real base money, Fig. 13.1.3 shows that when the interest rate is an important determinant of the real money supply, the *LM* schedule is more horizontal (interest elastic). This means that when the interest rate increases, for example, from R_1 to R_2, the level of real income increases from $(Y/P)_1$ to $(Y/P)_2$ if the interest rate is not considered an important determinant of real money supply. However, when the interest rate is considered important, the same increase in the interest rate increases real income from $(Y/P)_1$ to $(Y/P)_3 > (Y/P)_2$. Thus, it is important to know in evaluating the effects of policy whether or not the interest rate is an important determinant in the money creation process and to what extent it is important.

The policy implications are clear. Shifts in the *IS* schedule initiated by fiscal policies are more effective if the interest rate is an important determinant of the real money supply. For a given value of real base money, Fig. 13.1.4 shows the LM_{ex} schedule under the hypothesis that the interest rate *is not*

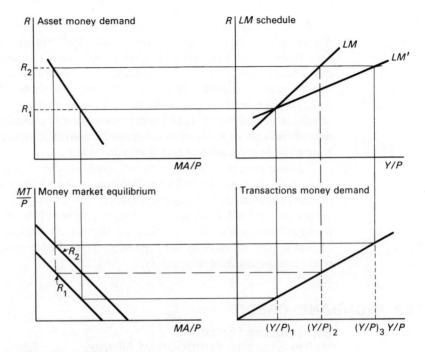

FIGURE 13.1.3

Endogenous Money Supply and the *LM* Schedule

FIGURE 13.1.4

Endogenous Money Supply and the Effectiveness of Fiscal Policies

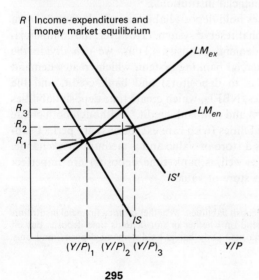

important in explaining the real money supply and the LM_{en} schedule under the hypothesis that the interest rate *is* an important determinant. Initial *IS–LM* equilibrium is shown by $((Y/P)_1, R_1)$. If, for example, government expenditures increase, the *IS* schedule shifts rightward to *IS'*, and the interest rate rises more and real income rises less along LM_{ex} than along LM_{en}. Hence, whether or not the interest rate is an important determinant of the real money supply is an important question in evaluating the effectiveness of fiscal policies. There is substantial empirical evidence to support the contention that the interest rate is very important.

However, the evidence does not diminish the ability of the Fed to control the quantity of real money balances in the economy. If the Fed can predict the movements in important market forces which explain both money supply and demand, it can use the money supply variables which it controls—nominal base money, etc.—to offset any undesirable changes in the quantity of real money balances in the economy. Thus, Fed control is compatible with an endogenous money supply.

13.2 NONBANK CREDIT

Substitutes for the Value Storage Function of Money

Financial institutions act as intermediaries of funds. Financial intermediation is the process of collecting current savings from some economic units and making them available to other economic units who wish to spend additional funds on current production. Financial intermediaries supply deeds to deposits (assets to depositors) in exchange for deposits (liabilities to financial institutions) and supply credit (liabilities to borrowers) in exchange for notes or bonds (assets to financial institutions).

All financial intermediaries hold deposit liabilities, which permits them to extend credit under a fractional reserve system. However, the commercial banking system alone holds demand deposits. Thus, we can divide the financial sector into the commercial banking system, which creates demand deposit liabilities (money assets to depositors) and bank credit, and the nonbank financial intermediaries, NBFIs, which create time deposit liabilities (nonmoney assets to depositors) and nonbank credit.[6] Although both create credit, only demand deposit liabilities (with rare exceptions) are perfect substitutes for legal money used as a store of value and a medium of exchange. NBFI time deposit liabilities (as well as bank time deposits) are imperfect substitutes for money used as a store of value.

---

[6] Commercial banks also hold time deposit liabilities. Whether or not a financial institution is a bank or nonbank does not depend on whether or not it holds time deposits but on whether or not it holds demand deposits. Only banks hold demand deposits, and only the banking system can create them.

Since World War II, in the United States the growth of NBFIs, such as savings and loan associations, insurance companies, pension funds, mutual savings banks, and credit unions, has been phenomenal. Their deposit liabilities have grown at an annual rate of about 8 percent, while commercial bank deposit liabilities have grown at an annual rate of about 4.7 percent. The relative growth of NBFIs prompted Professors J. G. Gurley, E. S. Shaw, and others to investigate the increasingly important role played by NBFIs in explaining money demand.

As an economy grows the highly liquid interest-bearing deposit liabilities of NBFIs increase. These deposits substitute for asset (or idle) money balances because they are better (more profitable) stores of value.[7] As a result, money is used less as a store of value and more as a medium of exchange. The released money balances augment the supply of loanable funds so that interest rates fall.

For simplification purposes we shall assume that all bonds are perfect substitutes, so that only one bond rate is important in determining money demand, and that all NBFI deposits are perfect substitutes, so that only one NBFI interest rate is important. Thus, the demand for asset money balances can be expressed as a function of the bond rate, R^B, and the interest rate on NBFI deposits, R^D. If we assume that the relationship is linear,

$$\frac{MA}{P} = c_0 \quad c_1 R^B - c_2 R^D \tag{13.2.1}$$

For any given NBFI deposit rate an increase in the bond rate decreases the quantity of money held as a store of value, $\partial(MA/P)/\partial R^B < 0$. For any given bond rate an increase in the NBFI deposit rate decreases the demand for money held as a store of value, $\partial(MA/P)/\partial R^D < 0$. You will remember that the bond rate is not only the yield on bonds but also the cost of borrowing funds by bond issues. For simplification purposes we shall assume that the bond rate represents the cost of borrowing all loanable funds including those made available by NBFIs.

Figure 13.2.1 shows the asset money demand function, $(MA/P)'$, for given values of the parameters and a fixed NBFI deposit rate, $\bar{R}^D$. For any given bond rate, say R_1^B, real asset money balances are $(MA/P)_2$. If the NBFI deposit rate increases from $\bar{R}^D$ to $\bar{\bar{R}}^D$, real deposits held by NBFIs

---

[7] The inclusion of the deposit liabilities of NBFIs in the theory of money demand is a logical extension of the theory of asset money demand developed in Chapter 5. However, instead of assuming that bonds and other nonmonetary assets are perfect substitutes, so that only one interest rate is important, we recognize that there are as many different interest rates as there are imperfect substitutes among nonmonetary assets. In the three-asset case of deciding how much to hold in money, bonds, and deposits held by NBFIs, relative interest rates of these imperfect substitutes are dependent on the relative quantities supplied.

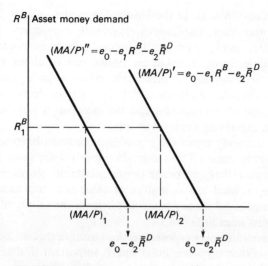

FIGURE 13.2.1

Impact of Changes in the NBFI Deposit Rate on the Demand for Asset Money Balances

FIGURE 13.2.2

Impact of Changes in the NBFI Deposit Rate on the *LM* Schedule

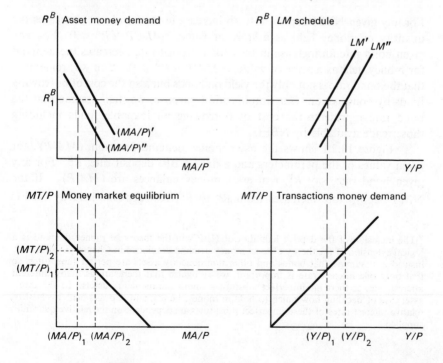

substitute for real asset money balances and the asset money demand curve decreases to $(MA/P)''$. For any given bond rate, say R_1^B, real asset money balances decrease from $(MA/P)_2$ to $(MA/P)_1$. Conversely, decreases in the NBFI deposit rate increase the asset money demand curve and increase real asset money balances for any given bond rate.

Figure 13.2.2 shows the influence of changes in the NBFI deposit rate on the LM schedule. The LM' schedule corresponds to the $(MA/P)'$ demand curve for asset money. For any given bond rate, say R_1^B, and the real money supply, real income is $(Y/P)_1$, real asset balances are $(MA/P)_2$, and real transactions balances are $(MT/P)_1$.

Now suppose that the NBFI deposit rate increases; real NBFI deposits will increase and the asset money demand curve will decrease to $(MA/P)''$. Correspondingly, the LM schedule shifts rightward to LM''. For any given bond rate, say R_1^B, real income increases to $(Y/P)_2$. As a result, real asset money balances decrease to $(MA/P)_1$ and real transactions money balances increase to $(MT/P)_2$. Thus, NBFIs can transfer idle money balances to active balances and expand output. The extent to which this is possible depends on the degree of substitutability between money, bonds, and the deposits of NBFIs.

Figure 13.2.3 illustrates the influence of NBFIs on output demand and the price level. Given the money stock, $\overline{MS}$, and the NBFI deposit rate, the LM', IS, S and D' curves indicate the initial equilibrium value of the price level, P_1, the bond or loan rate, R_2^B, real income, $(Y/P)_1$, real asset money balances, $(MA/P)_2$, and real transactions money balances, $(MT/P)_1$. Changes in the deposit rate and subsequent intermediation displace equilibrium. For example, an increase in the NBFI deposit rate shifts the asset money demand curve to $(MA/P)''$ and the LM schedule toward LM''. The decrease in money demand creates an excess supply of real money balances. As the bond or loan rate falls to eliminate the excess money supply, investment is stimulated, output demand rises to D'', and the price level rises to P_2.

Thus, NBFIs transfer idle money balances, $(MA/P)_2 - (MA/P)_1$, by raising the NBFI deposit rate and subsequent intermediation, i.e., augmenting the supply of loanable funds so as to decrease the rate at which investors borrow funds. Our diagram shows that in the absence of a wealth effect which would shift the IS leftward, small changes in the interest rate induce a relatively larger change in output demand. To the extent that this is true, NBFIs play an important role in increasing output demand and the price level. At close to full employment intermediation can feed the fires of inflation.

The creation of close substitutes for money through intermediation also affects the income velocity of money. As NBFI deposits substitute for idle money, money is transferred to active circulation. Hence, the income velocity of money increases. The growth of NBFIs helps to explain the secular increases in the income velocity of money (narrowly defined) in the United States since World War II.

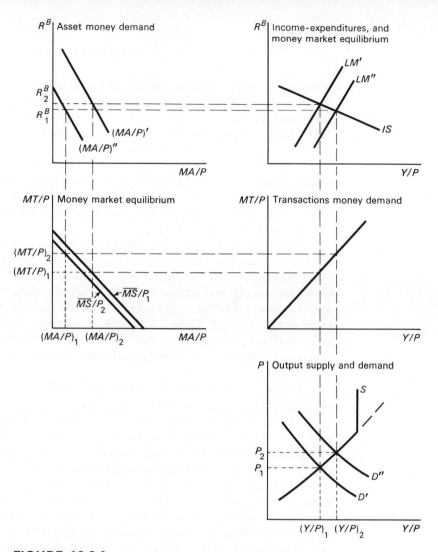

FIGURE 13.2.3

Impact of Changes in the NBFI Deposit Rate on Output Demand and the Price Level

Substitutes for the Medium of Exchange Function of Money

Another institutional development in the United States since World War II has been the increased use of other forms of credit, namely, credit card credit, installment credit, credit between businesses, and other short-term time payment plans issued by businesses whose primary function is not finance but the sale of goods. This type of credit, hereafter referred to as trade credit, has substantively reduced the need for individuals to hold money in order to transact their business.

Trade credit substitutes for the medium of exchange function of money not in terms of final exchange but in terms of intermediate exchange. Only money is a medium of final exchange. By helping to bridge the gap between receipts and payments, trade credit reduces the average required money balances for the period at a given level of income. Consequently, velocity increases. The spectacular growth in trade credit outstanding is still another factor that helps to explain the increase in the income velocity of money (narrowly defined). Moreover, for any given money supply the decrease in money demand means that the money market clears at a lower interest rate.

As increases (decreases) in trade credit occur, the same money stock will support a higher (lower) level of income. Therefore, we rewrite the real transactions money demand function to include real trade credit,

$$\frac{MT}{P} = g_1 \frac{Y}{P} - g_2 \frac{TC}{P} \tag{13.2.2}$$

where $\partial(MT/P)/\partial(Y/P) > 0$ and $\partial(MT/P)/\partial(TC/P) < 0$. We shall assume that trade credit is an exogenous variable. Since the price of trade credit is not known, we have included the availability of trade credit, rather than its price, in our transactions money demand function. Trade credit is frequently, if not usually, allocated on the basis of noninterest factors, such as the income class of the borrower, his race, and his previous repayment record.

For given values of the price level and the parameters in (13.2.2), Fig. 13.2.4 illustrates the impact of changes in trade credit on the transactions

FIGURE 13.2.4

Impact of Changes in Trade Credit
on the Demand for Transactions Money Balances

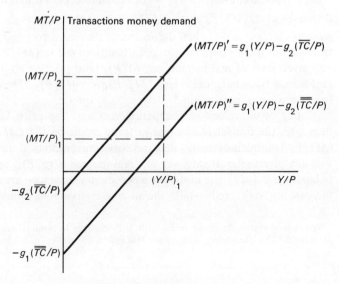

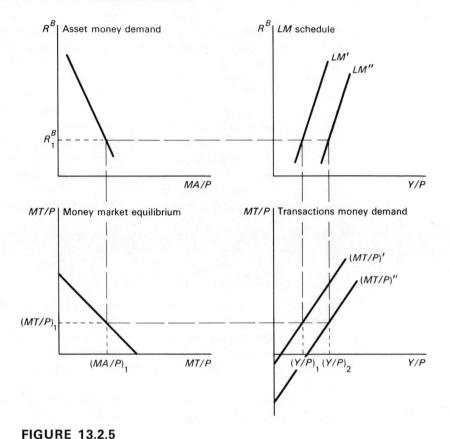

FIGURE 13.2.5

Impact of Changes in Trade Credit on the *LM* Schedule

money demand curve. For $TC = \overline{TC}$, the intercept of the transactions money demand curve, $(MT/P)'$, is $-g_2(\overline{TC}/P)$, and the slope is g_1. If trade credit were to increase to $\overline{\overline{TC}}$, then the intercept decreases to $-g_2(\overline{\overline{TC}}/P)$ and the transactions money demand curve shifts downward to $(MT/P)''$. That is, for any given level of real income, say $(Y/P)_1$ (and price level), the demand for real transactions balances is less, $(MT/P)_1 < (MT/P)_2$. The converse is true for decreases in trade credit.[8]

For given values of the parameters and the price level, Fig 13.2.5 illustrates the impact of changes in trade credit on the *LM* schedule. The $(MT/P)'$ transactions money demand curve corresponds to the *LM'* schedule. For any given interest rate, say R_1^B, real income is $(Y/P)_1$, real transactions balances are $(MT/P)_1$, and real asset money balances are $(MA/P)_1$. An increase in trade credit shifts the money transactions demand curve from

---

[8] Notice that real trade credit varies with both changes in nominal trade credit and the price level. The latter effect is called *the real indebtedness effect of trade credit.*

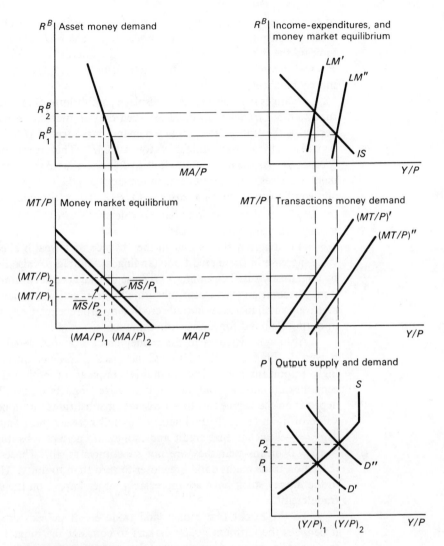

FIGURE 13.2.6

Impact of Changes in Trade Credit
on Output Demand and the Price Level

$(MT/P)'$ to $(MT/P)''$. Consequently, the LM schedule shifts rightward to
LM''. For any given interest rate, say R_1^B, real income increases to $(Y/P)_2$.
The same money stock supports a higher level of real income if trade credit
increases the efficiency or velocity of money balances. Conversely, decreases
in trade credit reduce real income. The same money stock supports a lower
level of real income and velocity falls.

For given values of the parameters and the other exogenous variables of the skeleton model, Fig. 13.2.6 illustrates the impact of changes in trade credit on output demand and the price level. The LM', IS, D', and S curves indicate the initial equilibrium values of the interest rate, R_2^B, the price level, P_1, real income, $(Y/P)_1$, real transactions balances, $(MT/P)_2$, and real asset money balances, $(MA/P)_1$.

Changes in trade credit can displace equilibrium. Suppose, for example, that nominal trade credit increases such that an increase in real trade credit decreases the transactions money demand curve from $(MT/P)'$ to $(MT/P)''$. As a result, the LM schedule shifts toward LM''. This creates an excess supply for money. As the interest rate falls to R_1^B to eliminate the excess, real investment increases, and output demand increases to D''. The price level rises to P_2 and equilibrium output increases to $(Y/P)_2$. The real money stock decreases to $\overline{MS}/P_2$, real transactions balances decrease to $(MT/P)_1$, and real asset money balances increase to $(MA/P)_2$.

Our diagram shows that in the absence of a wealth effect a relatively large increase in trade credit outstanding is required to raise output demand by a relatively small amount. As the use of trade credit continues to increase it may become an even closer substitute for transactions money balances, and relatively small increases in trade credit may produce relatively large increases in output demand for a given money stock.

Although increases in the money stock are considered a much more powerful stimulus to the economy, increases in trade credit play an increasingly important role. The qualitative impacts of both variables on the economy are similar, but their quantitative impacts differ. The difference depends on the degree to which trade credit substitutes for money, that is, the value of g_2 in (13.2.2). Estimates of g_2 fall between zero and unity, where $-g_2 = -1$ means that credit and money are perfect substitutes and where $-g_2 = 0$ means that they are not substitutes at all. The estimates of g_2 (based on trade credit data) are closer to zero than to unity. Hence, changes in the money stock have an appreciably larger impact on the economy than trade credit.

To the extent that money and trade credit policies are independent, it behoves the national policy makers to consider the impact of changes in trade credit on the economy and incorporate measures into their policy package which will curb any undesirable effects of changes in trade credit.

13.3 THE KEYNESIAN-MONETARIST CONTROVERSY

Throughout this text we have alluded to possible controversy over the most effective means of economic stabilization through aggregate demand management. Economists disagree about the nature, the history, and the boundaries of the controversy. Although it is not strictly accurate historically, we can describe the evolution of the controversy by breaking it down into three stages of development involving two basic positions. The first stage identifies the two polar (and naive) positions in the controversy. The extreme fiscalist position can be summarized by "money doesn't matter" (or "only fiscal policy matters") as an effective means of demand management. The extreme monetarist position can be summarized by "only money matters" (or "fiscal policy doesn't matter") as an effective means of demand management.

The second stage of the controversy identifies the areas of disagreement more clearly, and the opposing positions evolve into the fiscalist position that "money matters very little" as an effective means of demand management and the monetarist position that "money matters mostly".

The third stage of the controversy identifies an eclectic post-Keynesian position that "both monetary and fiscal policies matter" and the monetarist position that "money matters mostly."

The Extremes

The extreme positions can be explained within the framework of the *IS-LM* model under the assumption that investment demand is strictly determined by the rate of interest. The *extreme fiscalists* argue that investment demand is perfectly interest inelastic (vertical) so that the *IS* schedule is perfectly interest inelastic (vertical). This means that monetary policy (changes in the money stock which shift the *LM* schedule) has no effect on output demand. Thus, monetary policy is impotent and fiscal policy alone is the means whereby the economy can be controlled.[9]

The *extreme monetarists* argue that money demand is perfectly interest inelastic (vertical) so that the *LM* schedule is perfectly interest inelastic (vertical). This means that fiscal policies (changes in the tax parameters and government spending which shift the *IS* schedule) have no effect on output demand. Thus, fiscal policy is impotent and monetary policy alone is the means whereby the economy can be controlled.

Few economists today support the extreme monetarist position, and there is a question as to whether anyone has ever supported the extreme

[9] There are two other theoretical circumstances which have been used to argue that "money doesn't matter." If the money supply is perfectly interest elastic, the *LM* schedule will be perfectly interest elastic and only fiscal policy (shifts in the *IS* schedule) can change output demand. Thus, the monetary authority has no power to change output demand because it cannot change the money supply. The other circumstance is the liquidity trap case where the asset money demand curve is perfectly interest elastic (a theoretical possibility in a depressed economy). This means that the *LM* schedule is interest elastic and only fiscal policy (shifts in the *IS* schedule in the absence of a wealth effect) can change real income. Neither of these notions are supported by U.S. data with the possible exception of the liquidity trap case. If member bank excess reserves are included in the definition of asset money balances, then in the depression of the 1930s when banks held a very large volume of excess reserves the economy may have been in a liquidity trap, or, more precisely, "an excess reserve trap." However, this does not necessarily mean that changes in the money stock cannot increase real income, certainly not if the money stock can be increased beyond that which is necessary to arrest member bank fears of insolvency.

fiscalist position. The only reason that we mention them is that they identify the polar cases in the Keynesian-monetarist controversy over the effective means of demand management. Many economists consider themselves monetarists ("mostly money matters") on balance or fiscalists ("money matters very little") on balance, but very few align with the extremes. In fact, an increasing majority of economists supports the middle ground between the two extremes.

The Fiscalist Position

Fiscalists argue that changes in the interest rates which result from changes in the money supply are the most important means whereby monetary policy is transmitted to the real sector of the economy. They focus attention on a narrow and observable range of interest rates associated with financial assets such as government bonds, corporate bonds, saving and loan deposits, and mortgages.

The fiscalist transmission mechanism makes an important distinction between firms and households. Households hold only financial assets (nonmoney assets and money) in their asset portfolios (except for owner-occupied housing). Household income is used to purchase goods and services and to increase financial wealth. Firms hold the economy's real physical wealth (the real asset counterpart of nonmoney financial assets held by households). Consumer durables (excluding housing) are excluded from household asset portfolios and included in consumption expenditures. Changes in the interest rates alter both households' (financial) and firms' (real) asset holdings.

Changes in the interest rate displace equilibrium in financial asset portfolios of households. Subsequent adjustment has no effect on the real sector of the economy until firms change real investment in response to changes in interest rates. For example, an increase in the money stock through Fed purchases of government bonds means that holders of financial assets exchange government bonds for money. This initially creates an excess supply of money balances in household asset portfolios. Since financial assets substitute for the value storage function of money, households draw down excess money holdings and purchase nonmoney financial assets. The prices of nonmoney financial assets rise and interest rates fall. As households adjust their portfolio of financial assets, firms adjust their holdings of real assets through real investment. That is, the increase in prices of nonmoney financial assets such as corporate bonds encourages firms to sell new issues of these assets and use the receipts for real investment. In turn, the increase in real investment has a multiple effect on real income, consumption, additional investment, and net foreign expenditures. Since fiscalists believe that monetary policy is transmitted to the real sector indirectly through changes in interest rates, they argue that interest rates (on nonmoney financial assets) are the best indicator of *ease* or *tightness* of monetary policy.

Fiscalists argue that tangible real investment is highly interest inelastic so that the *IS* schedule is highly interest inelastic. In addition, they argue that since nonmoney financial assets are such close substitutes of money, changes in the interest rates on nonmoney financial assets change the quantity of money demanded by relatively larger amounts. This means that the *LM* schedule is very interest elastic. Thus, fiscal policy (shifts in the *IS* schedule) plays the most important role in changing output demand. Monetary policy (shifts in the *LM* schedule) plays a relatively minor role, i.e., "money matters very little."

Moreover, fiscalists argue that the appropriate time period of stabilization is the short run. Changes in thriftiness, exogenous bursts in investment opportunities and "animal spirits," wars, droughts, strikes, changes in preferences, and changes in expectations make the economy essentially unstable. Thus, short-run discretionary policies become appropriate. Even if disturbances are absorbed, the time interval is considered to be so long that economic welfare is greatly reduced if short-run actions are not taken. Since they believe that fiscal policies are more powerful and immediate and that monetary policy is relatively slow, fiscal policies are the preferred means of economic stabilization.

One final point is important. Fiscalists argue that since allocative effects (substitution relationships between financial assets in asset portfolios) are important in capturing the relationship between policy actions and economic activity, larger scale models are preferred. The closer the model is to approximating the real world, the greater the degree of explanatory and predictive ability of the model and the more useful the model for evaluating the full effects of short-run economic stabilization policies.

The Monetarist Position

The monetarist transmission mechanism of monetary policy is also based on asset portfolio adjustment. However, monetarists define the economy's physical wealth to include not only real assets held by firms but consumer durables held by households. Just as firms equate the marginal efficiency of investment to the appropriate rate of interest (or equate an asset's present value to its purchase cost given the appropriate interest rate) in the decision to change their holdings of real assets, households equate the (implicit) marginal efficiency of investment to the appropriate interest rate (or equate an asset's present value to its purchase cost given the appropriate interest rate) in the decision to increase their holdings of consumer durables (real assets of households which yield a flow of services over time).

Since all wealth yields rates of return, monetarists argue that changes in the money supply will affect the real asset holdings of households in the same way that they affect changes in the real asset holdings of firms. Thus, the effects of monetary policy are more widely diffused than believed by the fiscalist. Monetary policy changes interest rates (and therefore prices) and both households and firms adjust both financial and real asset holdings until the desired compositions of asset holdings are achieved. That is, households and firms desire some stock of money relative to income and monetary policy causes the actual stock to vary. Subsequent changes in rates of return and prices cause portfolio adjustments to occur until the actual and desired stocks are again equal. The adjustments directly affect the level of output demand, prices, and income because monetary policy directly influences investment expenditures as well as consumer durable expenditures.

Monetarists would agree that if the interest rate (the rate of return on the assets of both firms and households including consumer durables) on total wealth were observable, it would be an appropriate indicator of the ease or tightness of monetary policy. However, since the rate of return of consumer durables which more closely reflects the return on the flow of income to wealth is not observable, the "second best" indicator of monetary policy is the rate of change in the quantity of money.

Since monetarists argue that both consumer durable expenditures as well as business investment depend on the interest rate, these expenditures are highly interest elastic so that the *IS* schedule is highly interest elastic. Moreover, they argue that money demand and supply are highly interest inelastic so that the *LM* schedule is highly interest inelastic. Thus, monetary policy (shifts in the *LM* schedule) is the most important means whereby output demand can be changed. Fiscal policy (shifts in the *IS* schedule) plays a relatively minor role, i.e., "mostly money matters."

Moreover, monetarists argue that the appropriate time period of economic stabilization is the long run. And their theory is designed to explain long-run phenomena. Most of the exogenous shocks to the system emphasized by the fiscalists are mild and their impacts are of such short duration that the economy is essentially stable. Stability is ensured by market forces which change prices and rates of return in response to these exogenous shocks. Although market imperfections influence time patterns of response between economic variables and cause inefficient allocation of resources, they do not inhibit the stabilizing function of markets.

Although monetarists recognize that monetary policy has a mild short-run effect on real economic variables, they believe that the major impact of monetary policy is on long-run changes in nominal economic variables. In the long-run, they believe that changes in such factors as the labor force, the capital stock, the stock of raw materials, and technical progress account for major changes in real economic variables.

Monetarists view the short-run impact of fiscal policies as exerting little lasting impact on nominal economic variables. For example, government expenditures financed by borrowing from the public and taxation merely crowd out private expenditures. The long-run effects of fiscal policy change real output by changing the composition of output demand. A tax policy which stimulates investment provides for greater productive capacity (greater potential output) in the long run, and expansionary expenditure policy which provides stimulus for investment in human as well as nonhuman capital increases the productive ability of the economy by reallocating resources away from current consumption to investment.

The Current State of the Controversy

In the current state of the controversy we find that few economists can be labeled as being completely in the monetarist or fiscalist camps. However, two distinct bodies of ideas can be identified.

The post-Keynesian position attempts to select the best from the fiscalist and the monetarist positions. Post-Keynesians argue along with the fiscalists that the major impact of monetary policy is transmitted to the real sector indirectly through changes in the interest rates of nonmoney financial assets. Since they include consumer durable expenditures in consumption, monetary policy affects consumer durable expenditures indirectly through changes in real income.

Post-Keynesians argue with the monetarists that money demand is interest inelastic. However, they argue that since money supply is positively related to interest rate and is relatively interest elastic, the combined interest elasticities of money supply and demand make the *LM* schedule interest elastic.

In addition, the post-Keynesians argue with the monetarists that real business investment is highly interest elastic so that the *IS* schedule is highly interest elastic.

With both highly interest elastic *IS* and *LM* schedules the post-Keynesians conclude that both monetary and fiscal policies are viable means whereby the economy can be controlled through aggregate demand management ("money matters *and* fiscal policy matters"). They argue with the fiscalists that the short run is the appropriate time period for economic stabilization and that larger scale models are more helpful in evaluating the full effects of short-run policy alternatives.

The monetarist position has not changed significantly from that which has already been described. And although disagreement still exists over other perceived differences between the post-Keynesians and the monetarists, e.g., the appropriate definition of money, the appropriate concept of income and wealth, the degree of price and wage flexibility, the role of expectations, the degree of resource utilization, and the influences of market imperfections, at least some of the important issues in the continuing debate have been described in this section.

The Empirical Evidence

The empirical evidence indicates a significant inverse relationship between interest rates and money demand. However, the interest elasticity of money demand is very low; estimates range from approximately −.1 to −1.2. Thus, the extreme monetarist view (money demand is not sensitive to changes in the interest rates) and the fiscalist view (money demand is highly sensitive to changes in interest rates) are not supported by the data. The empirical evidence on the interest elasticity of money demand supports the monetarist contention that the *LM* schedule is interest inelastic.

However, the empirical evidence also indicates a significant positive relationship between interest rates and money supply. Estimates of the interest elasticity of money supply range from .1 to .7. Thus, by combining the empirical evidence on the interest elasticity of money demand and money supply, the post-Keynesian view that the *LM* schedule is relatively interest elastic is more consistent with the data than the monetarist view.

The empirical evidence indicates a significant inverse relationship between the interest rates and both business investment expenditures and housing (and a significant positive relationship between output and both business investment expenditures and housing). However, the estimates are low (see Chapter 11). This implies that the *IS* schedule is relatively interest inelastic. Thus, the extreme fiscalist, extreme monetarist, and monetarist views are not supported by the data.

However, the monetarists' expenditure theory and conclusions are not completely rejected if consumer durables are interest elastic. Also monetarist conclusions about the primary importance of monetary policy is supported if monetary policy largely has a direct effect (rather than a largely indirect effect through interest rates) on expenditures. The empirical evidence indicates a significant inverse relationship between consumer durables and interest rates as well as business investment expenditures. But the impact of monetary policy through changes in interest rates plays a relatively minor role when compared to the direct effects of monetary policy on household consumption. Although by no means conclusive, the evidence lends support to the contention that monetary policy causes change in income through the wealth effect on consumption expenditures and, in turn, on consumer durable expenditures. The effect of changes in the interest rate on consumer durables, as well as business investment, plays a relatively minor role.

Thus, the evidence supports the post-Keynesian view of the *IS* schedule, but not on the monetarist premise that business investment and consumer durable expenditures are relatively interest elastic. Rather, the *IS* schedule is very interest elastic because of the wealth effect on consumption expenditures (see Chapter 10). Although monetarist theory and the transmission mechanisms of the monetarist and fiscalists are weakened by the empirical evidence, the importance of the influences of monetary policy is strengthened by the empirical evidence.

13.4   SUMMARY

In this chapter we provided a few additional insights into the money sector of the economy.

First, we expanded the definition of the base money multiplier to include not only the variables directly controlled by the Fed (the required reserve ratios on demand and time deposits) but also the variables directly controlled by the public (the currency and time deposit ratio) and commercial banks (the net free reserve ratio). By developing a partial explanation of public and member bank behavior, we introduce an endogenous element into the base money multiplier and thereby recognized the endogenous character of money supply. Although changes in income exert some influence on the base money multiplier and therefore on the money supply through changes in the currency and time deposit ratios, changes in the interest rate appear to have a more important influence on money supply. An increase (decrease) in the interest rate decreases (increases) the desired time deposit ratio. As the public adjusts its actual time deposit ratio to the desired level, the base money multiplier rises (falls) and therefore the money supply increases (decreases). Similarly, an increase (decrease) in the interest rate decreases (increases) the desired net free reserve ratio. As banks adjust the actual to the desired net free reserve ratio, the base multiplier and therefore the money supply increase (decrease). Thus, the money supply depends on the interest rate because of public and commercial bank behavior and on base money and reserve requirements because of the behavior of the Fed. Since money supply is positively related to the interest rate, the more interest elastic the money supply, the more interest elastic is the *LM* schedule and the more effective is fiscal policy (shifts in the *IS* schedule) in changing output demand.

Second, we extended our theory of money demand to include the rate of return to owners of the highly liquid deposits of nonbank financial intermediaries. Increases (decreases) in the deposit rate means that the associated deposits substitute for the value storage function of money demand. The released money balances augment the supply of loanable funds and the interest rate falls, Thus, idle money is transferred to active money balances by intermediation, and output demand increases. Moreover, the increased use of trade credit substitutes for the exchange medium function of money and expands output demand.

Finally, we discussed the Keynesian-monetarist controversy by reference to variations in the interpretation of our skeleton model. The primary differences are based on the relative interest elasticities of the *IS* and *LM* schedules and the transmission mechanism whereby monetary policy affects the real sector of the model.

REVIEW QUESTIONS

1. Given:

$$C^P/DD = .26$$
$$r_D = .139$$
$$r_T = .1$$
$$TD/DD = .1$$
$$e = .02$$
$$br = .01$$
$$R = .05$$

(a) Calculate the real base money multiplier and the real money stock when real base money is $100.

(b) Suppose $(e - br) = l_0 - l_1 R$

where $l_0 = .015$ and $l_1 = .1$.

If the interest rate rises from .05 to .10 what will be the change in the real money stock?

2. Given:

$$MS/P = s_0 + s_1 R + s_2 B/P$$
$$MD/P = e_0 + g_1 Y/P - e_1 R$$

where $s_0 = \$40$, $s_1 = \$2$, $s_2 = .7$

$e_0 = \$50$, $g_1 = .8$, $e_1 = \$6$

show that the $\partial R/\partial (Y/P)$ is greater when the money stock is exogenous than when it is endogenous.

3. What determines the extent to which changes in NBFI deposits and trade credit change real income for any given interest rate?

4. If the Keynesians and Monetarists could agree on the definition of wealth, could they agree on the transmission mechanism for monetary policy? Explain.

SELECTED READINGS

ANDERSEN, L. C., "The State of the Monetarist Debate," *Federal Reserve Bank of St. Louis Review*, 55 (Sept. 1973), 2–8. Also read comments by L. R. Klein and K. Brunner in the same issue.

———, and A. E. BURGER, "Asset Management and Commercial Bank Portfolio Behavior: Theory and Practice," *Journal of Finance*, 24 (May 1969), 207–22.

———, and K. M. CARLSON, "A Monetarist Model for Economic Stabilization," *Federal Reserve Bank of St. Louis Review*, 52 (April 1970), 7–25.

ANDO, A., and F. MODIGLIANI, "The Relative Stability of Monetary Velocity and the Investment Multiplier," *American Economic Review*, 55 (Sept. 1965), 693–728.

BOWSHER, N. M., "Excess Reserves," *Federal Reserve Bank of St. Louis Review*, April 1963.

BRONFENBRENNER, M., and T. MAYER, "Liquidity Functions in the American Economy," *Econometrica*, 28 (Oct. 1960), 810–34.

BRUNNER, K., "A Schema for the Supply Theory of Money," *International Economic Review*, 2 (Jan. 1961), 79–109.

———, ed., *Targets and Indicators of Monetary Policy*, San Francisco: Chandler, 1969.

———, "The Role of Money and Monetary Policy," *Federal Reserve Bank of St. Louis Review*, 50 (July 1968), 8–24.

———, and A. H. MELTZER, "The Place of Financial Intermediaries in the Transmission of Monetary Policy," *American Economic Review*, 53 (May 1963), 372–82.

———, and A. H. MELTZER, "Predicting Velocity: Implications for Theory and Policy," *Journal of Finance*, 18 (May 1963), 319–54.

———, and A. H. MELTZER, "Some Further Investigations of Demand and Supply Functions for Money," *Journal of Finance*, 19 (May 1964), 240–83.

———, A. H. MELTZER, J. TOBIN, P. DAVIDSON, D. PATINKIN, and M. FRIEDMAN, "Symposium of Friedman's Theoretical Framework," *Journal of Political Economy*, 80 (Sept.–Oct. 1972), 837–950.

CARSON, D., and I. SCOTT, "Commercial Bank Attributes and Aversion to Risk," in *Banking and Monetary Studies*, D. Carson (ed.), Homewood, Ill.: Irwin, 1963, pp. 420–33.

CHOW, G., "On the Long-Run and Short-Run Demand for Money," *Journal of Political Economy*, 74 (April 1966), 111–31.

DEWALD, W., "Free Reserves, Total Reserves and Monetary Control," *Journal of Political Economy*, 71 (April 1963), 141–53.

DUESENBERRY, J. S., "The Portfolio Approach to the Demand for Money and Other Assets," *Review of Economics and Statistics*, 45 (Feb. 1963), 9–24.

FEIGE, E., *The Demand for Liquid Assets: A Temporal Cross Section Analysis*, Englewood Cliffs, N.J.: Prentice-Hall, 1964.

FRIEDMAN, M., "The Demand for Money: Some Theoretical and Empirical Results," *Journal of Political Economy*, 67 (Aug. 1959), 327–51.

———, "A Monetary and Fiscal Framework for Economic Stability," *American Economic Review*, 38 (June 1948), 245–64.

———, "The Quantity Theory of Money—A Restatement," in M. G. Mueller (ed.), *Readings in Macroeconomics*, New York: Holt, Rinehart and Winston, 1966, pp. 110–36.

———, "A Theoretical Framework for Monetary Analysis," *Journal of Political Economy*, 78 (March/April 1970), 193–238.

———, and A. J. SCHWARTZ, *A Monetary History of the United States, 1867–1960*, Princeton, N.J.: Princeton University Press, 1963.

GOLDFELD, S. M., and E. J. KANE, "The Determinants of Member Bank Borrowing: An Econometric Study," *Journal of Finance*, 21 (Sept. 1966), 499–514.

GURLEY, J. G., "The Radcliffe Report and Evidence," *American Economic Review*, 50 (Sept. 1960), 672–700.

——, and E. S. SHAW, *Money in a Theory of Finance*, Washington, D. C.: The Brookings Institution, 1960.

HAMBURGER, M. J., "The Demand for Money by Households, Money Substitutes and Monetary Policy," *Journal of Political Economy*, 74 (Dec. 1966), 600–23.

——, "Alternative Interest Rates and the Demand for Money: Comment," *American Economic Review*, 59 (June 1969), 407–12.

HELLER, H. R., "The Demand for Money—The Evidence from the Short-Run Data," *Quarterly Journal of Economics*, 79 (May 1965), 291–303.

JOHNSON, H., "The Keynesian Revolution and the Monetarist Counter-Revolution," *American Economic Review*, 61 (May 1971), 1–14.

——, "Monetary Theory and Policy," *American Economic Review*, 52 (June 1962), 335–84.

LAFFER, A. B., "Trade Credit and the Money Market," *Journal of Political Economy*, 78 (March/April 1970), 239–67.

LAIDLER, D., "The Rate of Interest and the Demand for Money—Some Empirical Evidence," *Journal of Political Economy*, 74 (Dec. 1966), 543–55.

——, *The Demand for Money: Theories and Evidence*, Scranton, Pa.: International Textbook Company, 1969.

LATANE, H. A., "Cash Balances and the Interest Rate—A Pragmatic Approach," *Review of Economics and Statistics*, 36 (Nov. 1954), 456–60.

LEE, T. H., "Alternative Interest Rates and the Demand for Money: The Empirical Evidence," *American Economic Review*, 57 (Dec. 1967), 1168–81.

DE LEEUW, F., "A Model of Financial Behavior," in *The Brookings Quarterly Econometric Model of the United States*, J. Duesenberry, G. Fromm, L. Klein, and E. Kuh (eds.), Skokie, Ill.: Rand McNally, 1965, pp. 7–18.

——, and E. M. GRAMLICH, "The Channels of Monetary Policy," *Journal of Finance*, 24 (May 1969), 265–90.

MEIGS, A. J., *Free Reserves and the Money Supply*, Chicago: University of Chicago Press, 1962.

MELTZER, A. H., "The Demand for Money: The Evidence from the Time Series," *Journal of Political Economy*, 71 (June 1963), 219–46.

——, "The Demand for Money: A Cross Section Study of Business Firms," *Quarterly Journal of Economics*, 77 (Aug. 1963), 405–22.

——, "Controlling Money," *Federal Reserve Bank of St. Louis Review*, 51 (May 1969), 16–24.

MODIGLIANI, F., "The Monetary Mechanism and Its Interaction with Real Phenomena," *Review of Economics and Statistics*, 45 (Feb. 1963), 79–107.

———, "Monetary Policy and Consumption: Linkages via Interest Rate and Wealth Effects in the FMP Model," in *Consumer Spending and Monetary Policy: The Linkages*, Boston: Federal Reserve Bank of Boston, 1971, pp. 9–84.

———, R. A. RASCHE, and J. P. COOPER, "Central Bank Policy, Money Supply, and the Short-term Rate of Interest," *Journal of Money, Credit, and Banking*, 2 (May 1970), 166–217.

MOTLEY, B., "A Demand-for-Money Function for the Household Sector—Some Preliminary Findings," *Journal of Finance*, 22 (Sept. 1967), 405–18.

———, "The Consumer's Demand for Money: A Neoclassical Approach," *Journal of Political Economy*, 77 (Sept./Oct. 1969), 817–26.

OKUN, A. M., "Rules and Roles for Fiscal and Monetary Policy," in *Issues in Fiscal Policy and Monetary Policy: The Eclectic Economist Views the Controversy*, J. J. Diamond (ed.), Chicago: DePaul University, 1971, pp. 102–20.

TEIGEN, R., "Demand and Supply Functions for Money in the American Economy," *Econometrica*, 32 (Oct. 1964), 476–509.

———, "A Critical Look at Monetarist Economics," *Federal Reserve Bank of St. Louis Review*, 54 (Jan. 1972), 10–26.

TOBIN, J., "Liquidity Preference and Monetary Policy," *Review of Economics and Statistics*, 29 (May 1947), 124–31.

———, "Money, Capital and Other Stores of Value," *American Economic Review*, 51 (May 1961), 26–37.

———, "Commercial Banks as Creators of 'Money'," in *Banking and Monetary Studies*, D. Carson (ed.), Homewood, Ill.: Irwin, 1963, pp. 408–19.

———, "The Monetary Interpretation of History," *American Economic Review*, 55 (June 1965), 464–85.

———, and W. C. Brainard, "Financial Intermediaries and the Effectiveness of Monetary Control," *American Economic Review*, 53 (May 1963), 383–400.

WEINTRAUB, R. E., *Introduction to Monetary Economics*, New York: Ronald, 1970, Chaps. 8, 9, and 18.

———, and W. R. HOSEK, "Further Reflections on and Investigations of Money Demand," *Journal of Finance*, 25 (March 1970), 109–25.

WRIGHT, C., "Saving and the Rate of Interest," in *The Taxation of Income from Capital*, A. C. Harberger and M. J. Bailey (eds.), Washington, D.C.: The Brookings Institution, 1969, pp. 275–99.

ZAHN, F., and W. R. HOSEK, "The Impact of Trade Credit on Velocity and the Market Rate of Interest," *Southern Economic Journal*, Oct. 1973.

Index